AMERICAN BATTLEFIELD TRUST ★ ★ ★

PRESERVE. EDUCATE. INSPIRE.

BATTLE MAPS OF THE CIVIL WAR: THE WESTERN THEATER
MAPS FROM THE AMERICAN BATTLEFIELD TRUST ⁓ VOLUME 2

FOREWORD

"I just love those maps you guys send to me.
Could you put them into a book for members?"

COUNTLESS TIMES OVER THE PAST TWENTY YEARS, , I have had members write, email, call, even pull me aside at conferences and events, and make the same request: Please publish the maps that the Trust includes in our battlefield fundraising mail and web appeals into a book! In late 2019, we created our first volume — *Battle Maps of the Civil War: The Eastern Theater* — and, being cautious with the funds entrusted to us by our members, printed a limited first run of the books to see if members would be truly interested in the book.

We ran out in less than a month.

Rushing back for a second print run, we blew through those in record time as well. To date, members like you have snapped up nearly 7,000 copies of Volume I! I am told that, in the history publishing world, any book that sells more than 5,000 copies is considered a runaway bestseller. So, if you were one of those who either made a generous donation to receive a copy, or simply bought one outright via our website or other bookseller, thank you. Thank you, 7,000 times, over.

With that recent history in mind, it is my honor to present *Volume 2 — Battle Maps of the Civil War: The Western Theater*.

As in Volume I, the maps — created by graphic designer and cartographer Steven Stanley, in close consultation with our battlefield preservation experts — are designed to show potential donors, at a glance, the specific piece of battlefield land we are attempting to save, and the historic significance of that hallowed ground. This particular volume is very important because we have found over the years that the crucial Western Theater battles are often overshadowed by their Eastern Theater brethren. As a national preservation and education organization, we have a duty to save hallowed ground wherever it may be, and it is my hope that this volume may help you learn about and appreciate some new part of the Civil War in the West.

As for the maps themselves, they have evolved into far more than just a depiction of regiments and brigades, charges and retreats, high ground and low points. These simple maps have established a personal connection between the generous supporters of this great cause like you, and the ground you have helped to save. Again, I cannot tell you how many times people have told me that they collected Trust maps in binders and had them in hand when they visited the battlefields, often to walk the very ground they have made personal gifts to preserve.

Next to the preserved land itself, these maps are the best visual evidence of the tangible and measurable nature of the mission of the American Battlefield Trust. Unlike most nonprofit organizations, we can show our supporters exactly — to the hundredth-of-an-acre — what their philanthropy is accomplishing, the precise land that their donations are helping to preserve forever, and why it is important.

As we noted in Volume I, with a pace of 30-40 land transactions each year, we know that any book of maps we publish is likely to be outdated before the delivery truck pulls away from the printer's loading dock. Still — until we stop saving hallowed ground, which will not happen for many years — we will simply have to live with the fact that any map book will be somewhat outdated. The troop movements won't change, of course, only the addition of newly saved parcels of land. I am confident that each map will still present a full understanding of how we are succeeding in our mission, thanks to our supporters.

I am grateful to all of the members of the Trust staff who have worked to create these first two volumes, but want to especially note Deputy Director of Education Kristopher White, who wrote the stellar text (it is wonderful to have a published author on staff), GIS Specialist Jon Mitchell, who oversaw the maps and offered key initial project management, and Deputy Director of Development Amanda Murray, who somehow gets everything printed and delivered on time and on budget.

We still envision a series of additional books highlighting more battles and theaters of the Civil War, as well as a book on the battles of the Revolutionary War, which is now a crucial part of our mission. My greatest hope is that this second volume will fill you with pride for all you have done for the cause of battlefield preservation, and that, by keeping it close at hand and referring to it often, it will inspire you to continue to make the preservation of American hallowed ground an important part of your personal legacy. Thank you.

David

David Duncan
President
American Battlefield Trust

WHAT GOES INTO MAKING A "NEW" MAP?

By Steven Stanley

THIS IS A TOPIC THAT COULD BE THE BASIS FOR AN ENTIRE BOOK in and of itself. Map creation is a topic that fascinates many history buffs. So much so that I have an entire 45-minute talk and PowerPoint presentation dedicated to how I create my battle maps. In a nutshell, the process is straightforward, but it's also labor and research intensive, while being wildly rewarding.

The first thing I do is actually find the battlefield. This might sound silly, but it is easier said than done for the majority of the battles I map. Granted, most people can locate Gettysburg, Vicksburg and Antietam, but do they know where the Natural Bridge Battlefield is located? I didn't either when I was first assigned the task of creating a battle map for land the Trust was preserving. I'll give you a hint, the battlefield is located in the Sunshine State.

Once I have located the battlefield, I then start pulling together all of the source materials I can find. For some battles, the list of materials is extensive; for others, not so much. I use primary sources first— letters, diaries, books—and then gather contemporary sources, too. After this step, I try to locate any existing maps; these are in the form of both primary and contemporary sources.

The existing maps help to get me started on locating the troops on the battlefield proper. Some of these maps are right on the money, and some are not. Now that I have this wealth of material spread across my office desk and floor, my wife knows that I am getting deeply involved in creating a new map by the mess around me.

Next, I will locate the oldest topographical (Topo) map of the battlefield. This topographical map gives me a better sense on how the battlefield looked around or at the time of the battle. As we all know, the topography of battlefields can change greatly after 150 or more years due to man and Mother Nature.

Using the old topographical map as a base, I then overlay a modern United States Geological Survey (USGS) map over the historical map. Before USGS reworked its modern Topo maps to be more user-friendly, I used to hand draw each and every Topo line on the maps. The Virginia Peninsula battles weren't too bad to draw because the terrain is fairly flat, but for the Shenandoah Valley battles you have mountains to contend with. Some maps take a couple of hours to hand draw, whereas others take a couple of days.

Using the historical and contemporary maps as guides, I start adding in the historical and modern roads, using different symbols for each. Sometimes the historical and modern roads coexist, which makes my job slightly easier. Then on to adding in the water features. They could be just small streams that were there at the time of the battle to huge rivers, bays, and sometimes, the Atlantic Ocean. After adding in the water, it is now time to add in historical features such as houses, commercial buildings, churches and other elements that make up the battlefield. Finally, I add in the historical treeline.

Once the base map is complete, I can truly add in the location of the troops. Using the sources I have collected, I add in where a unit entered the battle, and then follow the said unit's subsequent movements during the battle. The primary and contemporary resources I have collected get the troops moving in the correct direction.

After I feel I have the troops in the correct positions and moving the correct way, I send the maps to a historian for that battle and have them check my work. I will take any and all suggestions or corrections to heart and adjust the maps accordingly.

Once all the adjustments and corrections are made to the map, I deliver it to the American Battlefield Trust, which, in turn, delivers it to supporters and preservationists such as yourself.

INTRODUCTION

IN MANY WAYS, THE WESTERN THEATER OF THE AMERICAN CIVIL WAR was the decisive theater of operations. The Western Theater served as the training ground for some of the best Union generals—Ulysses S. Grant, William T. Sherman, and Philip H. Sheridan. And it served as a dumping ground for some of the worst Confederate generals—William W. Loring, William H.C. Whiting, and William B. Taliaferro— among many others. Unlike the Eastern Theater, where the two principal armies, the Army of the Potomac and Army of Northern Virginia, grappled over the same stretch of land for nearly four years, the Western Theater gave way to sweeping offensives that ended with decisive results.

The Western Theater encompassed more than 240,000 square miles of the United States. By the end of the war, the theater included the states of Kentucky, Mississippi, Tennessee, Alabama, Georgia, Florida, North Carolina, South Carolina, and parts of Louisiana. Some Western Theater campaigns crossed the Mississippi River (known as the Trans-Mississippi Theater) into Arkansas. Four major water bodies created the borders of this combat zone: the Atlantic Ocean to the east, the Gulf of Mexico to the south, the Mississippi River to the west, and the Ohio River to the north. Thus, the Union Navy played a vital role in taming these waterways and clearing them of Confederate resistance. More than in any other theater of the Civil War, the Union Navy played a decisive role in battle-after-battle. They created an early blueprint for later amphibious and joint operations of the Spanish American War and World War II. Military units from around the world still study the logistical and operational art of the Vicksburg Campaign. And the modern concept of the army group found its genesis in the 1864 Atlanta Campaign.

Yet, many Civil War buffs and some historians place a lesser emphasis on the Western Theater. They base their perceived importance of a battle or military campaign in terms of casualties. The bloodier the engagement, the more critical the action must have been. Thus, of the top five bloodiest battles of the Civil War, only one Western Theater battle—the Battle of Chickamauga—makes it onto this list. On the top ten list of bloodiest battles, four western actions sadly make the cut. But there is far more to war than casualty figures.

The Western Theater witnessed the Union Navy's dominance of the major waterways of the Ohio, Tennessee, and Mississippi Rivers—providing shipping highways for men and materials—and close-range support for battles and sieges along the brown watercourses. The fall of the rail centers at Corinth, Nashville, Chattanooga, and Atlanta immobilized Confederate arms and industry. Foreign commerce with the Confederacy was dealt a crippling blow with the fall of the south's largest city, New Orleans. While the Federal blockades of Mobile, Pensacola, Wilmington, and other Southern ports created a dire shortage of vital supplies. Major General William T. Sherman and his army group laid waste to the Cotton Belt. In the process, thousands of slaves were freed as Union forces drove relentlessly through the Deep South, causing $100 million in damages (in 1864 currency and $1.6 billion in 2020 dollars) during the March to the Sea—while stabbing at the heart of the Confederate economy, chattel slavery. The campaigns of the Western Theater changed the Deep South to this day culturally, economically, and politically.

Thus, while the armies in the Eastern Theater battled it out in the same corridor many times over the same exact land, the ground around the Southern Confederacy was ever-shrinking as Grant, Sherman, Henry Halleck, William Rosecrans, and a cadre of other Union generals and admirals were crippling the Confederacy's war-making abilities while securing tens of thousands of square miles of territory. As eastern newspapers lauded or lamented the exploits

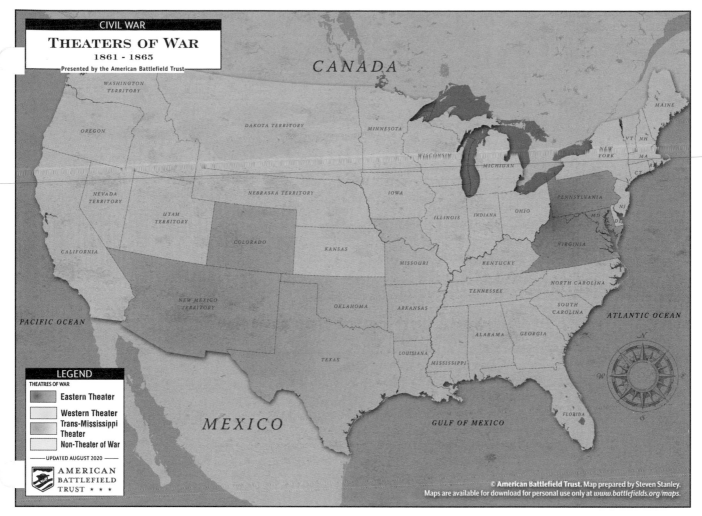

and tactical victories of Robert E. Lee, Jeb Stuart, James Longstreet, and Stonewall Jackson, the Federal armies in the west were amassing an impressive array of strategic victories at Forts Henry and Donelson, Perryville, Vicksburg, Chattanooga, Atlanta, and more. The true Achilles heel of the Confederacy was not the defeat of Lee's army at Gettysburg. It was the Western Theater, where Confederate President Jefferson Davis yearned to defend far too much with far too little. Davis, too, never secured a general on the level of Robert E. Lee in the west. Instead, the Confederate armies in the west were filled with capable soldiers, who were overwhelmingly led by unimpressive and sometimes woefully incompetent general officers.

The importance of what happened in the Western Theater cannot be understated. To that end—now more than 30 years ago—the American Battlefield Trust was created to preserve the battlefields associated with the Revolutionary War, War of 1812, and the American ivil War. Over the last three decades, the Trust and ..s members have preserved more than 53,000 acres of hallowed battlefield land in 24 states. And the Trust's

hallmark in land preservation has been our battle maps. Due to the sheer number of battlefields in the Western Theater, we cannot fit every map we have ever created into this work. Thus, we have focused on some of the significant actions of the Western Theater.

As in our first volume of this series, the battle maps are the real "star" of this work. We have provided the reader with some brief overview text to bring them up to speed on the battle action and then allowed the maps to tell the rest of the story.

It is our sincere hope that this collection of maps will give you a better understanding of the major actions of the Western Theater of the American Civil War. And an appreciation for the tens of thousands of acres of hallowed ground our members have helped to preserve over the last three decades.

Please visit our website **www.battlefields.org** for more maps and more information about America's defining conflicts.

BATTLE *of* FORT SUMTER

APRIL 9 - 12, 1861

THE CLOUDS OF WAR WERE SWIRLING ACROSS THE UNITED STATES in early 1861. The election of Abraham Lincoln as President of the United States in November of 1860 served as a catalyst for secession throughout the Deep South. After decades of short-lived but ultimately failed compromises largely revolving around the expansion of slavery in the United States and its territories, many people in the South felt when Lincoln assumed office on March 4, 1861, that his administration would try and end the institution of slavery, and "The slaveholding States will no longer have the power of self-government, or self-protection, and the Federal Government will have become their enemy." Others in the South claimed that their "position is thoroughly identified with the institution of slavery—the greatest material interest of the world…and a blow at slavery is a blow at commerce and civilization."

Thus, on December 20, 1860, South Carolina seceded from the United States, and by February 2, 1861, six more states followed suit. Rebel militia forces began seizing United States forts and property throughout the South. The crisis approached its boiling point, and war could erupt at any moment.

In Charleston, officials demanded the surrender of the Federal military instillations in the new "independent republic of South Carolina." President James Buchannan refused to back down. Meantime, the situation in Charleston grew tenser. On December 26, 1860, the Federal commander of the Charleston defenses, Maj. Robert Anderson moved his tiny garrison of fewer than 90 men from Fort Moultrie to Fort Sumter, situated in the middle of Charleston Harbor. Anderson's garrison was running low on supplies. On January 5, 1861, the Star of the West departed from New York with some 200 reinforcements and provisions for the Sumter garrison. As the ship approached Charleston Harbor on January 9, Confederates fired on the ship forcing the crew to abandon its mission.

On April 9, Confederate President Jefferson Davis and the Confederate cabinet decided to "strike a blow!" At 4:30 a.m. on April 12, Confederate Lt. Henry S. Farley pulled the lanyard of a ten-inch siege mortar. A flaming shot arched into the air and exploded over Fort Sumter. Upon this signal, Rebel guns from fortifications and floating batteries around Charleston Harbor roared to life. Anderson waited until around 7:00 a.m. to respond. His response was from a 32-pounder cannon commanded by Capt. Abner Doubleday.

For nearly 36 hours the two sides kept up this unequal contest. A shell struck the flag pole of Fort Sumter, and the American flag fell to the earth, only to be hoisted back upon the hastily repaired pole. Confederates fired hotshot into Fort Sumter. Buildings began to burn within Sumter. With supplies nearly exhausted, and in a no-win situation, Anderson surrendered Fort Sumter to Confederate forces at 2:30 p.m. on April 13. Anderson and his men were allowed to strike their colors, fire a 100-gun salute, and board a ship bound for New York. Sadly, the only casualties at Fort Sumter came during the 100-gun salute when a round exploded prematurely, killing Pvt. Daniel Hough and mortally wounding another soldier.

With the firing on Fort Sumter, the American Civil War was officially upon both the North and the South—a war that lasted four years and cost the lives of more than 620,000 Americans and freed 3.9 million people from the bondage of slavery.

✳ ✳ PRESERVATION ✳ ✳

To date, the **American Battlefield Trust** has not saved any land at Fort Sumter.

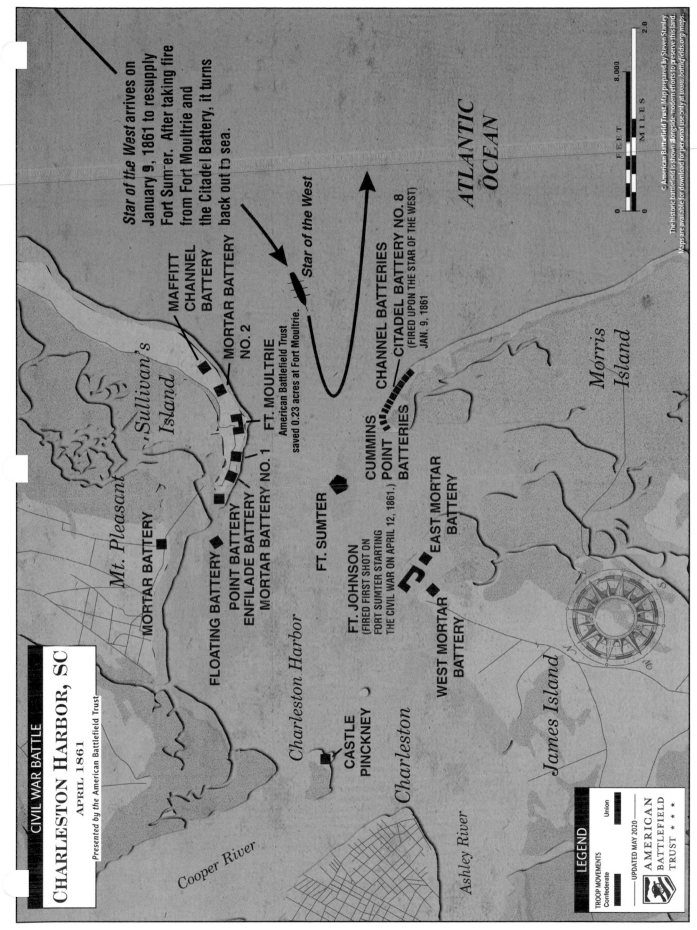

CIVIL WAR BATTLE

CHARLESTON HARBOR, SC

APRIL 1861

Presented by the American Battlefield Trust

Star of the West arrives on January 9, 1861 to resupply Fort Sumter. After taking fire from Fort Moultrie and the Citadel Battery, it turns back out to sea.

MAFFITT CHANNEL BATTERY

MORTAR BATTERY NO. 2

Star of the West

FT. MOULTRIE
American Battlefield Trust saved 0.23 acres at Fort Moultrie.

CHANNEL BATTERIES

CITADEL BATTERY NO. 8
(FIRED UPON THE STAR OF THE WEST)
JAN. 9, 1861

Sullivan's Island

Mt. Pleasant

MORTAR BATTERY

FLOATING BATTERY

POINT BATTERY
ENFILADE BATTERY
MORTAR BATTERY NO. 1

FT. SUMTER

CUMMINS POINT BATTERIES

FT. JOHNSON
(FIRED FIRST SHOT ON FORT SUMTER STARTING THE CIVIL WAR ON APRIL 12, 1861.)

EAST MORTAR BATTERY

WEST MORTAR BATTERY

Charleston Harbor

CASTLE PINCKNEY

Charleston

Cooper River

Ashley River

James Island

Morris Island

ATLANTIC OCEAN

FEET   8,001

0   MILES   2.0

© American Battlefield Trust. Map prepared by Steven Stanley. The historic battlefield is shown alongside modern efforts to preserve this land. Maps are available for download for personal use only at *www.battlefields.org/maps.*

LEGEND

TROOP MOVEMENTS
Confederate
Union

UPDATED MAY 2020

AMERICAN BATTLEFIELD TRUST ★ ★ ★

BATTLE *of* FORT HENRY

FEBRUARY 6, 1862

ON JANUARY 27, 1862, ABRAHAM LINCOLN ISSUED General War Order No. 1 directing all Federal armies to initiate offensive operations. Since the firing on Fort Sumter, both sides dramatically increased the size of their respective armies and navies. Clashes at Wilson's Creek, First Bull Run, and Ball's Bluff resulted in Confederate victories, while in western Virginia (modern-day West Virginia), the Union found sustained success.

While the Federal war machine lay idle in the Eastern Theater as it prepared for its offensive against the Confederate capital of Richmond, Virginia, the Federal army and navy sprang to life in the Western Theater. The Confederate border between the north and south in the Western Theater ran from the Appalachian Mountains across the Mississippi River into Arkansas and modern-day Oklahoma. General Albert S. Johnston was charged with the defense of this expansive line, and he only had roughly 71,000 Confederate soldiers and a cadre of unimpressive subordinates to employ for the defense of key strategic positions. This cordon strategy played into Federal hands.

Seeking to open river traffic on the Tennessee and Cumberland rivers, Federals targeted Fort Henry on the Tennessee River. The fort was situated on a low piece of ground and a thin peninsula of sorts created by the two rivers. Capturing Fort Henry and its sister, Fort Donelson, some five miles distant, would split Johnston's defensive line in two while opening the rivers to the Federals.

On February 2, 1862, Brig. Gen. Ulysses S. Grant and Flag Officer Andrew Foote moved a force of 15,000 soldiers, four ironclads, and three timberclad ships toward Fort Henry.

Some 3,000 Confederates commended by Brig. Gen. Lloyd Tilghman manned the defenses of Fort Henry. The poorly situated fort boasted 20-foot-high walls that were 20-feet thick at the base, but winter rains had swollen the river, leaving the parade ground submerged beneath two feet of water and much of the powder in the magazines damp.

On February 4–5, Grant's infantry disembarked out of range of Fort Henry's guns. Tilghman realized that he was woefully outmanned and outgunned. He withdrew his force manning the incomplete Fort Heiman, on the west bank of the river, and dispatched the majority of the force inside Fort Henry five miles overland to the more defensible Fort Donelson. Still, Tilghman determined to make a stand against the coming gunboats rather than abandon Fort Henry to the enemy.

At noon on February 6, 1862, Foote ordered his flotilla into position less than 300 yards from the fort. The point-blank range battle wreaked havoc on the Confederates. Before long, all four of the fort's heavy guns had been lost and 21 Southerners were casualties. A direct hit to the middle boiler knocked the ironclad USS *Essex* out of commission, causing 32 casualties in one shot and disabling her for the rest of the campaign. The *Cincinnati* took 32 hits, the *St. Louis* seven, and the *Carondelet* six. Confederates had the worst of it, though, and Tilghman asked Foote for terms. The sailor's response presaged Grant's 10 days later at Fort Donelson: "Your surrender will be unconditional." In a ceremony onboard the USS *Cincinnati*, 12 officers and 82 men surrendered.

With the Tennessee River now open before him, Foote dispatched his three timberclads, *Tyler*, *Conestoga* and *Lexington*, as far as Muscle Shoals, Alabama, destroying supplies and infrastructure as they went, even capturing the uncompleted Confederate ironclad *Eastport*. Grant eyed the next prizes, Fort Donelson and the Cumberland River.

✳ ✳ PRESERVATION ✳ ✳

The **American Battlefield Trust** has not saved any land at Fort Henry.

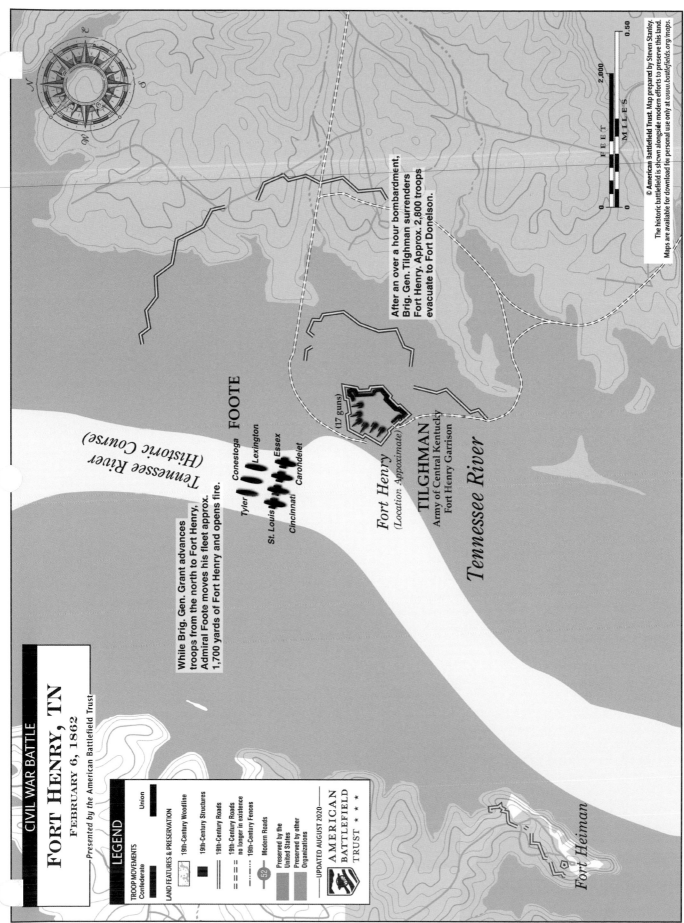

CIVIL WAR BATTLE
FORT HENRY, TN
FEBRUARY 6, 1862

Presented by the American Battlefield Trust

LEGEND

TROOP MOVEMENTS
Confederate
Union

LAND FEATURES & PRESERVATION
19th-Century Woodline
19th-Century Structures
19th-Century Roads
19th-Century Roads no longer in existence
19th-Century Fences
52 Modern Roads

Preserved by the United States
Preserved by other Organizations

— UPDATED AUGUST 2020 —

AMERICAN BATTLEFIELD TRUST ★ ★ ★

While Brig. Gen. Grant advances troops from the north to Fort Henry, Admiral Foote moves his fleet approx. 1,700 yards of Fort Henry and opens fire.

Tennessee River (Historic Course)

FOOTE
Conestoga
Tyler
Lexington
St. Louis
Essex
Cincinnati
Carondelet

(17 guns)

Fort Henry (Location Approximate)

After an over a hour bombardment, Brig. Gen. Tilghman surrenders Fort Henry. Approx. 2,800 troops evacuate to Fort Donelson.

TILGHMAN
Army of Central Kentucky
Fort Henry Garrison

Tennessee River

Fort Heiman

FEET
MILES

2,000
0.50

BATTLE *of* FORT DONELSON

FEBRUARY 15, 1862

AFTER THE FALL OF FORT HENRY, GRANT WAS DETERMINED TO MOVE QUICKLY onto the much larger Fort Donelson, located on the nearby Cumberland River. Grant's boast that he would capture Donelson by the 8th of February quickly ran into challenges. Poor winter weather, late-arriving reinforcements, and difficulties in moving the ironclads up the Cumberland all delayed Grant's advance on the fort.

Despite being convinced that no earthen fort could withstand the power of the Union gunboats, Confederate Gen. Albert Sidney Johnston allowed the garrison at Fort Donelson to remain and even sent new commanders and reinforcements there. On February 11, Johnston appointed Brig. Gen. John B. Floyd as the commander of Fort Donelson and the surrounding region. Nearly 17,000 Confederate soldiers, combined with improved artillery positions and earthworks convinced the inept Floyd that a hasty retreat was unnecessary.

By February 13, most of Grant's soldiers were positioned on the landward (western) side of the fort. The next day, Foote's ironclads moved upriver to bombard Fort Donelson. The subsequent duel between Foote's "Pook Turtles" and the heavier guns at the fort led to a Union defeat.

While Grant contemplated an extended siege, the Confederate leadership devised a bold plan to mass their troops against the Union right to force open a path of escape. Early on the morning of February 15, the Confederate assault struck the Union right and drove it back from its positions on Dudley's Hill. Brigadier General John McClernand's division attempted to reform their lines, but the ongoing Rebel attacks continued to drive his forces to the southeast. Disaster loomed for the Union army.

But inexplicably Confederate Brig. Gen. Gideon Pillow ordered the attacking force back to their earthworks, thereby abandoning the hard-fought gains of the morning.

Grant ordered McClernand and Brig. Gen. Lew Wallace to retake their lost ground and then rode to the Union left to order an attack upon the Confederate works opposite Brig. Gen. Charles F. Smith's division. Grant reasoned, correctly, that the Confederate right must be greatly reduced in strength given the heavy assault from the Confederate left. Smith's division surged forward and overwhelmed the lone Confederate regiment occupying the rifle pits in advance of the Confederate line. Capturing large stretches of the earthworks.

During the night of February 15 and 16, Confederate leaders discussed their options. It was determined that surrender was the only viable option for the garrison. Generals Floyd and Pillow abandoned their men and fled, while Lt. Col. Nathan Bedford Forrest, disgusted with the Confederate decision to surrender, took his cavalrymen and escaped down the Charlotte Road. Even with these defections, more than 13,000 Confederate soldiers remained in the fort.

Confederates hoisted white flags above their earthworks. Brigadier General Simon B. Buckner, now in command, met with Grant to determine the terms of surrender. Buckner, who was hoping for generous terms from his old friend, was disappointed at Grant's response: "No terms except unconditional and immediate surrender can be accepted. I propose to move immediately upon your works." Buckner surrendered.

The decisive Union victories at Forts Henry and Donelson thrust Grant into the national spotlight and opened the Tennessee and Cumberland Rivers to the Union navy. Tennessee was about to be cut in two.

✳ ✳ **PRESERVATION** ✳ ✳

To date, the **American Battlefield Trust** has saved **370 acres** at Fort Donelson.

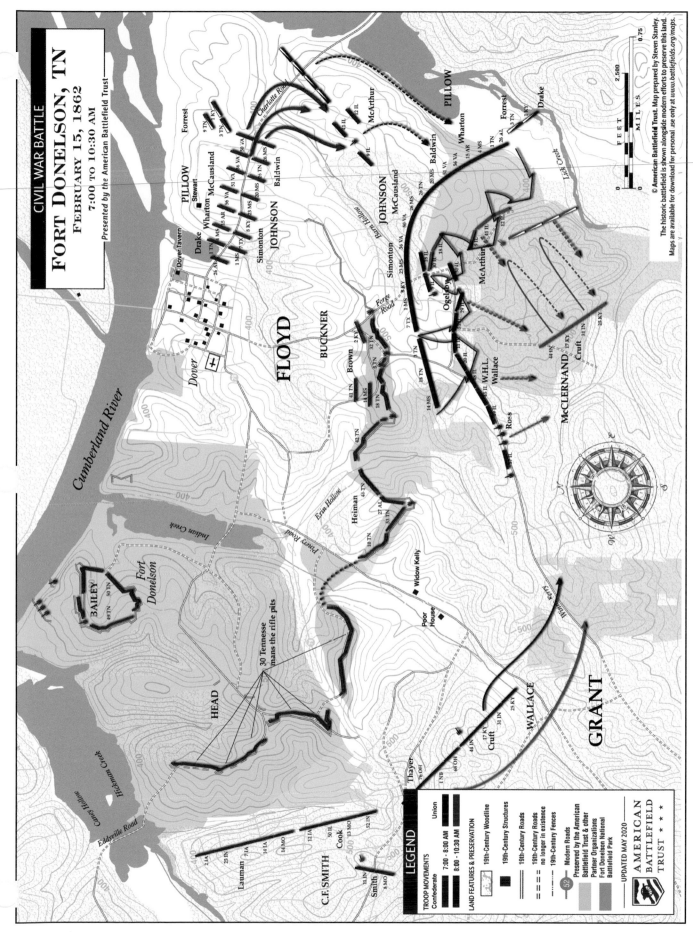

CIVIL WAR BATTLE

FORT DONELSON, TN

FEBRUARY 15, 1862
7:00 TO 10:30 AM

Presented by the American Battlefield Trust

LEGEND

TROOP MOVEMENTS

Confederate   Union

7:00 - 8:00 AM

8:00 - 10:30 AM

LAND FEATURES & PRESERVATION

19th-Century Woodline

19th-Century Structures

19th-Century Roads

19th-Century Roads no longer in existence

19th-Century Fences

Modern Roads

52

Preserved by the American Battlefield Trust & other Partner Organizations

Fort Donelson National Battlefield Park

AMERICAN BATTLEFIELD TRUST ★ ★ ★

— UPDATED MAY 2020 —

© American Battlefield Trust. Map prepared by Steven Stanley.
The historic battlefield is shown alongside modern efforts to preserve this land.
Maps are available for download for personal use only at *www.battlefields.org/maps*.

FEET

MILES

0   2,500   0.75

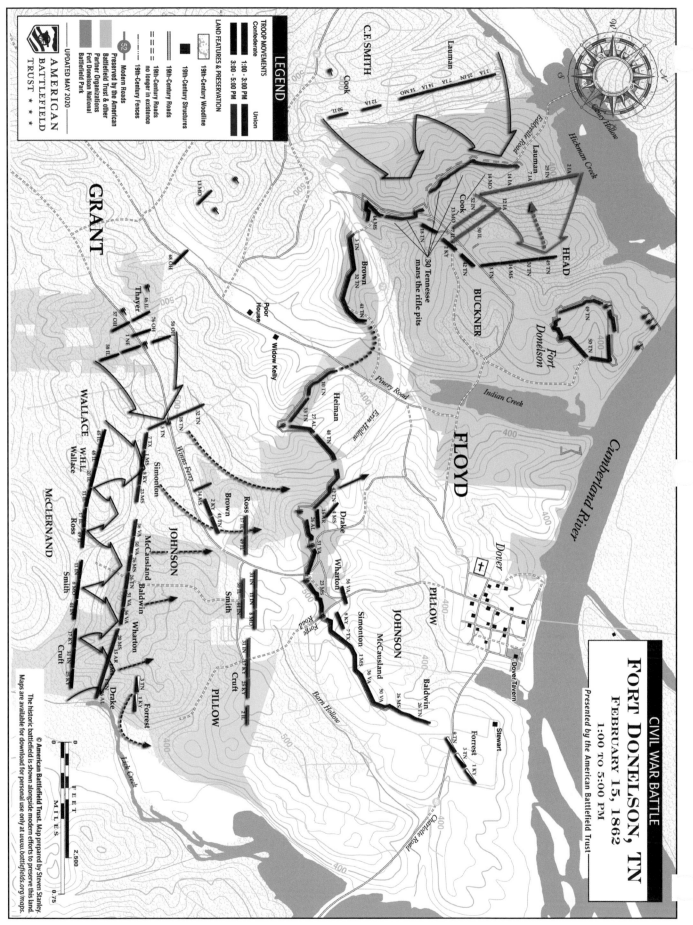

CIVIL WAR BATTLE

FORT DONELSON, TN

FEBRUARY 15, 1862
1:00 TO 5:00 PM
Presented by the American Battlefield Trust

LEGEND

TROOP MOVEMENTS
Confederate
Union

1:00 - 3:00 PM
3:00 - 5:00 PM

LAND FEATURES & PRESERVATION
19th-Century Woodline

19th-Century Structures

19th-Century Roads
19th-Century Roads
no longer in existence

19th-Century Fences

Modern Roads

Preserved by the American
Battlefield Trust & other
Partner Organizations
Fort Donelson National
Battlefield Park

AMERICAN BATTLEFIELD TRUST ★ ★ ★
UPDATED MAY 2020

© American Battlefield Trust. Map prepared by Steven Stanley.
The historic battlefield is shown alongside modern efforts to preserve this land.
Maps are available for download for personal use only at www.battlefields.org/maps.

FEET
0   2,500

MILES
0   0.75

30 Tennesse
mans the rifle pits

BATTLE *of* SHILOH

APRIL 6-7, 1862

FOLLOWING THE FALL OF FORTS HENRY AND DONELSON, Albert S. Johnston was compelled to withdraw from Kentucky, and leave much of western and middle Tennessee to the Federals. Major General Don Carlos Buell and his Army of the Ohio sliced into Middle Tennessee, capturing Nashville on February 25—the first Confederate state capital to fall—while Grant's Army of the Tennessee drove south toward Mississippi. Federal armies severed Confederate railroads, preventing reinforcements between the rebel armies in Virginia and those in the west, effectively splitting the Confederacy in two.

Johnston marshalled his forces at Corinth, Mississippi, a major railroad junction where the east-west rail lines met. Meantime, Grant prepared his army for its own offensive and camped at Pittsburg Landing 22 miles north of Corinth, where it spent time drilling recruits and awaiting the arrival of Buell's army.

Johnston planned to smash Grant's army at Pittsburg Landing before Buell could join him. Johnston placed his troops in motion on April 3, but heavy rains delayed his attack. By nightfall on April 5, his army was deployed for battle only four miles southwest of Pittsburg Landing.

At daybreak on Sunday, April 6, three corps of Confederate infantry stormed out of the woods and swept into the southernmost Federal camps. Most of the men were unprepared for the onslaught. Brigadier General William T. Sherman, the senior division commander at Pittsburg Landing had dismissed reports warning of a Confederates advance. Soon, the nearby divisions of generals McClernand, Benjamin Prentiss, and Stephen Hurlbut were hard pressed by the rebel attack. Intense fighting swirled around Shiloh Church as the Confederates swept Sherman's line from that area.

Near the center of the Union line was a thick grove of oak trees and dense underbrush bordered by a farm lane. During the morning, this was the scene of the most intense fighting of the battle. For six hours, Confederate brigades charged into Union defenders. Confederate attackers labeled the position "a hornets' nest." On the northwest edge of the field, Rebel division commander Brig. Gen. Daniel Ruggles assembled 62 artillery pieces to blast the Union line barely 400 yards away. After multiple attacks, the Confederates surrounded the position and forced nearly 2,300 Yankees to surrender, including Prentiss.

Around 2:30 p.m., while leading an attack on the left end of the Hornets' Nest line, Johnston was shot behind the right knee as he rode ahead of his troops. The bullet severed an artery, and Johnston was dead within minutes, and his second-in-command, Gen. P.G.T. Beauregard, took charge, calling a halt to the assaults.

On the night of April 5, the first units of Buell's army arrived. Grant ordered the establishment of a new defensive line bolstered with more than 50 pieces of heavy artillery. Undaunted by the day's events, Grant formed plans to go on the offensive. Sherman remarked, "Well, Grant, we've had the devil's own day, haven't we?" Grant, unmoved, drew from his cigar and proclaimed, "Yes. Lick em tomorrow, though."

Grant attacked at 6:00 a.m. on April 7. Beauregard immediately ordered a counterattack. Though his force was initially successful, Union resistance stiffened, and the Confederates were compelled to fall back. Around 3:00 p.m., Beauregard broke contact with the Yankees and retreated toward Corinth.

The Confederate defeat at Shiloh ended any hopes of blocking the Union advance into Mississippi, and the Federals set their sights on the railroad crossroads of Corinth.

✻ ✻ PRESERVATION ✻ ✻

To date, the **American Battlefield Trust** has saved **1,400 acres** at Shiloh Battlefield.

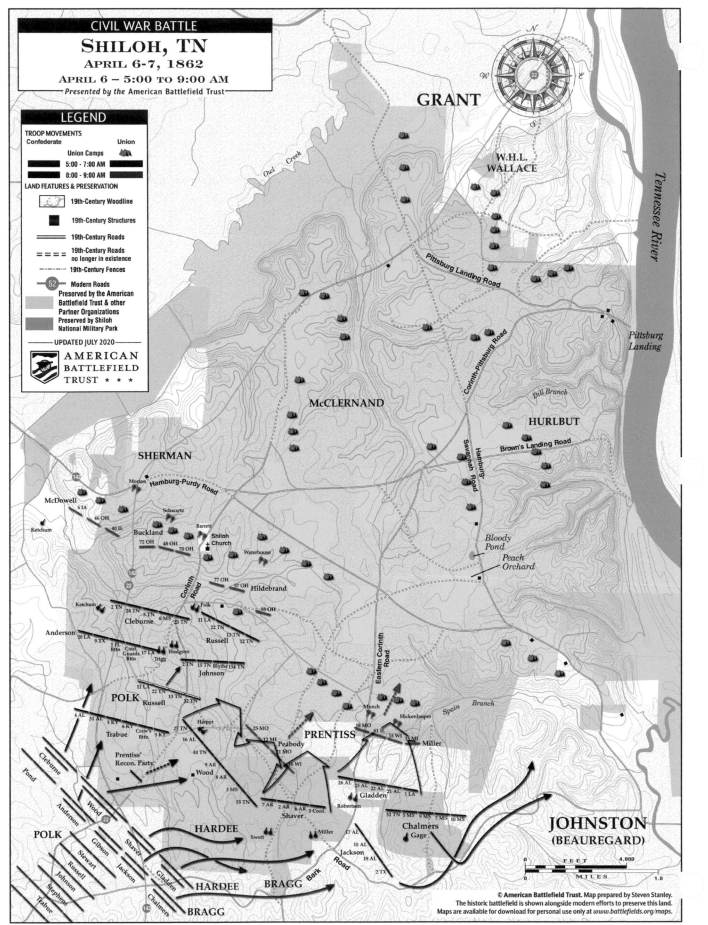

CIVIL WAR BATTLE
SHILOH, TN
APRIL 6-7, 1862
APRIL 6 – 5:00 TO 9:00 AM
Presented by the American Battlefield Trust

LEGEND

TROOP MOVEMENTS
Confederate   Union
           Union Camps
5:00 - 7:00 AM
8:00 - 9:00 AM

LAND FEATURES & PRESERVATION
19th-Century Woodline
19th-Century Structures
19th-Century Roads
19th-Century Roads no longer in existence
19th-Century Fences
52 Modern Roads
Preserved by the American Battlefield Trust & other Partner Organizations
Preserved by Shiloh National Military Park

— UPDATED JULY 2020 —

AMERICAN BATTLEFIELD TRUST ★ ★ ★

GRANT

W.H.L. WALLACE

Tennessee River

Owl Creek

Pittsburg Landing Road

Corinth-Pittsburg Road

Pittsburg Landing

McCLERNAND

Dill Branch

HURLBUT

Brown's Landing Road

Hamburg-Savannah Road

SHERMAN

Hamburg-Purdy Road

Morton

McDowell
6 IA
46 OH
Ketchum
40 IL

Schwartz
Barrett
Buckland
72 OH   48 OH
70 OH
Shiloh Church
Waterhouse

Bloody Pond

Peach Orchard

77 OH   57 OH   Hildebrand

Corinth Road

Ketchum
2 TN   24 TN
5 TN   6 MS
Cleburne   23 TN
Anderson   20 LA   9 TX   1 FL   Conf.
Bttn   Guards
Bttn   17 LA
Trigg   Hodgson

Polk
11 LA
53 OH
Russell
13 TN
12 TN

Eastern Corinth Road

Spain Branch

2 TN   15 TN Blythe 154 TN
Johnson

POLK
11 LA   22 TN   13 TN
Russell   13 TN
12 TN

4 AL   31 AL   3 KY
Trabue   5 KY

Harper   25 MO
27 TN
16 AL   12 MI   Peabody
44 TN   21 MO
9 AR   16 WI
Wood   8 AR

Munch   Hickenlooper
18 MO   61 IL
18 WI   12 MI
Miller

PRENTISS

Prentiss' Recon. Party

3 MS
55 TN   7 AR   2 AR   6 AR
Shaver   3 Conf.
Robertson

26 AL   25 AL   22 AL   21 AL   1 LA
Gladden

52 TN   5 MS   9 MS   7 MS   10 MS

POLK

Cleburne
Pond
Anderson
Wood
Gibson
Stewart
Shaver
Russell
Jackson
Johnson
Gladden
Stephens
Trabue
Chalmers

HARDEE
Swett   Miller

17 AL
18 AL
Jackson   19 AL
Bark Road
2 TX

Chalmers
Gage

JOHNSTON
(BEAUREGARD)

HARDEE   BRAGG

BRAGG

0   FEET   4,000
0   MILES   1.0

© American Battlefield Trust. Map prepared by Steven Stanley.
The historic battlefield is shown alongside modern efforts to preserve this land.
Maps are available for download for personal use only at *www.battlefields.org/maps*.

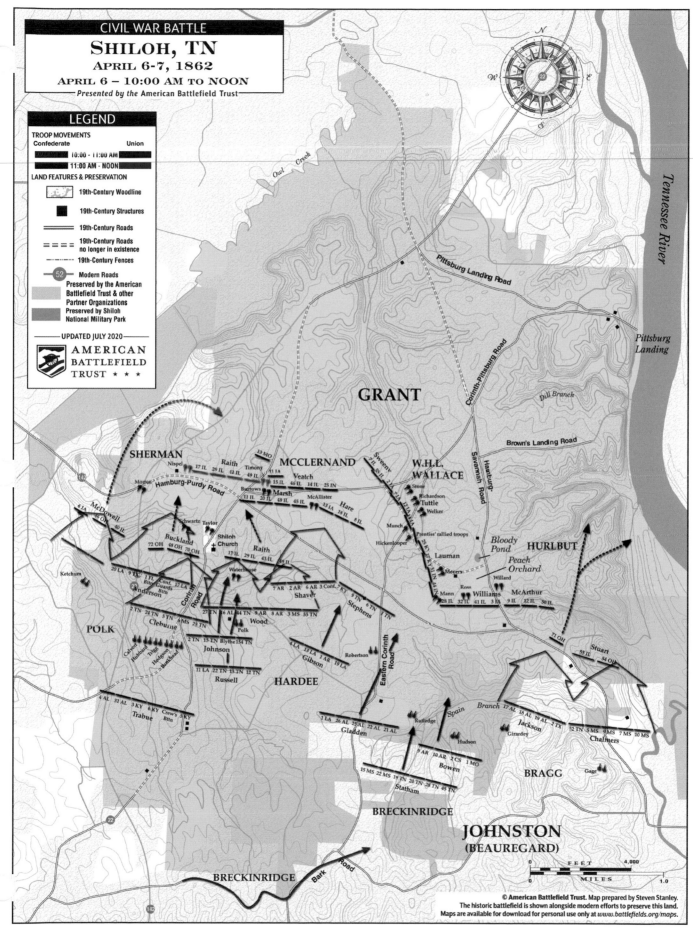

CIVIL WAR BATTLE

SHILOH, TN
APRIL 6-7, 1862
APRIL 6 – 10:00 AM TO NOON
Presented by the American Battlefield Trust

LEGEND

TROOP MOVEMENTS
Confederate   Union
10:00 – 11:00 AM
11:00 AM - NOON

LAND FEATURES & PRESERVATION

19th-Century Woodline

19th-Century Structures

19th-Century Roads

19th-Century Roads no longer in existence

19th-Century Fences

52   Modern Roads

Preserved by the American Battlefield Trust & other Partner Organizations

Preserved by Shiloh National Military Park

— UPDATED JULY 2020 —

AMERICAN
BATTLEFIELD
TRUST ★ ★ ★

Owl Creek

Pittsburg Landing Road

Tennessee River

Corinth-Pittsburg Road

GRANT

Dill Branch

Brown's Landing Road

Pittsburg Landing

Hamburg-Savannah Road

SHERMAN

Nispel   17 IL   Raith   13 MO

Morgas   29 IL   13 IL   Timony

Hamburg-Purdy Road   49 IL

McCLERNAND

Veatch   46 IL   14 IL   25 IN

15 IL

Sweeny   2 IL   8 IL

W.H.L. WALLACE

Stone   7 IL   9 IL   12 IL   14 IL

Burrows   **Marsh**

McDowell   6 IA   40 IL

11 IL   20 IL   48 IL   45 IL

McAllister   **Hare**   13 IA   18 IL   8 IL

Richardson   **Tuttle**

Welker

Munch   Prentiss' rallied troops

Hickenlooper   25 IA   3 IA   31 IN

Buckland   Schwartz   Taylor

72 OH   48 OH   70 OH

Shiloh Church

Raith

17 IL   29 IL   43 IL   49 IL

Waterhouse

Ketchum

20 LA   9 TX   1 FL   Conf.   17 LA

Bttn. Guards   Bttn.

Anderson

2 TN   24 TN   5 TN   23 TN

Clebume

4 MS

POLK

Lauman

Bloody Pond

Peach Orchard

HURLBUT

Meyers

Mann   Ross   **Williams**   **McArthur**

28 IL   32 IL   41 IL   3 IA   9 IL   12 IL   50 IL

Willard

7 AR   2 AR   6 AR   3 Conf.   7 KY   6 TN

Shaver

Stephens

71 OH

27 TN   16 AL   44 TN   9 AR   8 AR   3 MS   55 TN

Wood

Polk

2 TN   15 TN   Blythe   154 TN

Johnson

55 IL   54 OH

Stuart

Calvert   Hubbard   Trigg   Jackson   Bankhead

11 LA   22 TN   13 TN   12 TN

Russell

4 LA   13 LA   1 AR   19 LA

Gibson

Robertson

Eastern Corinth Road

HARDEE

4 AL   31 AL   3 KY   6 KY   5 KY

Crew's Bttn

Trabue

Branch   17 AL   16 AL   19 AL   2 TX

Jackson

1 LA   26 AL   25 AL   22 AL   21 AL

Spain

Rutledge

Girardey

52 TN   5 MS   9 MS   7 MS   10 MS

Chalmers

Gladden

9 AR   10 AR   2 CS   1 MO

Hudson

Bowen

Gage

15 MS   22 MS   19 TN   20 TN   28 TN   45 TN

Statham

BRAGG

BRECKINRIDGE

JOHNSTON
(BEAUREGARD)

Bark Road

BRECKINRIDGE

FEET   0   4,000

MILES   0   1.0

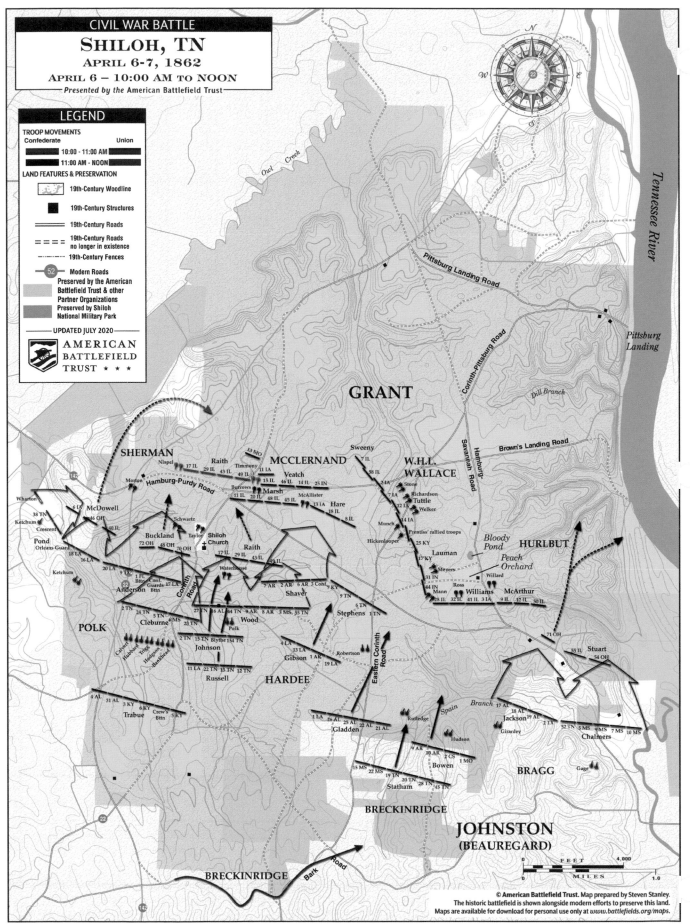

CIVIL WAR BATTLE

SHILOH, TN
APRIL 6-7, 1862
APRIL 6 – 10:00 AM TO NOON
Presented by the American Battlefield Trust

LEGEND

TROOP MOVEMENTS
Confederate   Union

10:00 - 11:00 AM
11:00 AM - NOON

LAND FEATURES & PRESERVATION

19th-Century Woodline

19th-Century Structures

19th-Century Roads

19th-Century Roads no longer in existence

19th-Century Fences

52 Modern Roads

Preserved by the American Battlefield Trust & other Partner Organizations

Preserved by Shiloh National Military Park

— UPDATED JULY 2020 —

AMERICAN BATTLEFIELD TRUST ★ ★ ★

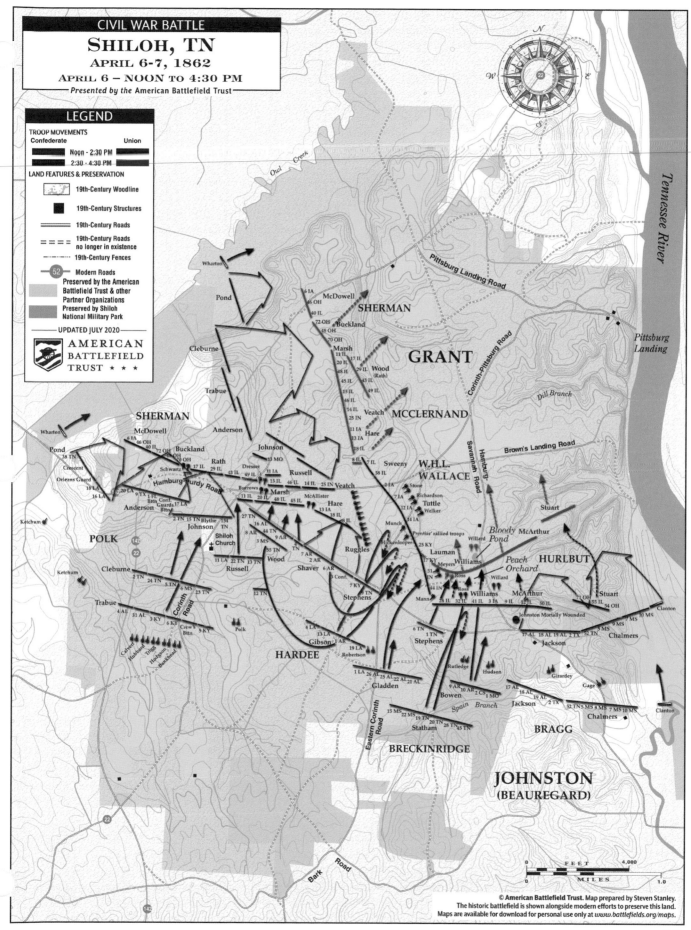

CIVIL WAR BATTLE
SHILOH, TN
APRIL 6-7, 1862
APRIL 6 – NOON TO 4:30 PM
Presented by the American Battlefield Trust

LEGEND

TROOP MOVEMENTS

Confederate	Union
Noon - 2:30 PM	
2:30 - 4:30 PM	

LAND FEATURES & PRESERVATION

- 19th-Century Woodline
- 19th-Century Structures
- 19th-Century Roads
- 19th-Century Roads no longer in existence
- 19th-Century Fences
- 52 Modern Roads
- Preserved by the American Battlefield Trust & other Partner Organizations
- Preserved by Shiloh National Military Park

— UPDATED JULY 2020 —

AMERICAN BATTLEFIELD TRUST ★ ★ ★

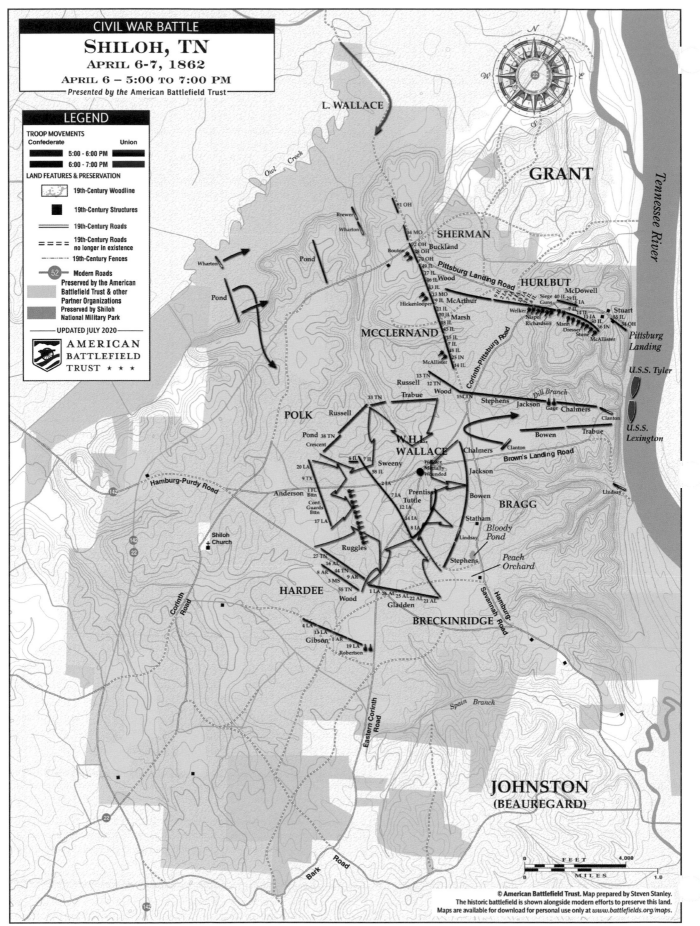

CIVIL WAR BATTLE
SHILOH, TN
APRIL 6-7, 1862
APRIL 6 – 5:00 TO 7:00 PM
Presented by the American Battlefield Trust

LEGEND

TROOP MOVEMENTS
Confederate   Union
5:00 - 6:00 PM
6:00 - 7:00 PM

LAND FEATURES & PRESERVATION

19th-Century Woodline

19th-Century Structures

19th-Century Roads

19th-Century Roads no longer in existence

19th-Century Fences

52 Modern Roads

Preserved by the American Battlefield Trust & other Partner Organizations

Preserved by Shiloh National Military Park

UPDATED JULY 2020

AMERICAN BATTLEFIELD TRUST ★ ★ ★

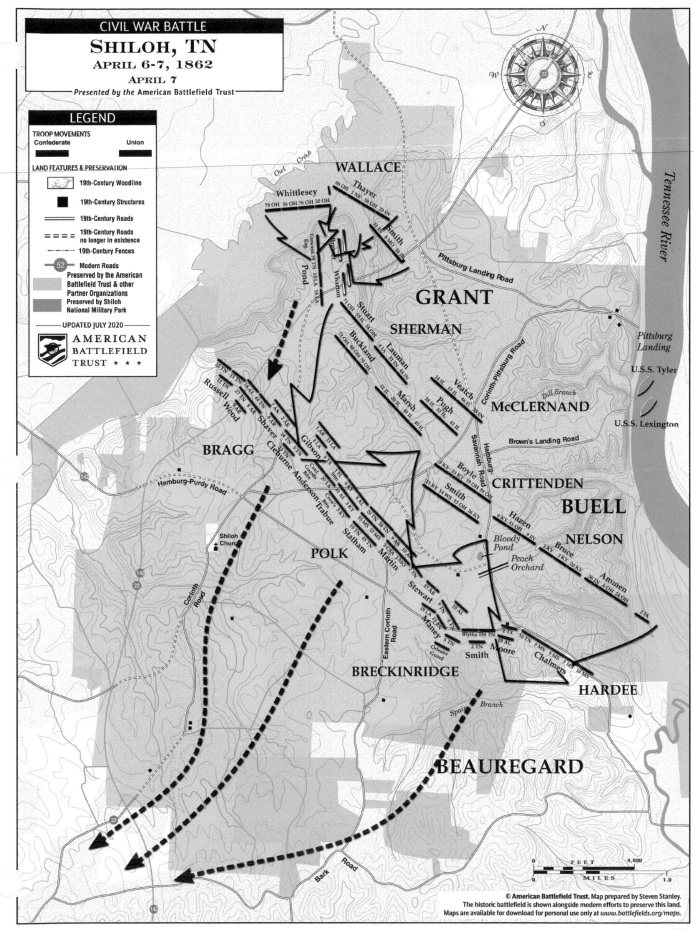

CIVIL WAR BATTLE
SHILOH, TN
APRIL 6-7, 1862
APRIL 7
Presented by the American Battlefield Trust

LEGEND

TROOP MOVEMENTS
Confederate   Union

LAND FEATURES & PRESERVATION

19th-Century Woodline

19th-Century Structures

19th-Century Roads

19th-Century Roads
no longer in existence

19th-Century Fences

52   Modern Roads

Preserved by the American
Battlefield Trust & other
Partner Organizations

Preserved by Shiloh
National Military Park

UPDATED JULY 2020

AMERICAN
BATTLEFIELD
TRUST ★ ★ ★

Tennessee River

Owl Creek

WALLACE

Whittlesey   Thayer
78 OH 56 OH 76 OH 20 OH   6th OH 1 NE 58 OH 23 IN
Smith
9 IN 8 MO 2 IN

Pittsburg Landing Road

GRANT

SHERMAN

Stuart
71 OH 55 IL 54 OH
Lauman
Buckland   8 IL 31 IN 44 IN
72 OH 48 OH 70 OH
Marsh
11 IL 20 IL 45 IL
Veatch   14 IL 15 IL 46 IL
Pugh   25 IL 32 IL 41 IL

McCLERNAND

Dill Branch

Pittsburg
Landing

U.S.S. Tyler

U.S.S. Lexington

Brown's Landing Road

Russell
Wood   21 TN 13 TN 16 AL 44 TN
12 TN 2 AR
9 AS 2 AR
Shaver   6 TN 5 TN
Gibson   1 AR 11 LA
BRAGG   9 TX 1 AR
Cleburne Anderson Trabue
Confed
Guards   20 LA 4 TN Stanford
Crews 5 KY
Statham   4 AL 1 KY
25 MS 22 MS 9 AR
79 TN 45 TN 3 MS 1 MO
Martin   20 TN 26 TN 9 AR

Hamburg-Purdy Road

Shiloh
Church

POLK

142

22

Corinth
Road

Savannah Road

Hamburg

Boyle
9 KY 23 KY 19 IN

CRITTENDEN

BUELL

Smith
11 KY 14 WS 13 OH 26 KY

Hazen
6 KY 41 OH 9 IN   NELSON

Bloody
Pond   Bruce
1 KY 2 KY 20 KY

Peach
Orchard   Ammen
36 IN 6 OH 24 OH

21 IL

Stewart   R AR
11 LA 9 TN 25 AL

Maney 5 TN
19 AL

Eastern Corinth
Road

Blythe 154 TN 2 TX 32 TN 5 MS 5 MS
Orleans
Guard   2 IN   Moore Chalmers 2 MS 10 MS
Smith

BRECKINRIDGE

HARDEE

Spain Branch

BEAUREGARD

Bark Road

142

FEET
0   4,000
MILES
0   1.0

© **American Battlefield Trust**. Map prepared by Steven Stanley.
The historic battlefield is shown alongside modern efforts to preserve this land.
Maps are available for download for personal use only at *www.battlefields.org/maps*.

SECOND BATTLE *of* CORINTH

OCTOBER 4, 1862

IN THE WAKE OF SHILOH, UNION ARMIES SCORED VICTORIES in the Western Theater at a rapid rate. Major General John Pope made a name for himself with his success at Island Number 10 on April 8. The siege of Fort Pulaski resulted in Union victory on April 11. New Orleans, the largest city in the south, surrendered to the Federals on April 28. The city of Memphis fell to Federals on June 6. And in the midst of these victories, Maj. Gen. Henry W. Halleck captured the "the vertebrae of the Confederacy", the vital railroad crossing of Corinth, Mississippi, where the east-west Memphis & Charleston Railroad met the north-south Mobile & Ohio. From April 29-May 30, Halleck besieged Beauregard's Army of Mississippi there, capturing the town on May 30.

The stunning string of victories forced the Union high command to slow its operations during the summer of 1862 in order to shore up their defenses and supply lines. Halleck was promoted to General-in-Chief of all Union armies and transferred to Washington, while Buell dealt with an extended Confederate offensive orchestrated by Gen. Braxton Bragg that carried the two armies into Kentucky. Grant, meanwhile, attempted to destroy two Confederate armies in Mississippi.

After the Union victory at the Battle of Iuka, on September 19, 1862, Maj. Gen. Sterling Price's Confederate Army of the West marched to join Maj. Gen. Earl Van Dorn's Army of West Tennessee. Van Dorn was senior officer and took command of the combined force numbering about 22,000 men. With this combined force, Van Dorn and Price hoped to seize Corinth, sweep into Middle Tennessee, and relieve pressure on Bragg's army in Kentucky.

Since the Siege of Corinth in the spring, Union forces had erected various fortifications, an inner and intermediate line, to protect the town and its vital rail lines. Thus, when Van Dorn and Price targeted Corinth, 23,000 Federals stood poised to meet the Confederate threat. Van Dorn arrived near Corinth at 10:00 a.m. on October 3.

Confederates launched a determined assault on the left of the Federal line, which occupied the outer defenses. A gap opened between two Union brigades that the Confederates exploited around 1:30 p.m. As the Federals fell back, an opportunity presented itself. One Federal division was perfectly situated to attack the left rear of the advancing Confederate line. But a botched order thwarted the Federals.

By evening, Van Dorn was sure that he could finish the Federals off during the next day. This confidence—combined with the heat, fatigue, and water shortages—persuaded him to cancel any further operations that day. Union Maj. Gen. William S. Rosecrans regrouped his men in the fortifications to be ready for the attack to come the next morning. Van Dorn had planned to attack at daybreak, but one of his subordinates, Brig. Gen. Louis Hébert, fell ill, postponing the attack until 9:00 a.m. As the Confederates moved forward, Union artillery swept the field, causing heavy casualties, but the Rebels continued onward. They stormed Battery Powell and closed on Battery Robinett, where desperate hand-to-hand fighting ensued. A few Rebels fought their way into Corinth, but the Federals quickly drove them out. The Federal counterattack continued on, recapturing Battery Powell and forcing Van Dorn into a general retreat.

Rosecrans postponed any pursuit until the next day. As a result, Van Dorn was defeated, but not destroyed. And Bragg was left on his own accord in Kentucky.

✳ ✳ PRESERVATION ✳ ✳

To date, the **American Battlefield Trust** has saved **791 acres** at Corinth Battlefield.

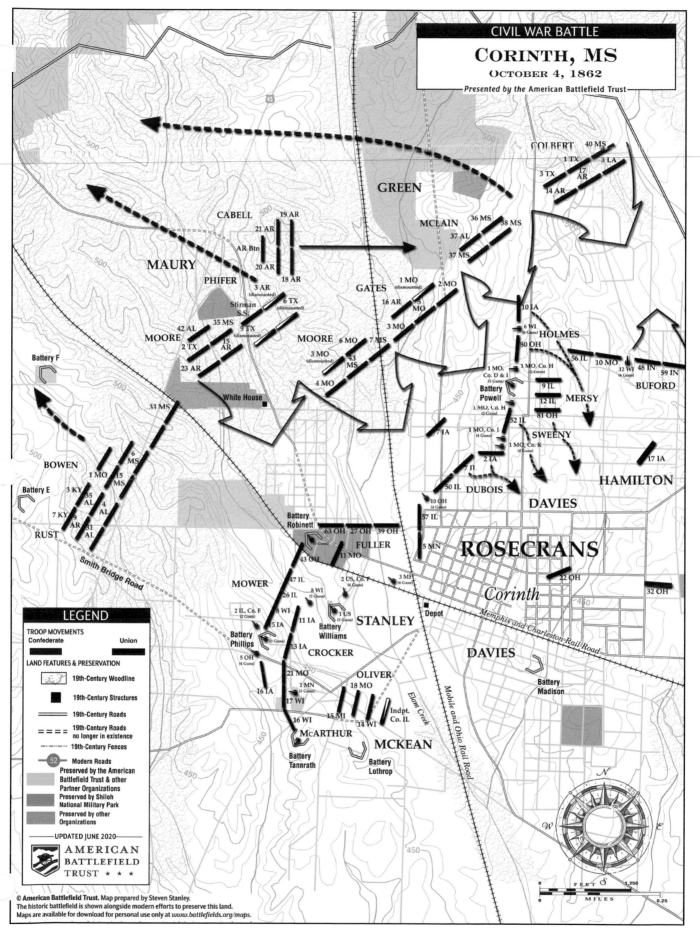

CIVIL WAR BATTLE

CORINTH, MS
OCTOBER 4, 1862

Presented by the American Battlefield Trust

GREEN

COLBERT 40 MS
1 TX 3 LA
3 TX 17 AR
14 AR

CABELL 19 AR
21 AR
AR Btn
20 AR
MAURY 18 AR

MCLAIN 36 MS
37 AL 38 MS
37 MS

PHIFER
3 AR (dismounted)
Stirman S.S.
6 TX (dismounted)
9 TX (dismounted)

GATES
1 MO (dismounted) 2 MO
16 AR 5 MO
3 MO

10 IA
6 WI (6 Guns)
HOLMES

MOORE 42 AL 35 MS
2 TX 15 AR
23 AR

MOORE 6 MO 7 MS
3 MO (dismounted) 33 MS
4 MO

80 OH
56 IL 10 MO
12 WI (6 Guns) 48 IN 59 IN
BUFORD

1 MO, Co. D & I (5 Guns)
1 MO, Co. H (2 Guns)
Battery Powell
1 MO, Co. H (2 Guns)
9 IL
12 IL
81 OH
MERSY

Battery F

White House

33 MS

BOWEN
1 MO 6 MS
15 MS

Battery E
3 KY
35 AL
7 KY 4 AL
9 AR 31 AL
RUST

Smith Bridge Road

52 IL
1 MO, Co. I (4 Guns)
7 IA
2 IA
7 IL
50 IL
10 OH (4 Guns)
57 IL

1 MO, Co. K (4 Guns)
SWEENY

DUBOIS

DAVIES

HAMILTON
17 IA

Battery Robinett
63 OH 27 OH 39 OH
FULLER
43 OH 11 MO

5 MN
ROSECRANS

MOWER
47 IL
26 IL
2 IL, Co. F (2 Guns) 8 WI
15 IA 11 IA
Battery Phillips (3 Guns)
13 IA
CROCKER

8 WI (2 Guns)
2 US, Co. F (6 Guns)
1 US (3 Guns)
Battery Williams
STANLEY

Depot

3 MI (4 Guns)

22 OH
32 OH

Corinth

Memphis and Charleston Rail Road

DAVIES

Battery Madison

5 OH (4 Guns)
21 MO
1 MN (3 Guns)
16 IA
17 WI
16 WI

OLIVER
18 MO

15 MI
14 WI
Indpt. Co. IL

Elam Creek

Mobile and Ohio Rail Road

McARTHUR
Battery Tannrath
MCKEAN
Battery Lothrop

N
W   E
S

FEET 0   1,250
MILES 0   0.25

BATTLE *of* PERRYVILLE

(CHAPLIN HILLS)

OCTOBER 8, 1862

AFTER THE SIEGE OF CORINTH (APRIL 29-MAY 30, 1862), Jefferson Davis replaced Beauregard with Gen. Braxton Bragg as the commander of the Army of Mississippi. In turn, Bragg launched an extended campaign that carried Confederate forces from Tupelo, Mississippi, through Mobile, Alabama, into north Georgia, and into the Union-held border state of Kentucky via Middle Tennessee. Bragg and other southern leaders hoped to gain support for the southern cause and bring the Bluegrass State into the war on the side of the Confederacy. He also hoped to supply his army and to fill its ranks with Kentuckians. A victorious Confederate army in Kentucky would not only complicate the state's neutrality but could threaten Union cities and shipping all along the Ohio River.

At first Bragg coordinated his movements with Maj. Gen. Edmund Kirby Smith. Smith was a proponent of the "Heartland Offensive," but it soon became evident to Bragg that the Floridian had illusions of grandeur and higher command rather than the best interests of the Confederacy in his heart—and the cooperation between the two officers broke down.

As a result of the Confederate incursion into Kentucky, Maj. Gen. Don Carlos Buell and his Union Army of the Ohio broke off their attempts to take Chattanooga, Tennessee, and shadowed Bragg's army. Buell station his army in Louisville, Kentucky, blocking any Confederate move across the Ohio River.

On October 7, Buell's 55,000-man army converged on the small crossroads town of Perryville, Kentucky. Union cavalry first skirmished with Rebel infantry where the Springfield Pike crossed Bull Run Creek. As more gray-clad infantry arrived, the fighting became more general on Peters Hill further west on the turnpike. Movement and fighting on both sides were hampered by the lack of water in the area; Kentucky was in the midst of the worst drought in years, and the small pools of water in the nearly dry creek beds around Perryville drew both armies to the area.

At dawn the next morning, fighting reignited around Peters Hill as the Union division of Brig. Gen. Lovell H. Rousseau advanced and met the Confederate battle line. After noon, Brig. Gen. Benjamin F. Cheatham's Confederate division crossed Doctor's Creek, striking the Union left flank and forcing it to fall back. When more Confederate divisions joined the fray, the Union defenders made a stubborn stand near the Open Knob along the Benton Road and counterattacked Cheatham's brigades, but finally fell back with many regiments completely routed. Although his I Corps, commanded by Maj. Gen. Alexander M. McCook, had been fully committed and fought hard all day, Buell did not know of the happenings on the field. An earlier fall from his horse kept the general immobile throughout October 8. During the day's fight, only minor elements of Buell's other two corps made contact with the enemy. Even so, McCook's left flank, reinforced by two brigades, stabilized its line and the Rebel attacks sputtered to a halt. Major General William J. Hardee's men struck the Union right near Squire Henry Bottom's family farm, but the undulating terrain and well-placed Union artillery slowed his progress.

Late in the afternoon, a single Rebel brigade under Col. Samuel Powel assaulted Brig. Gen. Phillip H. Sheridan's Union division on the Springfield Pike but was repulsed and fell back into Perryville. Although he had won a tactical victory, Bragg, short of men and water, withdrew during the night and, after pausing at Harrodsburg, retreated into eastern Tennessee. The Confederate Heartland Offensive was over, and the Union would control Kentucky for the rest of the war.

✳ ✳ PRESERVATION ✳ ✳

To date, the **American Battlefield Trust** has saved **1,150 acres** at Perryville Battlefield.

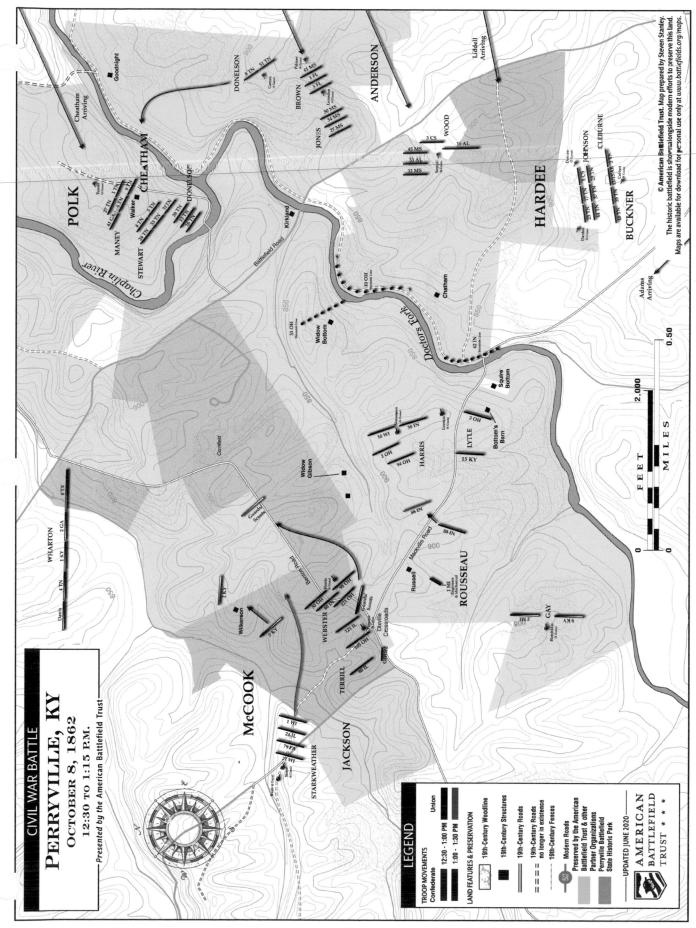

CIVIL WAR BATTLE
PERRYVILLE, KY
OCTOBER 8, 1862
12:30 TO 1:15 P.M.
Presented by the American Battlefield Trust

© American Battlefield Trust. Map prepared by Steven Stanley. The historic battlefield is shown alongside modern efforts to preserve this land. Maps are available for download for personal use only at www.battlefields.org/maps.

LEGEND

TROOP MOVEMENTS
Confederate | Union
12:30 - 1:00 PM
1:00 - 1:30 PM

LAND FEATURES & PRESERVATION
19th-Century Woodline
19th-Century Structures
19th-Century Roads
19th-Century Roads no longer in existence
19th-Century Fences
52 Modern Roads
Preserved by the American Battlefield Trust & other Partner Organizations
Perryville Battlefield State Historic Park

UPDATED JUNE 2020

AMERICAN BATTLEFIELD TRUST ★ ★ ★

FEET 0   2,000
MILES 0   0.50

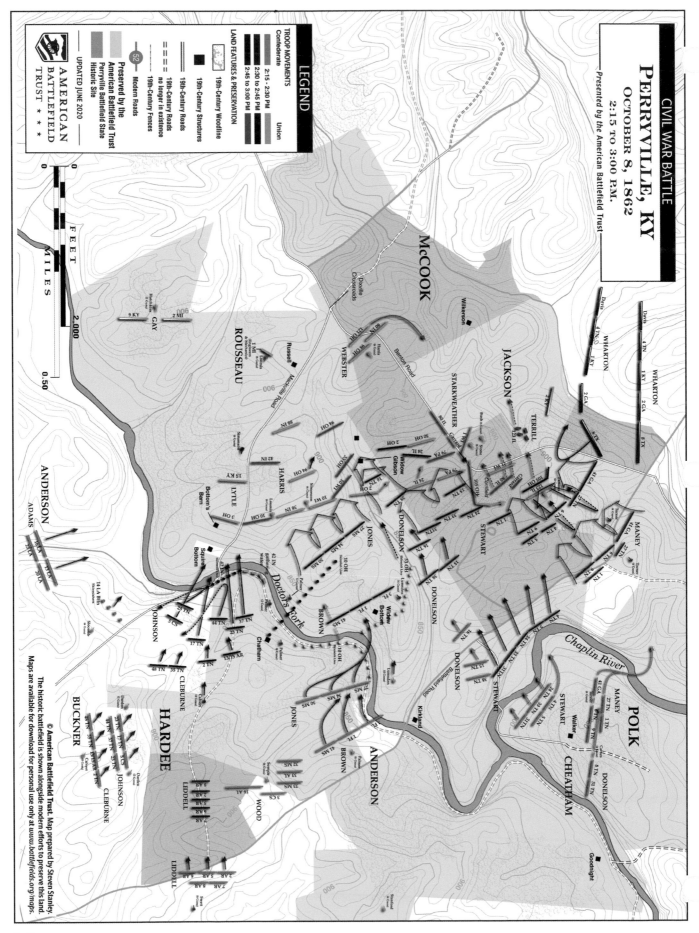

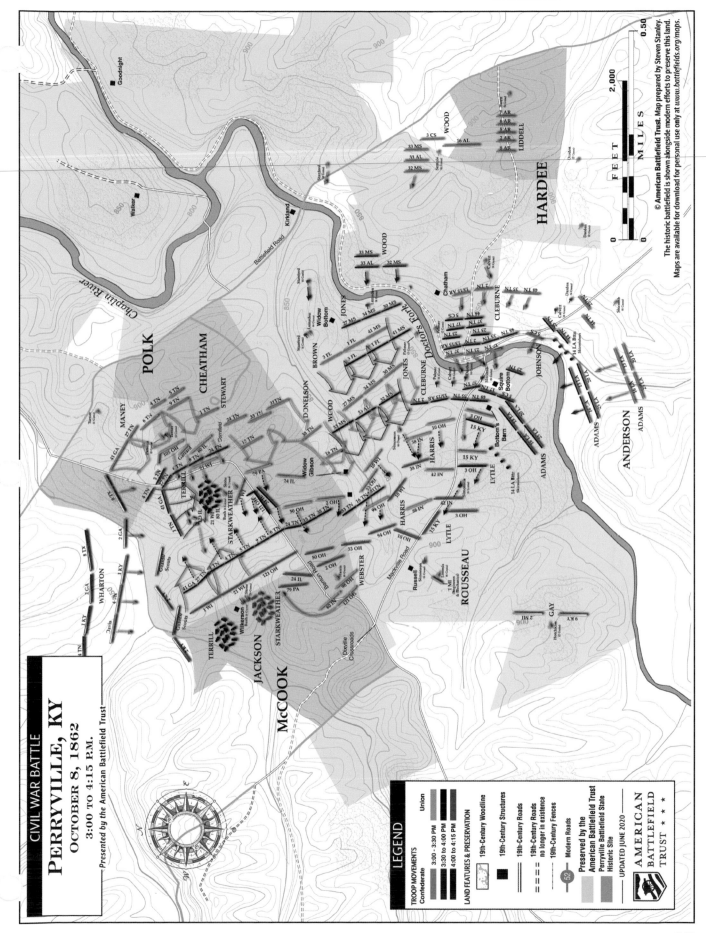

CIVIL WAR BATTLE

PERRYVILLE, KY
OCTOBER 8, 1862
3:00 TO 4:15 P.M.

Presented by the American Battlefield Trust

LEGEND

TROOP MOVEMENTS

Confederate | Union

3:00 – 3:30 PM
3:30 to 4:00 PM
4:00 to 4:15 PM

LAND FEATURES & PRESERVATION

19th-Century Woodline

19th-Century Structures

19th-Century Roads

19th-Century Roads no longer in existence

19th-Century Fences

52 — Modern Roads

Preserved by the American Battlefield Trust

Perryville Battlefield State Historic Site

— UPDATED JUNE 2020

AMERICAN BATTLEFIELD TRUST ★ ★ ★

© American Battlefield Trust. Map prepared by Steven Stanley.

The historic battlefield is shown alongside modern efforts to preserve this land.
Maps are available for download for personal use only at *www.battlefields.org/maps.*

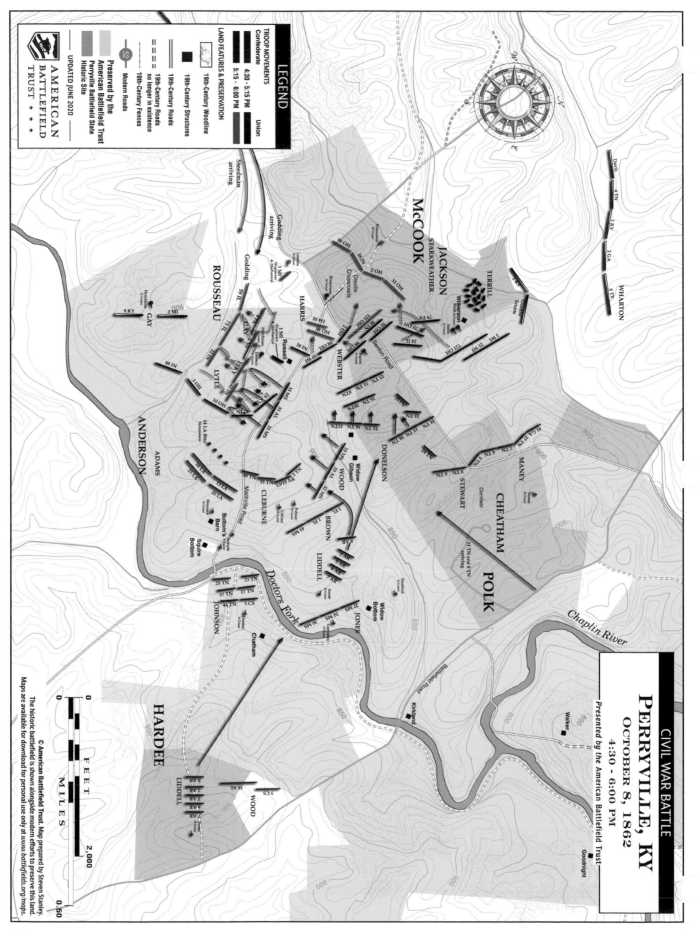

CIVIL WAR BATTLE

PERRYVILLE, KY

OCTOBER 8, 1862
4:30 - 6:00 PM

Presented by the American Battlefield Trust

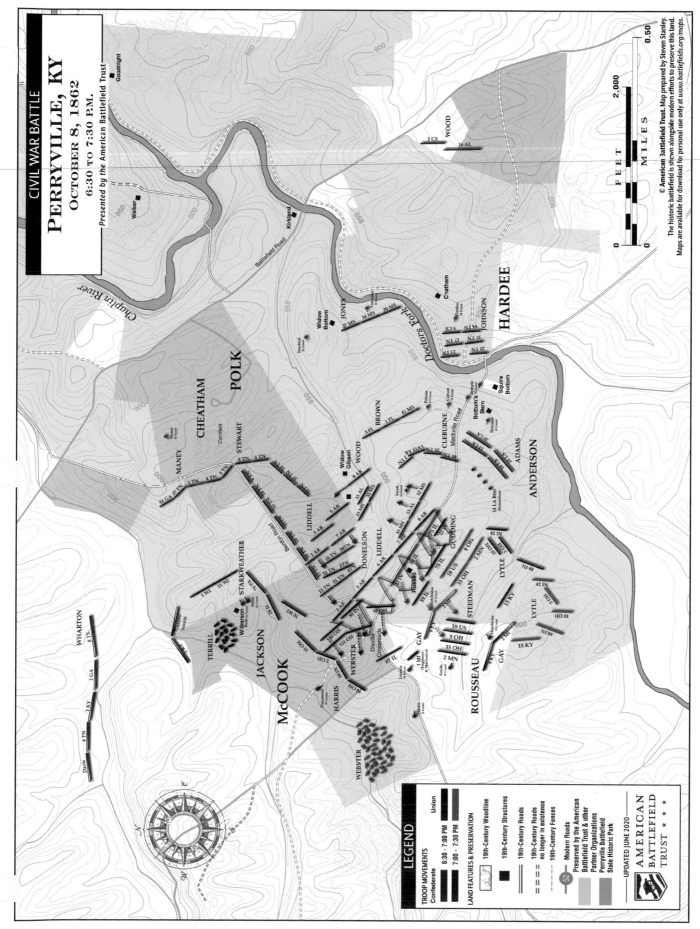

CIVIL WAR BATTLE

PERRYVILLE, KY
OCTOBER 8, 1862
6:30 TO 7:30 P.M.

Presented by the American Battlefield Trust

LEGEND

TROOP MOVEMENTS

Confederate | Union
6:30 - 7:00 PM
7:00 - 7:30 PM

LAND FEATURES & PRESERVATION

19th-Century Woodline
19th-Century Structures
19th-Century Roads
19th-Century Roads no longer in existence
19th-Century Fences
Modern Roads
Preserved by the American Battlefield Trust & other Partner Organizations
Perryville Battlefield State Historic Park

UPDATED JUNE 2020

AMERICAN BATTLEFIELD TRUST ★ ★ ★

© American Battlefield Trust. Map prepared by Steven Stanley.
The historic battlefield is shown alongside modern efforts to preserve this land.
Maps are available for download for personal use only at *www.battlefields.org/maps.*

0   FEET   2,000

0   MILES   0.50

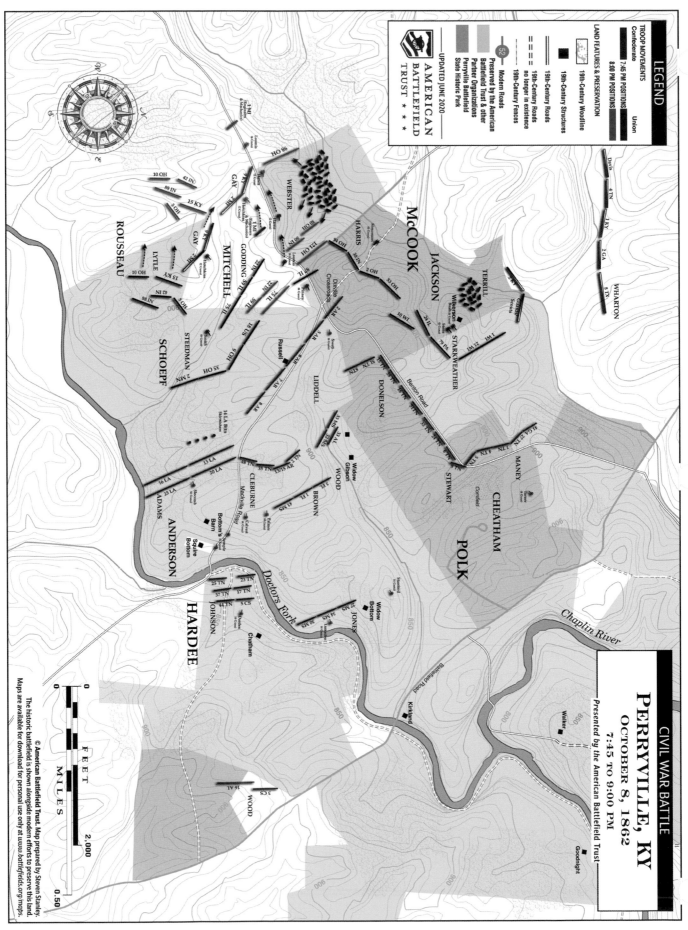

LEGEND

TROOP MOVEMENTS
Confederate
Union

7:45 PM POSITIONS
8:00 PM POSITIONS

LAND FEATURES & PRESERVATION
19th-Century Woodline
19th-Century Structures
19th-Century Roads
19th-Century Roads no longer in existence
19th-Century Fences
Modern Roads
Preserved by the American Battlefield Trust & other Partner Organizations
Perryville Battlefield State Historic Park

UPDATED JUNE 2020

AMERICAN BATTLEFIELD TRUST ★★★

CIVIL WAR BATTLE

PERRYVILLE, KY

OCTOBER 8, 1862
7:45 TO 9:00 PM

Presented by the American Battlefield Trust

0 — FEET — 2,000

0 — MILES — 0.50

© American Battlefield Trust. Map prepared by Steven Stanley.
The historic battlefield is shown alongside modern efforts to preserve this land.
Maps are available for download for personal use only at www.battlefields.org/maps.

BATTLE *of* STONES RIVER

(MURFREESBORO)

DECEMBER 31, 1862 — JANUARY 2, 1863

AN EXTENDED LULL FELL OVER THE WESTERN ARMIES FOLLOWING the Battle of Perryville in the fall of 1862. Although victorious, Buell lacked the initiative to follow up on his victory and was soon relieved of command by Lincoln. Major General William S. Rosecrans assumed command of the Army of the Ohio and reconstituted it as the Army of the Cumberland. On September 22, 1862, Lincoln issued the preliminary Emancipation Proclamation, and the President expected his generals to bring home as many victories as possible by January 1, 1863—when he would officially sign the act—to give this new measure backbone.

The day after Christmas 1862, Rosecrans's Army of the Cumberland departed Nashville with 44,000 men, marching toward Confederate Gen. Braxton Bragg's Army of Tennessee at Murfreesboro, 30 miles to the south. The overly cautious and plodding Rosecrans left some 40,000 men in and around the Tennessee capital to guard his communication and supply routes—nearly evening the odds in favor of Bragg.

The two armies gathered on the banks of Stones River on the evening of December 30 within 700 yards of one another. Rosecrans' army on the northwest side of the river was organized into three wings with three divisions each. Bragg's 35,000 men were arranged into two corps of infantry.

Both commanders formulated a nearly identical battleplan for December 31: strike their opponent's right flank. While a portion of Rosecrans's army would have to cross the river to accomplish this goal, the Confederates faced no such problem, and at 6 a.m., Maj. Gen. William J. Hardee's corps smashed into the Union right flank. The Federals were sent reeling backward, and many Union cannon fell into Confederate hands. The stout resistance of Maj. Gen. George Thomas's wing, the omnipresent Rosecrans, and the failure of Bragg's army to coordinate its attacks saved the Army of the Cumberland from utter destruction.

By the evening of December 31, the Army of the Cumberland was cornered against Stones River, and Bragg crowed to Richmond, "God has granted us a happy New Year." A hiatus on January 1 gave both sides time to shore up their battle lines. Rosecrans shifted men eastward across the river and established a formidable line along a hilltop. Bragg, too, focused on the east side of the river, and near 4 p.m. on January 2, the Confederate leader renewed his efforts to dislodge the Army of the Cumberland. Men of Hardee's corps drove many Federals back across Stones River. The Federal line was once again salvaged, this time due to the courageous efforts of Capt. John C. Mendenhall, who positioned nearly 50 cannon hub-to-hub and blasted away at the Confederate attackers. The artillery, coupled with a Union counterattack, proved too much for Bragg's men.

Braxton Bragg gave up the field on January 3 and withdrew his forces southward to Tullahoma. While Rosecrans held the initiative, his army was so battered from the battle that it would not campaign again for another six months. In the meantime, Rosecrans consolidated his battered army and established a fortified supply base at Murfreesboro, which would serve the Army of the Cumberland later that year in its drive toward Chattanooga.

✳ ✳ PRESERVATION ✳ ✳

To date, the **American Battlefield Trust** has saved **32 acres** at Stones River Battlefield.

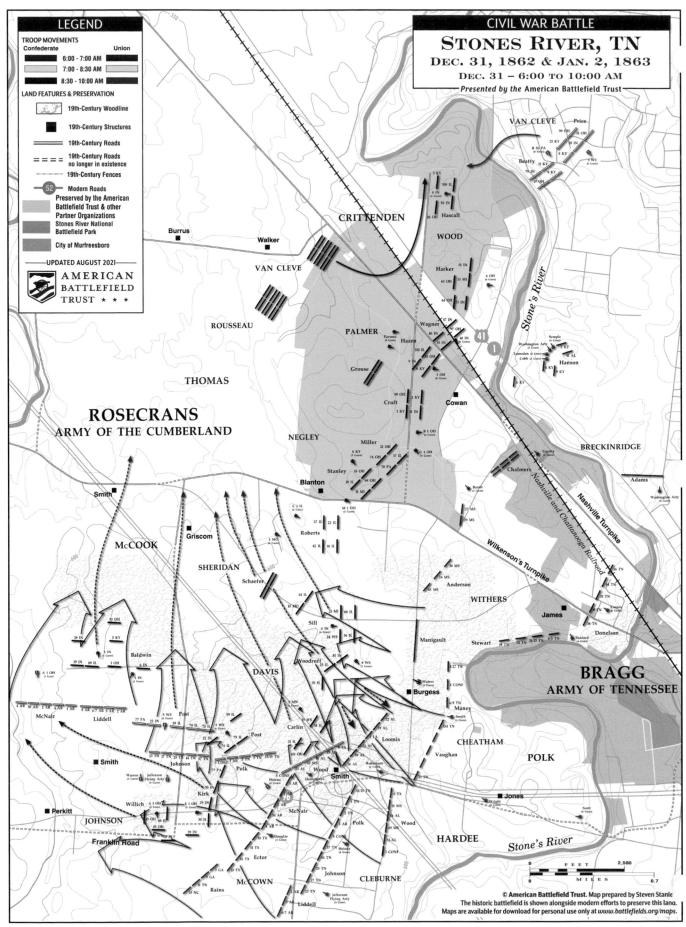

LEGEND

TROOP MOVEMENTS

Confederate	Union
6:00 – 7:00 AM	
7:00 – 8:30 AM	
8:30 – 10:00 AM	

LAND FEATURES & PRESERVATION

- 19th-Century Woodline
- 19th-Century Structures
- 19th-Century Roads
- 19th-Century Roads no longer in existence
- 19th-Century Fences
- 52 Modern Roads
- Preserved by the American Battlefield Trust & other Partner Organizations
- Stones River National Battlefield Park
- City of Murfreesboro

—UPDATED AUGUST 2021—

AMERICAN BATTLEFIELD TRUST ★ ★ ★

CIVIL WAR BATTLE
STONES RIVER, TN
DEC. 31, 1862 & JAN. 2, 1863
DEC. 31 – 6:00 TO 10:00 AM
Presented by the American Battlefield Trust

ROSECRANS
ARMY OF THE CUMBERLAND

BRAGG
ARMY OF TENNESSEE

© **American Battlefield Trust**. Map prepared by Steven Stanle
The historic battlefield is shown alongside modern efforts to preserve this land.
Maps are available for download for personal use only at *www.battlefields.org/maps.*

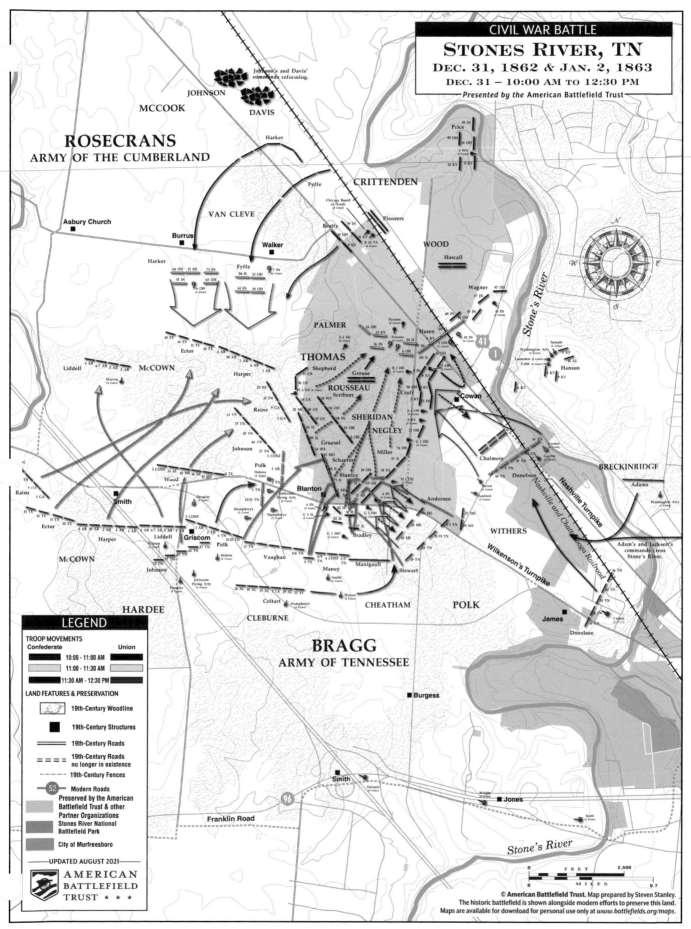

CIVIL WAR BATTLE

STONES RIVER, TN

DEC. 31, 1862 & JAN. 2, 1863

DEC. 31 – 10:00 AM TO 12:30 PM

Presented by the American Battlefield Trust

LEGEND

TROOP MOVEMENTS

Confederate	Union	
		10:00 – 11:00 AM
		11:00 – 11:30 AM
		11:30 AM – 12:30 PM

LAND FEATURES & PRESERVATION

19th-Century Woodline

19th-Century Structures

19th-Century Roads

19th-Century Roads no longer in existence

19th-Century Fences

52 Modern Roads

Preserved by the American Battlefield Trust & other Partner Organizations

Stones River National Battlefield Park

City of Murfreesboro

UPDATED AUGUST 2021

AMERICAN BATTLEFIELD TRUST ★ ★ ★

© American Battlefield Trust. Map prepared by Steven Stanley.
The historic battlefield is shown alongside modern efforts to preserve this land.
Maps are available for download for personal use only at *www.battlefields.org/maps*.

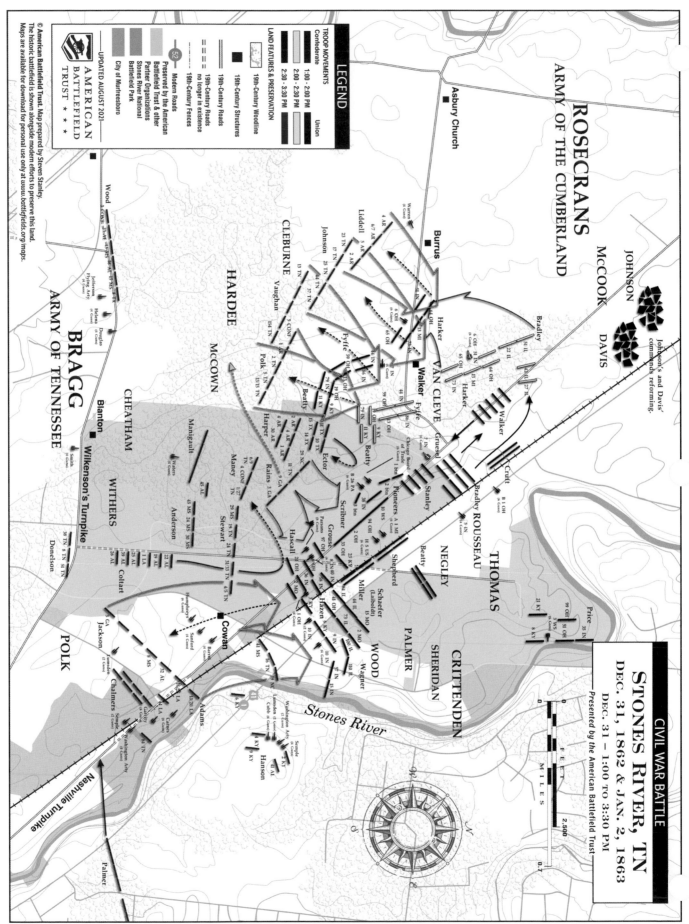

CIVIL WAR BATTLE

STONES RIVER, TN

DEC. 31, 1862 & JAN. 2, 1863

DEC. 31 – 1:00 TO 3:30 PM

Presented by the American Battlefield Trust

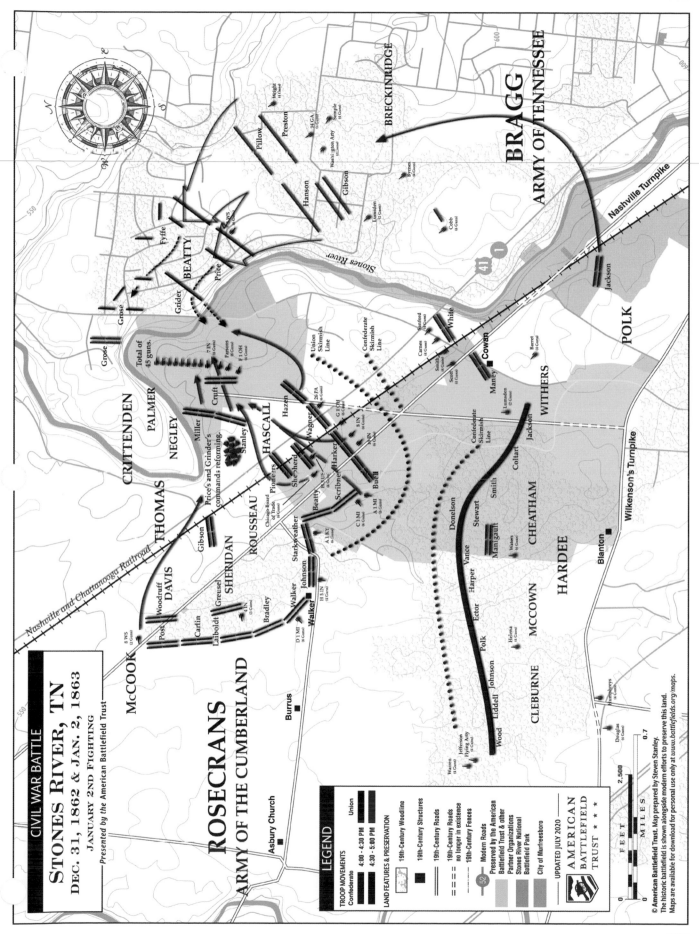

STONES RIVER, TN

CIVIL WAR BATTLE

DEC. 31, 1862 & JAN. 2, 1863

JANUARY 2ND FIGHTING

Presented by the American Battlefield Trust

LEGEND

TROOP MOVEMENTS

	Confederate	Union
4:00 - 4:30 PM		
4:30 - 5:00 PM		

LAND FEATURES & PRESERVATION

19th-Century Woodline

19th-Century Structures

19th-Century Roads

19th-Century Roads no longer in existence

19th-Century Fences

Modern Roads

Preserved by the American Battlefield Trust & other Partner Organizations

Stones River National Battlefield Park

City of Murfreesboro

UPDATED JULY 2020

AMERICAN BATTLEFIELD TRUST ★ ★ ★

FEET   0   2,500

MILES   0   0.7

© American Battlefield Trust. Map prepared by Steven Stanley.
The historic battlefield is shown alongside modern efforts to preserve this land.
Maps are available for download for personal use only at www.battlefields.org/maps.

BATTLE *of* PORT GIBSON

MAY 1, 1863

OBTAINING THE FULL CONTROL OF THE MISSISSIPPI RIVER was an early and vital war aim for the Federals. The Mississippi served as a highway to move men and materials from places as far as way as Pittsburgh to New Orleans and the Gulf of Mexico, and in early 1863, only two Confederate strong points stood between the Federals and dominance of the mighty river.

The first strong point on the Mississippi was the "Gibraltar of the Confederacy," Vicksburg. Situated atop dominate bluffs overlooking a sweeping bend of the river, Vicksburg was a tough nut to crack. Time and again Ulysses S. Grant tried and failed to approach the bastion city. A late 1862 advance south from Tennessee ended with Confederates severing Grant's supply lines. William T. Sherman attempted to storm the city but came up short at Chickasaw Bayou. Canals were dug and abandoned. Levees were blown up to create flood plains only to carry the boats too high in the water, literally among the branches of the trees. Nothing seemed to work. In late April, Grant finally struck gold. Utilizing some diversions, he marched his army down the western side of the river while Rear Adm. David Dixon Porter ran his flotilla of gunboats and transports past the Confederate guns of Vicksburg. The two forces reunited some 30 miles south of the city, and on April 29-30, Porter's sailors were transporting Grant's army across the river into Bruinsburg, Mississippi—unopposed.

Now on the Vicksburg side of the river, Grant's men marched toward their first objective, Port Gibson, situated roughly ten miles east of Bruinsburg, which commanded the local road network. The road over which the blue soldiers now marched led to the Shaifer House, roughly 1.5 miles from Port Gibson.

Confederate Brig. Gen. Martin E. Green was inspecting his picket line at the Shaifer House as the Confederate pickets spotted movement in the distance. The stillness of the night was shattered as a volley of musketry. Fighting in the scattered fields and forest around the Shaifer House intensified as more Union regiments and batteries came into action. By 3:00 a.m., the fighting petered out.

At dawn the battle was renewed as Maj. Gen. John A. McClernand threw most of his XIII Corps toward Green's thin line. Green called for reinforcements from Brig. Gen. Edward Tracy, who anchored the Confederate right flank roughly a mile and half to the northwest. Tracy dispatched infantry and artillery to Green's assistance minutes before cannons began to pound his own line, signaling the advance of a new Union column under Brig. Gen. Peter Osterhaus. Soon after, Tracy was killed by a sniper's bullet.

Despite the reinforcements, Green was still heavily outnumbered, and at around 10:00 a.m., his line collapsed. As Green's men scrambled to the rear, Brig. Gen. John Bowen, in overall Confederate command on the field, worked feverishly to restore his line. The brigades of Brig. Gen. William Baldwin, just arriving from Vicksburg, and Col. Francis Cockrell's from Grand Gulf, were placed into position astride the road at White and Irwin's Branches of Willow Creek, a mile and a half east of Magnolia Church.

The Confederate right did not last long. The Union troops pushed forward all along the line, and fierce fighting continued throughout the afternoon. A desperate Confederate counterattack by Cockrell's Missourians was repulsed, and Bowen ordered a retreat. The remaining garrison at Grand Gulf was evacuated the next day. The Battle of Port Gibson was a resounding Union victory that secured Grant's beachhead east of the Mississippi River and cleared the way to the Southern Railroad supplying Vicksburg.

✳ ✳ PRESERVATION ✳ ✳

To date, the **American Battlefield Trust** has saved **645 acres** at Port Gibson Battlefield.

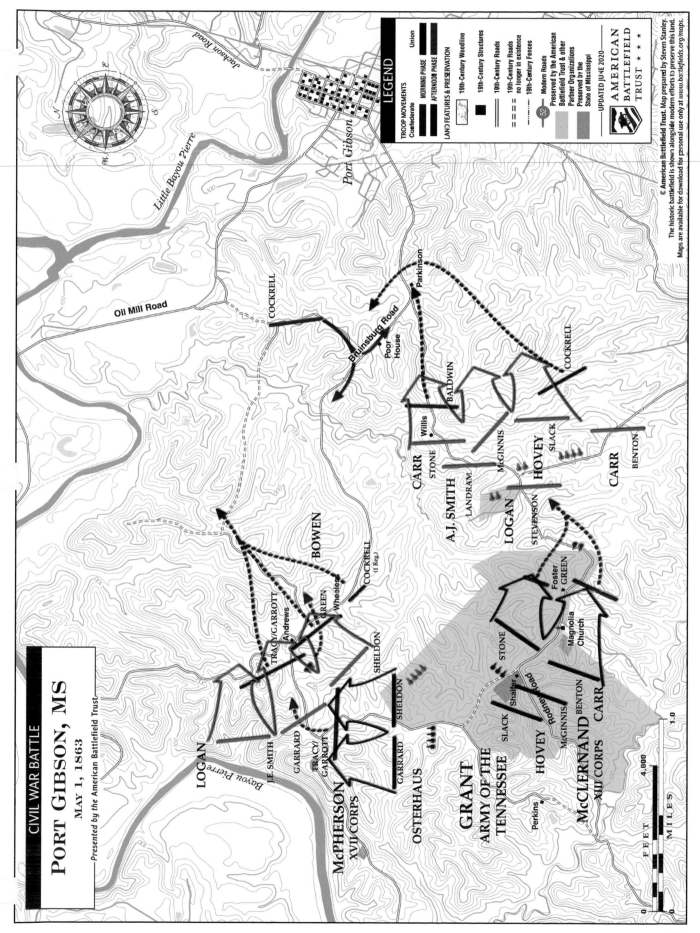

CIVIL WAR BATTLE

PORT GIBSON, MS

MAY 1, 1863

Presented by the American Battlefield Trust

LEGEND

TROOP MOVEMENTS
Confederate   Union
MORNING PHASE
AFTERNOON PHASE

LAND FEATURES & PRESERVATION
19th-Century Woodline
19th-Century Structures
19th-Century Roads
19th-Century Roads no longer in existence
19th-Century Fences
52 Modern Roads
Preserved by the American Battlefield Trust & other Partner Organizations
Preserved by the State of Mississippi

UPDATED JUNE 2020

AMERICAN BATTLEFIELD TRUST ★ ★ ★

© American Battlefield Trust. Map prepared by Steven Stanley.
The historic battlefield is shown alongside modern efforts to preserve this land.
Maps are available for download for personal use only at www.battlefields.org/maps.

Jackson Road

Little Bayou Pierre

Port Gibson

Oil Mill Road

COCKRELL

Bruinsburg Road

Poor House

Parkinson

BALDWIN

COCKRELL

Willis

CARR

STONE

A.J. SMITH

LANDRAM

McGINNIS

LOGAN

STEVENSON

HOVEY

SLACK

CARR

BENTON

BOWEN

COCKRELL (1 Reg.)

Wheeless

GREEN

Andrews

TRACY/GARROTT

Foster

GREEN

Magnolia Church

STONE

Shaifer

Rodney Road

SLACK

McGINNIS

HOVEY

BENTON

CARR

McCLERNAND
XIII CORPS

GRANT
ARMY OF THE TENNESSEE

Perkins

OSTERHAUS

SHELDON

GARRARD

SHELDON

GARRARD

McPHERSON
XVII CORPS

LOGAN

J.E. SMITH

GARRARD

TRACY/GARROTT

Bayou Pierre

FEET   4,000

MILES   1.0

BATTLE *of* RAYMOND

MAY 12, 1863

RATHER THAN MOVE DIRECTLY ON VICKSBURG, **GRANT AND** his Army of the Tennessee drove along a northeastern axis of advance. Grant's ultimate goal was to isolate Confederate Gen. John C. Pemberton and Vicksburg from the rest of the Confederacy. Grant aimed to take the state capital of Jackson, while eliminating the threat Gen. Joseph E. Johnston and his Confederate forces in and around the city. The Federal commander, too, sought to disrupt the railroads and communications lines in and out of the capital. The destruction of the Southern Railroad in central Mississippi was a vital target.

Grant's army advanced over a broad front. As it moved eastward from Port Gibson, McClernand's XIII Corps held the left, closest to the Big Black River; Sherman's XV Corps moved in the center; and Maj. Gen. James B. McPherson's XVII Corps advanced on the right, farthest removed from the enemy—or so it was thought.

On May 12, Grant directed his three corps to various crossings of Fourteenmile Creek to secure a source of water for his men and animals. It would also move his army into position for the planned lunge against the railroad.

Confederate Brig. Gen. John Gregg had been dispatched to Raymond with 3,000 men and orders to strike the Federals in flank or rear as they advanced. Faulty intelligence led him to believe that he would only face a small contingent of Union troops. Gregg's intention was to hold the enemy in check with one regiment where the Utica Road bridged the Fourteenmile Creek while his other regiments attacked en echelon to the left, turned the Federal flank, and destroyed the enemy in his front. However, rather than the single brigade Gregg expected, McPherson's powerful 10,000-man corps confronted him.

Confederate Militia harassed the Federals throughout their morning's march toward Raymond, and were no match for the Federals, so they grudgingly fell back toward Raymond.

Just before 10 a.m., a skirmish line of Union infantry swept over a low ridge and moved cautiously into the valley of Fourteenmile Creek. As they neared the belt of timber that lined the stream, a volley ripped into their ranks. Almost at the same time, the three guns of Capt. Hiram Bledsoe's Missouri battery sent shells crashing among the Union skirmishers. With battle joined, Union Maj. Gen. John A. "Black Jack" Logan led the long blue column, deployed his lead brigade, and called up his artillery, which soon joined the fray.

Although outnumbered, Gregg ordered an attack. While the 7th Texas, engaged the Federals along the Utica Road at the bridge, Gregg's other regiments splashed en echelon across the creek and slammed into the Federals. The blue line began to waver and break in places, but Logan rode forward and, with "the shriek of an eagle," turned the men back to their places.

Union resistance stiffened, and by noon, as McPherson directed fresh troops to extend his line both left and right, the Confederate attack faltered. By 1:30 p.m., the tide of battle shifted as Gregg's battered troops were confronted by five Union brigades with still more Federals arriving on the field. McPherson launched a counterattack that compelled Gregg to abandon the field and retreat through Raymond toward Jackson.

With a victory in hand, Grant divided his columns and continue north toward the Southern Railroad, while also pressing eastward toward Jackson.

✳ ✳ **PRESERVATION** ✳ ✳

To date, the **American Battlefield Trust** has saved **106 acres** at Raymond Battlefield.

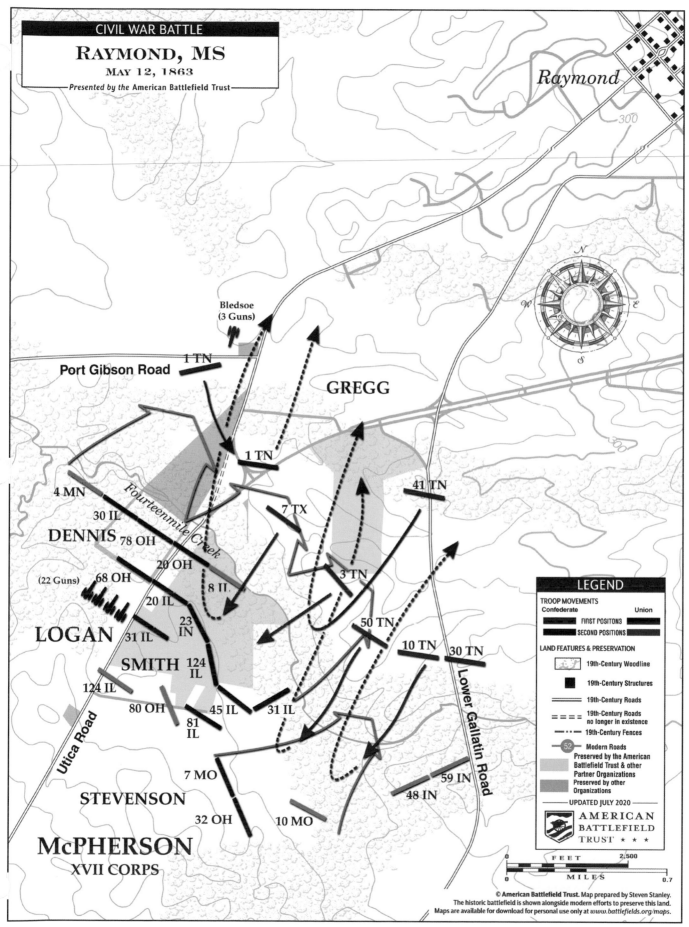

CIVIL WAR BATTLE

RAYMOND, MS

May 12, 1863

Presented by the American Battlefield Trust

Raymond

Bledsoe
(3 Guns)

1 TN

Port Gibson Road

GREGG

1 TN

41 TN

4 MN

Fourteenmile Creek

30 IL

7 TX

DENNIS 78 OH

20 OH

(22 Guns) 68 OH

8 IL

3 TN

20 IL

23 IN

50 TN

LOGAN 31 IL

SMITH 124 IL

10 TN 30 TN

124 IL

Lower Gallatin Road

80 OH 45 IL 31 IL

81 IL

7 MO

59 IN

STEVENSON 48 IN

32 OH 10 MO

McPHERSON

XVII CORPS

LEGEND

TROOP MOVEMENTS
Confederate   Union

FIRST POSITONS

SECOND POSITIONS

LAND FEATURES & PRESERVATION

19th-Century Woodline

19th-Century Structures

19th-Century Roads

19th-Century Roads
no longer in existence

19th-Century Fences

52 Modern Roads

Preserved by the American
Battlefield Trust & other
Partner Organizations

Preserved by other
Organizations

— UPDATED JULY 2020 —

**AMERICAN
BATTLEFIELD
TRUST ★ ★ ★**

Utica Road

FEET   2,500

0

0   MILES   0.7

© **American Battlefield Trust.** Map prepared by Steven Stanley.
The historic battlefield is shown alongside modern efforts to preserve this land.
Maps are available for download for personal use only at *www.battlefields.org/maps.*

BATTLE *of* CHAMPION HILL
(CHAMPION'S HILL/BAKERS CREEK)

MAY 16, 1863

AS THE FIRST STREAKS OF DAWN APPEARED IN THE EASTERN SKY on May 16, 1863, a train heading east neared Clinton, Mississippi, and found the tracks ahead destroyed. The brakeman and the baggage-master were escorted by Union soldiers into the presence of Maj. Gen. Ulysses S. Grant. When questioned, they informed the Union commander that the Confederate army defending Vicksburg, which they estimated numbered 25,000 men with ten batteries, was in Edwards Station and preparing to attack the rear of Grant's army. This was not a bad estimate of the Confederate army, which consisted of 23,000 men and 15 batteries. Grant ordered his troops, 32,000 in all, to march on Edwards along three parallel roads.

Although the opening shots of the Battle of Champion Hill were fired along the lower road around 7:00 a.m., it was not until 9:45 that the Union vanguard of Brig. Gen. Alvin Hovey's division turned a bend in the upper road and reached the country home of Sid and Matilda Champion. A half-mile southwest of the house was the bald crest of Champion Hill, which dominated a strategic crossroads that would be vital to the final assault on Vicksburg.

Hovey quickly swung his men into line of battle, supported by the men of Maj. Gen. John A. Logan's division. Grant arrived on the field shortly after 10 a.m.. and ordered this powerful battle line to advance. With a mighty cheer, the Federals slammed into the Confederates at the base of the hill and a wild hand-to-hand brawl ensued.

Union soldiers swept over the crest of Champion Hill and drove hard toward the crossroads only 600 yards farther south. Despite a murderous fire of musketry and artillery, Hovey's division seized the crossroads and the Union army was on the verge of victory.

Confederate Gen. John Pemberton ordered a desperate counterattack by Brig. Gen. John S. Bowen's Division. Around 2 p.m., Bowen's Missourians and Arkansans slammed into Hovey's men before they consolidated their hold on the crossroads. Bowen's soldiers surged over the crest of Champion Hill and pushed the Federals back to the Champion House. Their success, however, was short-lived, as two more Union divisions charged the hill. Threatened in flank and rear, Bowen was compelled to fall back. When the Federals again seized the crossroads, Pemberton ordered his army off of the field and back toward the defenses of Vicksburg. Union victory was at hand.

Brig. Gen. Lloyd Tilghman's brigade was left behind to cover the Confederate retreat. The Federals advanced in force against Tilghman, and he was mortally wounded, struck in the body by a Federal artillery shell while directing the fire of Capt. James Cowen's Mississippi battery covering the bridge over Baker's Creek. Tilghman's brigade was forced from the field, but his sacrifice enabled most of Pemberton's army to safely withdraw towards Vicksburg, with the exception of Maj. Gen. William W. Loring's Division, which was cut off. Loring's men managed to escape and join Joe Johnston's forces elsewhere.

Casualties for both sides totaled around 6,300, making the battle of Champion Hill the bloodiest of the Vicksburg Campaign. The Union victory at Champion Hill, and the next day at the Big Black River Bridge, forced the Confederates into a doomed position inside the fortifications of Vicksburg.

✳ ✳ PRESERVATION ✳ ✳

To date, the **American Battlefield Trust** has saved **869 acres** at Champion Hill Battlefield.

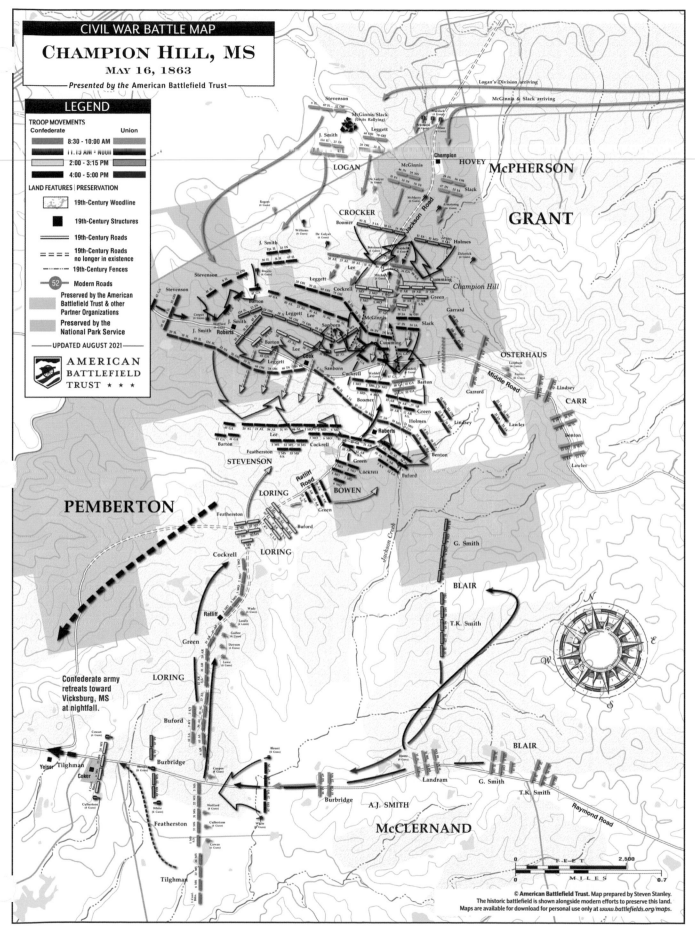

CIVIL WAR BATTLE MAP

CHAMPION HILL, MS

MAY 16, 1863

Presented by the American Battlefield Trust

LEGEND

TROOP MOVEMENTS

Confederate	Union
8:30 - 10:00 AM	
11:15 AM - Noon	
2:00 - 3:15 PM	
4:00 - 5:00 PM	

LAND FEATURES | PRESERVATION

19th-Century Woodline

19th-Century Structures

19th-Century Roads

19th-Century Roads no longer in existence

19th-Century Fences

Modern Roads

Preserved by the American Battlefield Trust & other Partner Organizations

Preserved by the National Park Service

— UPDATED AUGUST 2021 —

AMERICAN BATTLEFIELD TRUST ★ ★ ★

Confederate army retreats toward Vicksburg, MS at nightfall.

BATTLES *and* SEIGE *of* VICKSBURG

MAY 18-JULY 4, 1863

BY MID-MAY 1863, ULYSSES S. GRANT FINALLY APPROACHED the Confederate defenses of Vicksburg. On the evening of May 17, John C. Pemberton's beleaguered army poured into their lines around Vicksburg after their defeats at Champion Hill and along the Big Black River. Looking for a quick victory and not wanting to give Pemberton time to settle in, Grant ordered an immediate assault. Of his three corps, only Maj. Gen. William T. Sherman's XV Corps northeast of the city was in position to attack on the 19th. Sherman's assault focused on the Stockade Redan.

Sherman's men moved forward down the road at 2 p.m. and were immediately slowed by the ravines and obstructions in front of the redan. Bloody combat ensued outside the Confederate works. The 13th United States Infantry, once commanded by Sherman, planted their colors on the redan but could advance no farther. Capt. Edward C. Washington, the grandnephew of George Washington, commanding the regiment's 1st Battalion, was mortally wounded in the attack. After fierce fighting, Sherman's men pulled back.

Undaunted by his failure, Grant ordered another assault on May 22. Early on the morning of May 22, Union artillery opened fire and for four hours bombarded the city's defenses. At 10 a.m. the guns fell silent and Union infantry advanced on a three-mile front.

Sherman attacked again down the Graveyard Road, McPherson's Corps moved against the center along the Jackson Road, and McClernand's Corps attacked to the south at the 2nd Texas Lunette and the Railroad Redoubt. Surrounded by a ditch 10 feet deep and walls 20 feet high, the redoubt offered enfilading fire for rifles and artillery. After bloody hand-to-hand fighting, Federals breached the Railroad Redoubt, capturing a handful of prisoners. The victory, however, was the only Confederate position captured that day.

Grant's unsuccessful attacks gave him no choice but to invest Vicksburg in a siege. Pemberton's defenders suffered from shortened rations, exposure to the elements, and constant bombardment from Grant's army and navy gunboats. Reduced in number by sickness and casualties, the garrison of Vicksburg was spread dangerously thin. Civilians were particularly hard hit. Many were forced to live underground in crudely dug caves due to the heavy shelling.

By early June, Grant had established his own line of circumvallation surrounding the city. At thirteen points along his line, Grant ordered tunnels dug under the Confederate positions where explosives could be placed to destroy the rebel works. On June 25, 2,200 pounds of black powder was detonated under the Confederate lines, producing a massive explosion. Union soldiers attacked. After more than 20 hours of hand-to-hand fighting in the 12-foot deep crater left by the blast, the Union regiments were unable to advance out of it and withdrew back to their lines. The siege continued.

By July, the situation was dire for Confederates. Grant and Pemberton met between the lines on July 3. Grant insisted on an unconditional surrender, but Pemberton refused. Rebuffed, Grant later that night offered to parole the Confederate defenders. At 10:00 a.m. the next day, Independence Day, some 29,000 Confederates marched out of their lines, stacked their rifles and furled their flags. The 47-day siege of Vicksburg was over. With the loss of Pemberton's army and a Union victory at Port Hudson five days later, the Union controlled the entire Mississippi River, and the Confederacy was split in half.

✷ ✷ PRESERVATION ✷ ✷

To date, the **American Battlefield Trust** has saved **14 acres** at Vicksburg Battlefield.

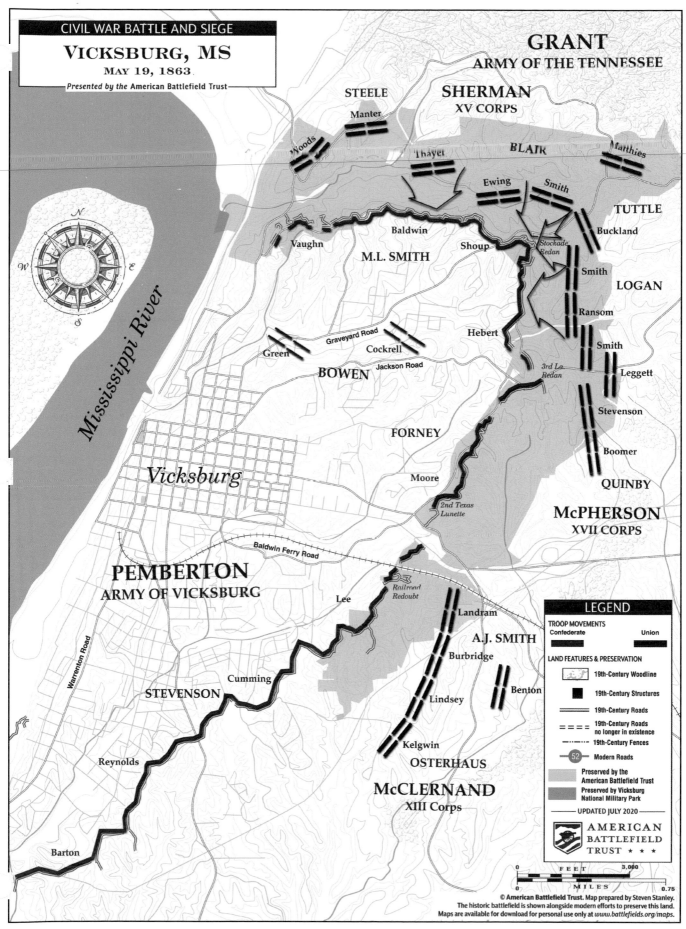

CIVIL WAR BATTLE AND SIEGE
VICKSBURG, MS
MAY 19, 1863
Presented by the American Battlefield Trust

GRANT
ARMY OF THE TENNESSEE

SHERMAN
XV CORPS

STEELE

Manter

Woods

Thayer

BLAIR

Matthies

Ewing

Smith

TUTTLE

Baldwin

Buckland

Vaughn

Shoup

Stockade Redan

M.L. SMITH

Smith

LOGAN

Ransom

Hebert

Smith

Graveyard Road

Green

Cockrell

Leggett

Jackson Road

3rd La. Redan

BOWEN

Stevenson

Mississippi River

Boomer

FORNEY

Moore

QUINBY

2nd Texas Lunette

McPHERSON
XVII CORPS

Vicksburg

Baldwin Ferry Road

PEMBERTON
ARMY OF VICKSBURG

Lee

Railroad Redoubt

Landram

A.J. SMITH

Burbridge

Benton

Cumming

STEVENSON

Lindsey

Warrenton Road

Reynolds

Kelgwin

OSTERHAUS

Barton

McCLERNAND
XIII Corps

LEGEND
TROOP MOVEMENTS
Confederate   Union

LAND FEATURES & PRESERVATION
- 19th-Century Woodline
- 19th-Century Structures
- 19th-Century Roads
- 19th-Century Roads no longer in existence
- 19th-Century Fences
- 52 Modern Roads
- Preserved by the American Battlefield Trust
- Preserved by Vicksburg National Military Park

UPDATED JULY 2020

AMERICAN BATTLEFIELD TRUST ★★★

0 FEET 3,000
0 MILES 0.75

© American Battlefield Trust. Map prepared by Steven Stanley.
The historic battlefield is shown alongside modern efforts to preserve this land.
Maps are available for download for personal use only at www.battlefields.org/maps.

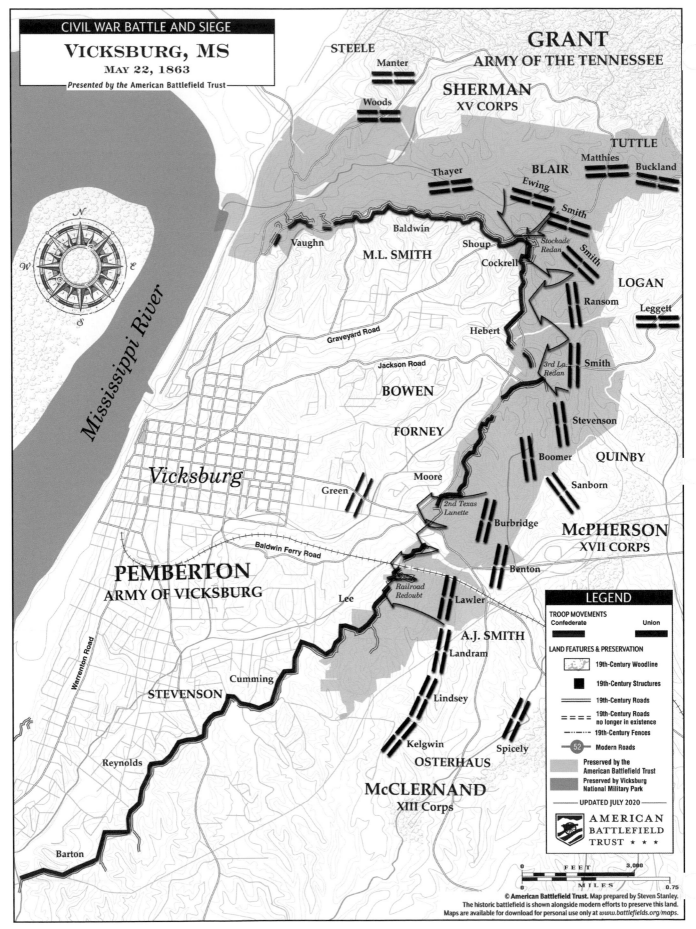

CIVIL WAR BATTLE AND SIEGE

VICKSBURG, MS

MAY 22, 1863

Presented by the American Battlefield Trust

GRANT
ARMY OF THE TENNESSEE

STEELE
Manter

SHERMAN
XV CORPS

Woods

TUTTLE
Matthies   Buckland

Thayer   **BLAIR**
              Ewing
                    Smith

Baldwin   Smith

Vaughn   Shoup   *Stockade Redan*
                              Smith
        M.L. SMITH   Cockrell

                              LOGAN
                         Ransom
                                  Leggett

Graveyard Road   Hebert

                    3rd La. Redan   Smith
Jackson Road

        BOWEN   Stevenson

        FORNEY

                              Boomer   **QUINBY**
        Moore
                              Sanborn
Green
        2nd Texas Lunette
                    Burbridge
Vicksburg   **McPHERSON**
                                        XVII CORPS
                              Benton

Baldwin Ferry Road

PEMBERTON
ARMY OF VICKSBURG

Lee   *Railroad Redoubt*   Lawler

                    A.J. SMITH
                    Landram

Warrenton Road

Cumming   Lindsey

STEVENSON

                    Kelgwin   Spicely

Reynolds   **OSTERHAUS**

        McCLERNAND
        XIII Corps

Barton

Mississippi River

LEGEND

TROOP MOVEMENTS
Confederate   Union

LAND FEATURES & PRESERVATION

19th-Century Woodline

19th-Century Structures

19th-Century Roads

19th-Century Roads no longer in existence

19th-Century Fences

52 Modern Roads

Preserved by the American Battlefield Trust

Preserved by Vicksburg National Military Park

— UPDATED JULY 2020 —

AMERICAN BATTLEFIELD TRUST ★★★

0   FEET   3,000
0   MILES   0.75

© **American Battlefield Trust**. Map prepared by Steven Stanley.
The historic battlefield is shown alongside modern efforts to preserve this land.
Maps are available for download for personal use only at *www.battlefields.org/maps*.

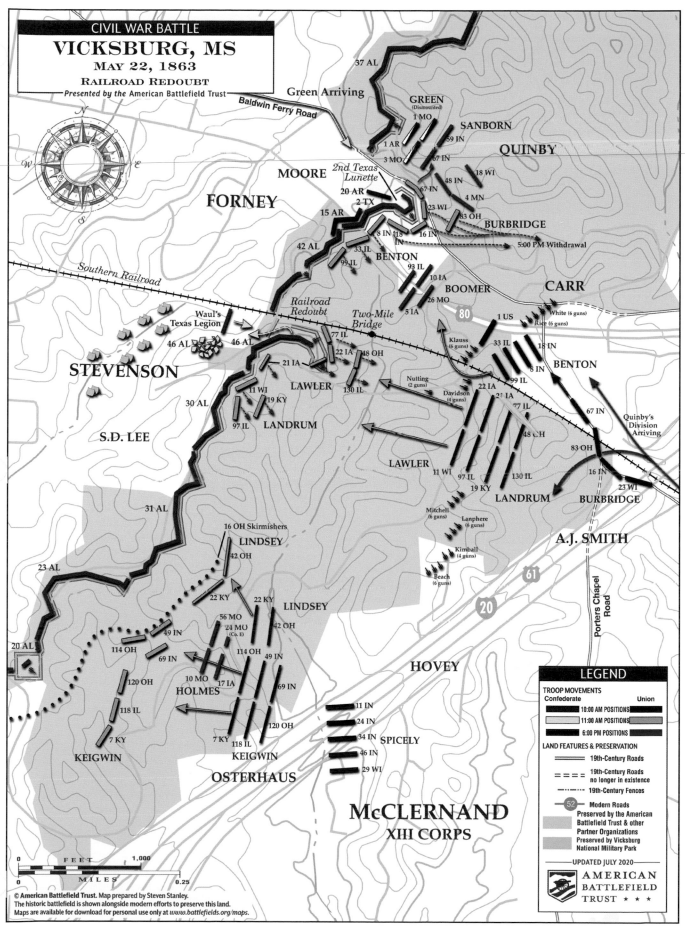

CIVIL WAR BATTLE
VICKSBURG, MS
MAY 22, 1863
RAILROAD REDOUBT
Presented by the American Battlefield Trust

BATTLE *and* SEIGE *of* PORT HUDSON

MAY 27, 1863

VICKSBURG WAS NOT THE LAST REMAINING CONFEDERATE BASTION on the Mississippi in the summer of 1863. Some 120 miles south of Vicksburg and 25 miles north of Baton Rouge, as the crow flies, sat Port Hudson, Louisiana. In many ways, Port Hudson was a mirror image of Vicksburg. Situated on high bluffs overlooking the east bank of river, and above a hairpin turn, Port Hudson was the last major obstacle between the Federal navy and its dominance of the mighty Mississippi.

A naval foray in March 1863 headed by Rear Adm. David G. Farragut from New Orleans came to grief, illustrating the necessity for a combined Army-Navy effort against the stronghold. Farragut, who was one of the most capable officers in the United States Navy, was joined by one of the least capable Union army commanders, Maj. Gen. Nathaniel Banks. A political general through-and-through.

On May 11, Banks learned that a significant portion of the Confederate garrison at Port Hudson had been transferred to support the southern forces defending Vicksburg. Hoping to take advantage of this southern manpower shortage, Banks drove his forces toward Port Hudson. Banks divided his forces into two columns: one column of three divisions approached Port Hudson from Alexandria, Louisiana, to the north, and a second column of two divisions advanced north from Baton Rouge. By May 21, the columns had combined, and Banks's force numbered nearly 40,000 men. The Federal army at Port Hudson enjoyed a four-to-one manpower advantage over their enemy, yet Banks delayed nearly a week organizing his forces for an assault.

Banks's opponent was a New Yorker and graduate of the West Point class of 1843, Maj. Gen. Franklin Gardner. The experienced Gardner was up to the task before him, and he and his men worked hard to improve their defenses before Banks unleashed his assault.

Boasting five division of infantry, an oversized brigade of cavalry, and a navy, Banks failed miserably to coordinate his assaults on the Confederate fortifications when he finally attacked on May 27. Two Federal divisions assaulted the north side of the rebel works near dawn, which was repulsed after nearly three hours of fighting. At noon, two more Federal divisions thrust themselves upon the rebel works from the east. For another three hours, fighting raged on this front. The Confederate works were so impressive and their fortifying moats so deep that Federal commanders ordered forward volunteers and engineers—including the 1st Louisiana Engineers Corps D'Afrique to fill the dry moats with bridging materials.

In a desperate attempt to break the Confederate lines, Union Brig. Gen. William Dwight ordered the 1st and 3rd Louisiana Native Guards into action. The units consisted of newly freed Black troops and were acting as pioneers (construction troops) during the battle, but were nevertheless pressed into action. The Guards' attack route was perhaps the deadliest, as it skirted the river that ran along their right flank and, on their left, was an enfilading line of Confederate infantry and artillery. This attack, too, failed.

Another Union attack on June 13 was beaten back, so Banks settled in for a siege. Soon the defenders exhausted their food and ammunition, and fighting and disease greatly reduced the number of men able to defend the trenches. When Gardner learned that Vicksburg had surrendered on July 4, he realized his situation was hopeless and surrendered his garrison on July 9. The Mississippi was open to Union navigation for the rest of the war.

✳ ✳ PRESERVATION ✳ ✳

To date, the **American Battlefield Trust** has saved **256 acres** at Port Hudson Battlefield.

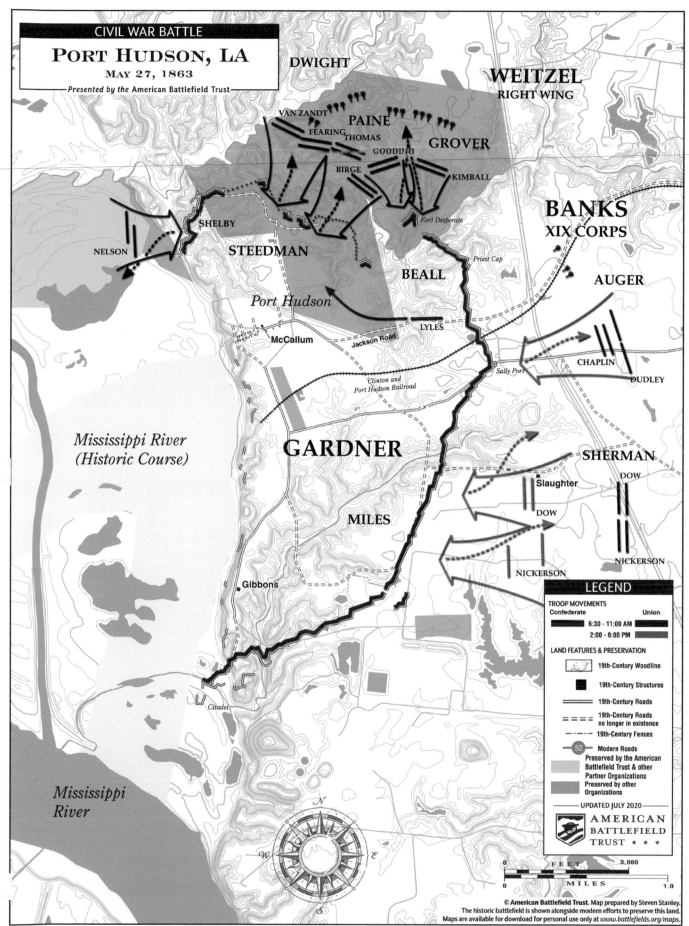

CIVIL WAR BATTLE

PORT HUDSON, LA

MAY 27, 1863

Presented by the American Battlefield Trust

DWIGHT

WEITZEL
RIGHT WING

VAN ZANDT

PAINE

FEARING

THOMAS

GOODING

GROVER

BIRGE

KIMBALL

Fort Desperate

BANKS
XIX CORPS

SHELBY

NELSON

STEEDMAN

Priest Cap

BEALL

AUGER

Port Hudson

LYLES

Sally Port

CHAPLIN

DUDLEY

McCallum

Jackson Road

*Clinton and
Port Hudson Railroad*

*Mississippi River
(Historic Course)*

GARDNER

SHERMAN

Slaughter

DOW

DOW

MILES

NICKERSON

NICKERSON

Gibbons

Citadel

*Mississippi
River*

N

W E

S

LEGEND

TROOP MOVEMENTS

Confederate	Union
6:30 – 11:00 AM	
2:00 – 6:00 PM	

LAND FEATURES & PRESERVATION

- 19th-Century Woodline
- 19th-Century Structures
- 19th-Century Roads
- 19th-Century Roads no longer in existence
- 19th-Century Fences
- 52 Modern Roads
- Preserved by the American Battlefield Trust & other Partner Organizations
- Preserved by other Organizations

— UPDATED JULY 2020 —

**AMERICAN
BATTLEFIELD
TRUST** ★ ★ ★

FEET 3,000

MILES 1.0

© **American Battlefield Trust**. Map prepared by Steven Stanley.
The historic battlefield is shown alongside modern efforts to preserve this land.
Maps are available for download for personal use only at *www.battlefields.org/maps*.

47

BATTLE *of* FORT WAGNER

(BATTERY WAGNER)

JULY 18, 1863

THE CITY OF CHARLESTON, SOUTH CAROLINA, STOOD AS A SYMBOL to people in the north and the south throughout the Civil War. To many northerners, it was the symbol of secession. To many southerners, it stood as their birthplace of independence. While Charleston was an important port city before the war, its strategic importance after the firing on Fort Sumter was questionable. By 1863, a Union blockading squadron sat off of the coast, largely sealing off the harbor. The city lacked major industry to supply the south with goods and war materials, and it was situated far from the front lines of war. Yet, the fall of Charleston was always in the fore of Federal war planners.

Brigadier General Quincy Gillmore was assigned to lead the 1863 campaign against the city of Charleston. Gillmore's plan, supported by a heavy naval presence, was to seize Morris Island so he could place heavy rifled guns on Cummings Point that would, in turn, neutralize Fort Sumter. Once Sumter was reduced, the army and the navy could move swiftly to capture Charleston.

On July 10, Gillmore's Federal soldiers crossed from adjacent Folly Island to the south and secured a foothold on the southern tip of Morris Island. The Confederate defenders held the northern portion of the island, which included the formidable earthen Fort Wagner, a stronghold created out of sand, earth, and palmetto logs.

A Federal assault on July 11 was easily repulsed by Wagner's defenders. The undeterred Federals prepared for a new and better coordinated attack upon Fort Wagner. The new plan included a close-range land and sea bombardment of the fort, followed by a land assault of some 5,000 soldiers.

Facing the renewed Federal onslaught were more than 1,620 Confederate soldiers under the command of Brig. Gen. William Taliaferro, a cast-away from Lee's Army of Northern Virginia but an experienced leader nonetheless. Fort Wagner bristled with 14 heavy guns, mortars, carronades, and field pieces situated among a well-laid-out fortress, designed to withstand modern rifled artillery fire.

On July 18, Gillmore sent forward his Federal regiments. The assault was led by the 54th Massachusetts, a Boston regiment filled with free Blacks. As the Federal soldiers neared the fort, they were subjected to artillery and musket fire that shredded their exposed ranks. Despite their heavy losses, the remnants of the 54th Massachusetts reached and scaled the earthen walls of Fort Wagner. Descending into the fort, the 54th engaged in a bloody hand-to-hand struggle with the Confederate defenders only to be thrown back with heavy losses

Subsequent assaults by nine other Union regiments led to nothing but more futile bloodshed. The hard-fighting Confederate defenders were stretched to their limits, but the Federals failed to take the fort. Federal casualties reached 1,515, with the 54th Massachusetts losing 42% of its ranks in the attack. Brigadier General George Strong and three colonels, including the leader of the 54th Massachusetts, Col. Robert G. Shaw, were killed or mortally wounded in the attack. Light by comparison, Confederate losses numbered just 174 men.

After this bloody repulse, Gillmore's men settled into their Morris Island positions for a lengthy siege that finally led to the Confederate abandonment of Fort Wagner on September 7, 1863—yet even after all of the effort and bloodshed, the Federals were no closer to securing Charleston.

✳ ✳ PRESERVATION ✳ ✳

To date, the **American Battlefield Trust** has saved **118 acres** at Fort Wagner Battlefield.

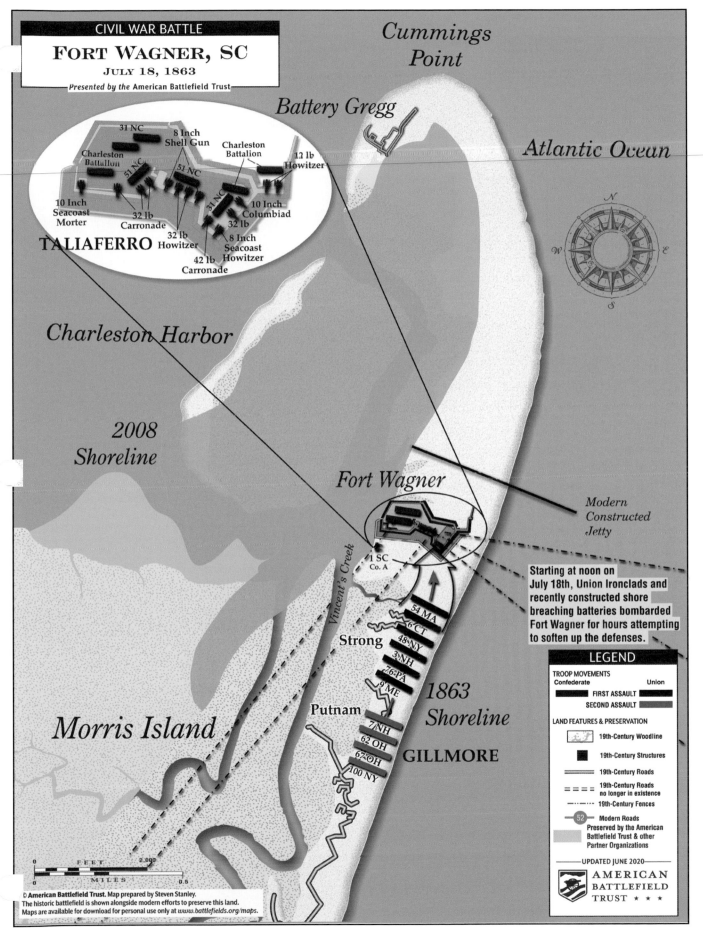

CIVIL WAR BATTLE
FORT WAGNER, SC
JULY 18, 1863
Presented by the American Battlefield Trust

31 NC

Charleston Battalion

8 Inch Shell Gun

Charleston Battalion

12 lb Howitzer

51 NC

51 NC

31 NC

10 Inch Seacoast Morter

32 lb Carronade

32 lb Howitzer

42 lb Carronade

8 Inch Seacoast Howitzer

32 lb

8 Inch Columbiad

10 Inch Columbiad

TALIAFERRO

Cummings Point

Battery Gregg

Atlantic Ocean

Charleston Harbor

2008 Shoreline

Fort Wagner

1 SC Co. A

Vincent's Creek

54 MA

6 CT

Strong

48 NY

3 NH

76 PA

9 ME

Putnam

7 NH

62 OH

67 OH

100 NY

1863 Shoreline

GILLMORE

Morris Island

Modern Constructed Jetty

Starting at noon on July 18th, Union Ironclads and recently constructed shore breaching batteries bombarded Fort Wagner for hours attempting to soften up the defenses.

LEGEND
TROOP MOVEMENTS
Confederate   Union

FIRST ASSAULT

SECOND ASSAULT

LAND FEATURES & PRESERVATION

19th-Century Woodline

19th-Century Structures

19th-Century Roads

19th-Century Roads no longer in existence

19th-Century Fences

52 Modern Roads

Preserved by the American Battlefield Trust & other Partner Organizations

— UPDATED JUNE 2020 —

AMERICAN BATTLEFIELD TRUST ★ ★ ★

FEET   2,000

MILES   0.5

© American Battlefield Trust. Map prepared by Steven Stanley.
The historic battlefield is shown alongside modern efforts to preserve this land.
Maps are available for download for personal use only at *www.battlefields.org/maps.*

BATTLE *of* CHICKAMAUGA

SEPTEMBER 18-20, 1863

WILLIAM S. ROSECRANS AND HIS ARMY OF THE CUMBERLAND SPENT THE SIX months following the Battle of Stones Rover licking their wounds, reorganizing, and resupplying while "Old Rosey" prepared for his offensive south to Chattanooga. From June 24–July 3, Rosecrans's army out-maneuvered Braxton Bragg's Army of Tennessee during the Tullahoma Campaign. By mid-September, Chattanooga was in Federal hands, and Union soldiers were spread across south Tennessee, north Alabama, and north Georgia. All seemed to be coming up aces for William Rosecrans, but Braxton Bragg was determined to put up a fight.

Bragg concentrated his forces in LaFayette, Georgia, and determined to reoccupy Chattanooga. By September 17, Bragg had been reinforced with the eastern divisions of Maj. Gens. John Bell Hood, Lafayette McLaws, and the Mississippi division under Brig. Gen. Bushrod Johnson. With renewed confidence that Chattanooga could be recaptured, Bragg marched his army to the west bank of Chickamauga Creek, hoping to position his troops between Chattanooga and the Federal army, cutting off their line of retreat. As Bragg's infantry crossed the creek on the 18th, they skirmished with Federals.

The Battle of Chickamauga began in earnest shortly after dawn on September 19. Throughout the day, Bragg's men gained ground but could not break the extended Union line despite a series of aggressive attacks. Confederate luck changed when, reinforcements arrived at Chickamauga. Bragg divided his army into two wings: Lieutenant General James Longstreet commanded the left; Lt. Gen. Leonidas K. Polk took charge of the right. The battle resumed at 9:30 a.m. the next morning, with coordinated Confederate attacks on the Union left flank.

About an hour later, Rosecrans, believing a gap existed in his line, ordered Brig. Gen. Thomas Wood's division to fill the gap. Wood, however, knew that the order was a mistake; no such gap existed in the Federal line, and moving his division would, in turn, open a large swath in the Union position. However, Wood had already been berated twice in the campaign for not promptly following orders. To avoid further reprimand, he immediately moved, creating a division-wide hole in the Union line. This was the chance that the Confederates needed. Longstreet massed a striking force, led by Hood. Longstreet's men surged through the gap that Wood had created, and Union resistance at the southern end of the battlefield evaporated as Federal troops, including Rosecrans himself, were driven off the field and back to Chattanooga.

Union Maj. Gen. George H. Thomas, in an action that earned him the nom de guerre "The Rock of Chickamauga," took command of scattered Federal forces on the field and consolidated them on Horseshoe Ridge and Snodgrass Hill. Thomas and his men formed a defensive position, and although Confederates continued to assault, the Federals held firm. Thomas withdrew as darkness fell. Bragg's victorious army followed toward Chattanooga and occupied the heights surrounding the town, blocking Federal supply lines—but they did not pursue Rosecrans further.

While Chickamauga was a decided Confederate victory, the results of the battle were staggering. With more than 16,000 Union and 18,000 Confederate casualties, Chickamauga reached the highest losses of any battle in the Western Theater. Although the Confederates had driven Rosecrans from the field, they had not succeeded in Bragg's goals of destroying Rosecrans's army or reoccupying Chattanooga.

✳ ✳ PRESERVATION ✳ ✳

To date, the **American Battlefield Trust** has saved **141 acres** at Chickamauga Battlefield.

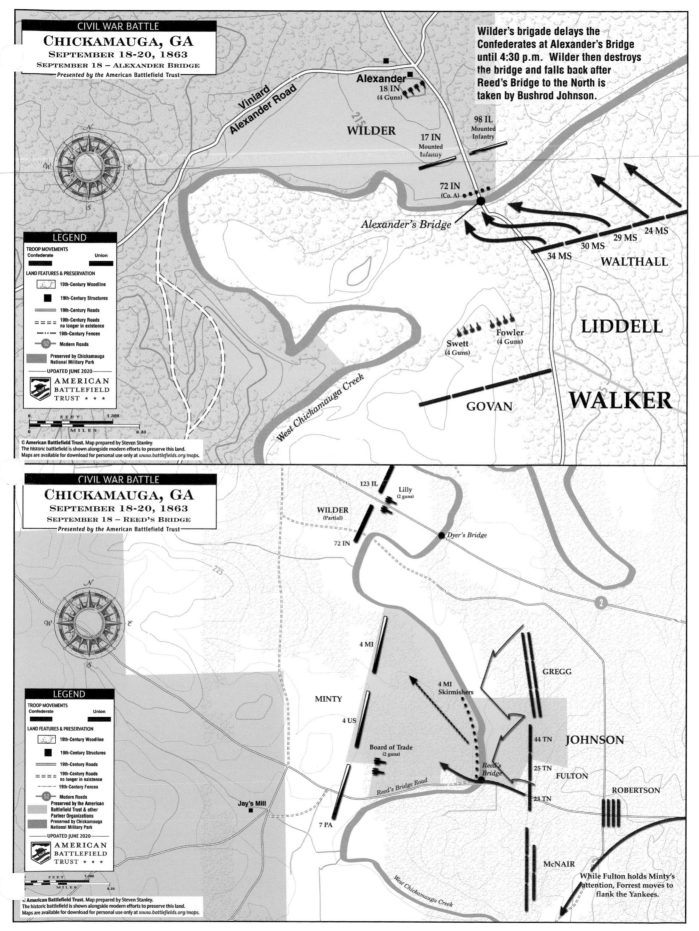

CIVIL WAR BATTLE
CHICKAMAUGA, GA
SEPTEMBER 18-20, 1863
SEPTEMBER 18 – ALEXANDER BRIDGE
Presented by the American Battlefield Trust

Wilder's brigade delays the Confederates at Alexander's Bridge until 4:30 p.m. Wilder then destroys the bridge and falls back after Reed's Bridge to the North is taken by Bushrod Johnson.

Viniard Alexander Road

Alexander
18 IN
(4 Guns)

WILDER

17 IN
Mounted
Infantry

98 IL
Mounted
Infantry

72 IN
(Co. A)

Alexander's Bridge

24 MS
29 MS
30 MS
34 MS

WALTHALL

LIDDELL

Swett
(4 Guns)

Fowler
(4 Guns)

GOVAN

WALKER

LEGEND
TROOP MOVEMENTS
Confederate   Union

LAND FEATURES & PRESERVATION
19th-Century Woodline
19th-Century Structures
19th-Century Roads
19th-Century Roads no longer in existence
19th-Century Fences
52 Modern Roads
Preserved by Chickamauga National Military Park
— UPDATED JUNE 2020 —

AMERICAN BATTLEFIELD TRUST ★ ★ ★

FEET   1,800
MILES   0.33

© American Battlefield Trust. Map prepared by Steven Stanley.
The historic battlefield is shown alongside modern efforts to preserve this land.
Maps are available for download for personal use only at *www.battlefields.org/maps.*

CIVIL WAR BATTLE
CHICKAMAUGA, GA
SEPTEMBER 18-20, 1863
SEPTEMBER 18 – REED'S BRIDGE
Presented by the American Battlefield Trust

123 IL
Lilly
(2 guns)

WILDER
(Partial)

72 IN

Dyer's Bridge

2

4 MI

GREGG

4 MI
Skirmishers

MINTY

4 US

JOHNSON

44 TN

Board of Trade
(2 guns)

*Reed's
Bridge*

25 TN

FULTON

23 TN

ROBERTSON

Jay's Mill

Reed's Bridge Road

7 PA

McNAIR

West Chickamauga Creek

While Fulton holds Minty's attention, Forrest moves to flank the Yankees.

LEGEND
TROOP MOVEMENTS
Confederate   Union

LAND FEATURES & PRESERVATION
19th-Century Woodline
19th-Century Structures
19th-Century Roads
19th-Century Roads no longer in existence
19th-Century Fences
52 Modern Roads
Preserved by the American Battlefield Trust & other Partner Organizations
Preserved by Chickamauga National Military Park
— UPDATED JUNE 2020 —

AMERICAN BATTLEFIELD TRUST ★ ★ ★

FEET   1,000
MILES   0.25

© American Battlefield Trust. Map prepared by Steven Stanley.
The historic battlefield is shown alongside modern efforts to preserve this land.
Maps are available for download for personal use only at *www.battlefields.org/maps.*

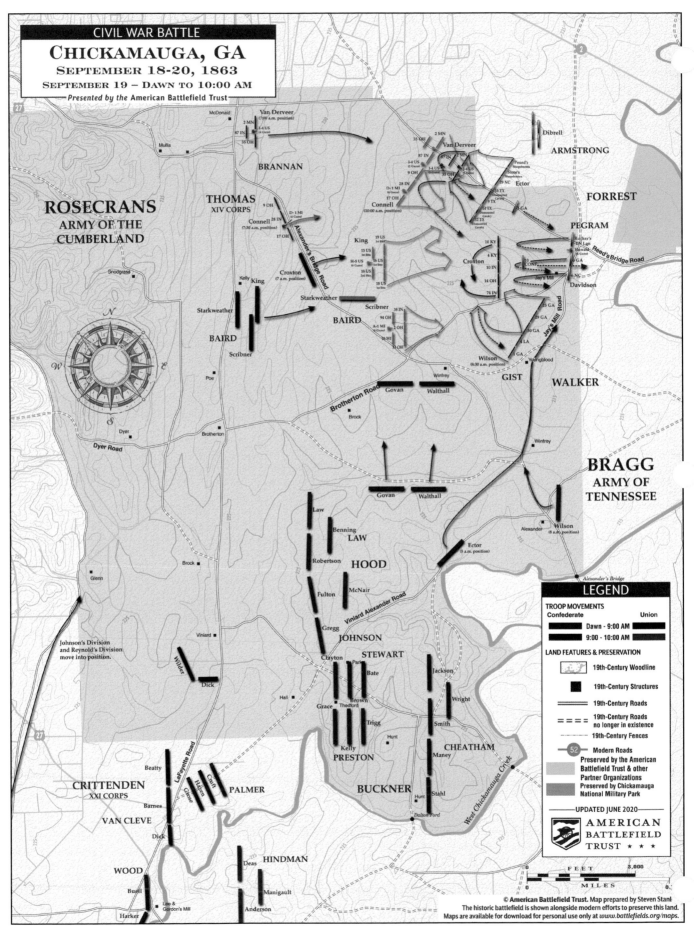

CIVIL WAR BATTLE
CHICKAMAUGA, GA
SEPTEMBER 18-20, 1863
SEPTEMBER 19 – DAWN TO 10:00 AM
Presented by the American Battlefield Trust

ROSECRANS
ARMY OF THE
CUMBERLAND

BRAGG
ARMY OF
TENNESSEE

LEGEND

TROOP MOVEMENTS
Confederate — Union

Dawn - 9:00 AM
9:00 - 10:00 AM

LAND FEATURES & PRESERVATION

19th-Century Woodline

19th-Century Structures

19th-Century Roads

19th-Century Roads no longer in existence

19th-Century Fences

52 — Modern Roads

Preserved by the American Battlefield Trust & other Partner Organizations

Preserved by Chickamauga National Military Park

—UPDATED JUNE 2020—

AMERICAN BATTLEFIELD TRUST ★★★

FEET 3,000

MILES

© American Battlefield Trust. Map prepared by Steven Stanl
The historic battlefield is shown alongside modern efforts to preserve this land.
Maps are available for download for personal use only at www.battlefields.org/maps.

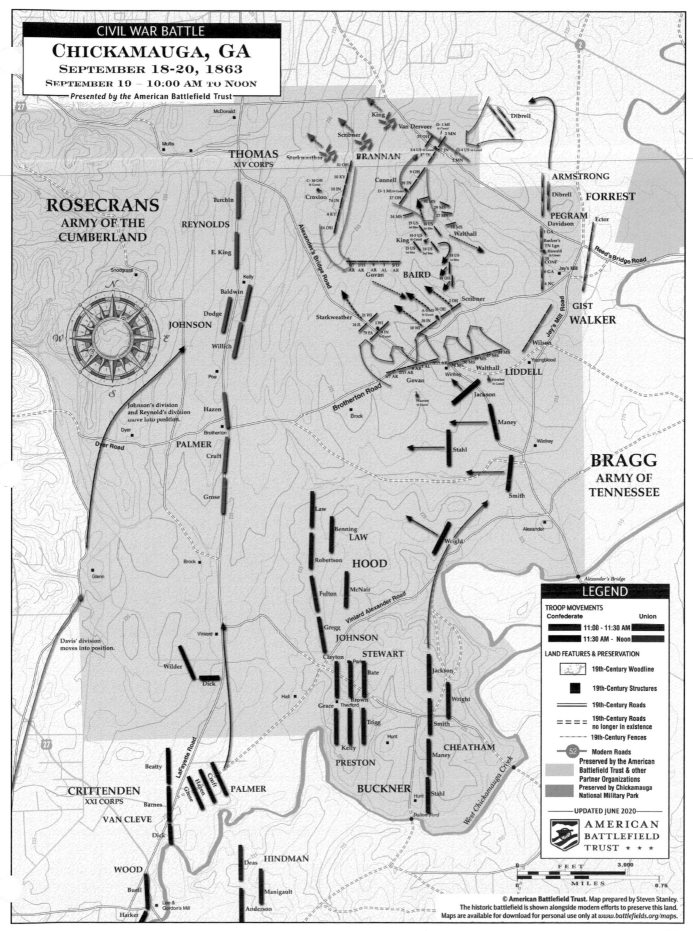

CIVIL WAR BATTLE
CHICKAMAUGA, GA
SEPTEMBER 18-20, 1863
SEPTEMBER 19 – 10:00 AM TO NOON
Presented by the American Battlefield Trust

ROSECRANS
ARMY OF THE
CUMBERLAND

THOMAS
XIV CORPS

BRAGG
ARMY OF
TENNESSEE

FORREST

ARMSTRONG

GIST
WALKER

LIDDELL

HOOD

LAW

JOHNSON

STEWART

PRESTON

BUCKNER

CHEATHAM

CRITTENDEN
XXI CORPS

VAN CLEVE

WOOD

HINDMAN

PALMER

Johnson's division
and Reynold's division
move into position.

Davis' division
moves into position.

LEGEND
TROOP MOVEMENTS
Confederate   Union
11:00 - 11:30 AM
11:30 AM - Noon

LAND FEATURES & PRESERVATION
19th-Century Woodline
19th-Century Structures
19th-Century Roads
19th-Century Roads
no longer in existence
19th-Century Fences
52 Modern Roads
Preserved by the American
Battlefield Trust & other
Partner Organizations
Preserved by Chickamauga
National Military Park

UPDATED JUNE 2020

AMERICAN
BATTLEFIELD
TRUST ★★★

FEET   3,000
MILES   0.75

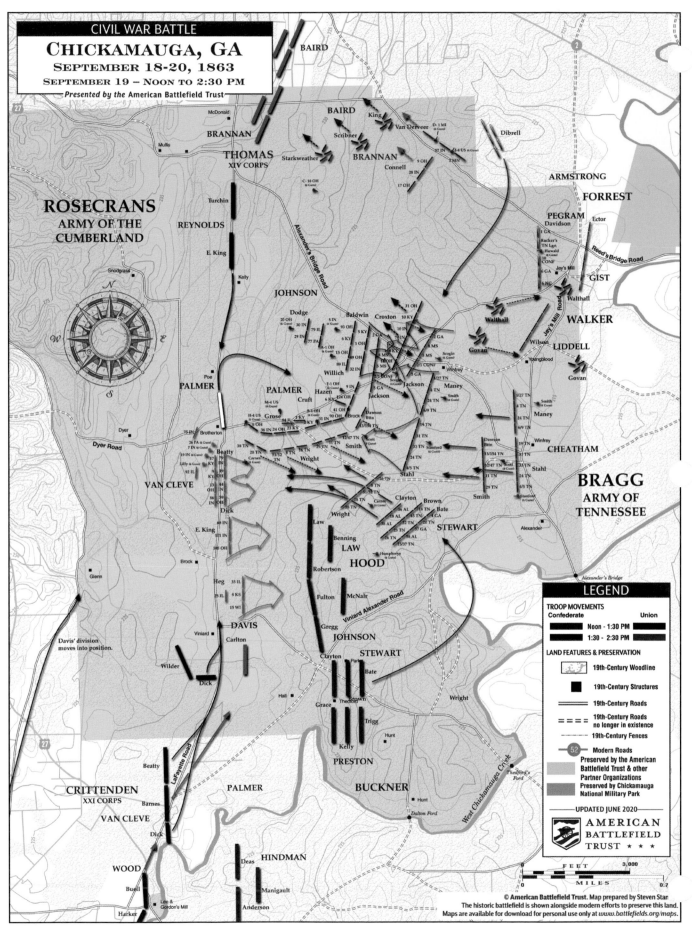

CIVIL WAR BATTLE
CHICKAMAUGA, GA
SEPTEMBER 18-20, 1863
SEPTEMBER 19 – NOON TO 2:30 PM
Presented by the American Battlefield Trust

ROSECRANS
ARMY OF THE
CUMBERLAND

BRAGG
ARMY OF
TENNESSEE

LEGEND

TROOP MOVEMENTS
Confederate   Union

Noon - 1:30 PM
1:30 - 2:30 PM

LAND FEATURES & PRESERVATION

19th-Century Woodline

19th-Century Structures

19th-Century Roads

19th-Century Roads no longer in existence

19th-Century Fences

52 Modern Roads

Preserved by the American Battlefield Trust & other Partner Organizations

Preserved by Chickamauga National Military Park

UPDATED JUNE 2020

AMERICAN
BATTLEFIELD
TRUST ★ ★ ★

FEET   3,000
0

MILES   0.7
0

© American Battlefield Trust. Map prepared by Steven Stan
The historic battlefield is shown alongside modern efforts to preserve this land.
Maps are available for download for personal use only at www.battlefields.org/maps.

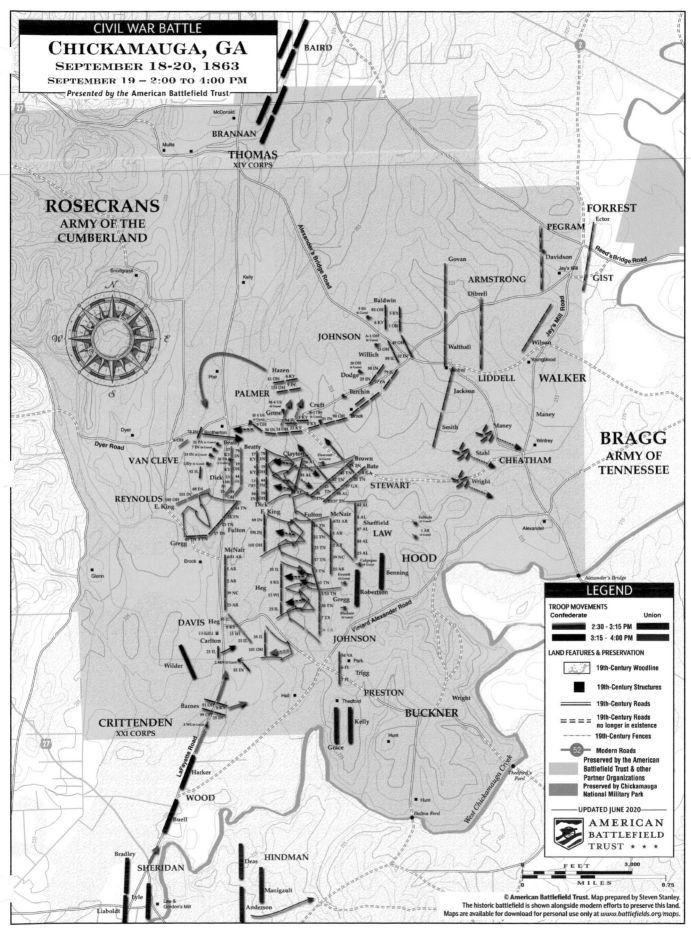

CIVIL WAR BATTLE
CHICKAMAUGA, GA
SEPTEMBER 18-20, 1863
SEPTEMBER 19 – 2:00 TO 4:00 PM
Presented by the American Battlefield Trust

BAIRD

McDonald

BRANNAN

Mullis

THOMAS
XIV CORPS

ROSECRANS
ARMY OF THE
CUMBERLAND

Snodgrass

Kelly

Poe

Hazen
41 OH 6 KY
124 IN

PALMER

Dyer

Dyer Road

VAN CLEVE

REYNOLDS
E. King

Gregg

Brock

Glenn

DAVIS

Wilder

Barnes 51 OH 8 KY
99 OH 35 IN
3 WI (6 Guns)

CRITTENDEN
XXI CORPS

Lafayette Road

Harker

WOOD
Buell

Bradley

SHERIDAN
Lyle
Liaboldt
Lee & Gordon's Mill

Deas HINDMAN

Manigault

Anderson

FORREST
Ector

PEGRAM

Davidson
Jay's Mill

GIST

Govan

ARMSTRONG
Dibrell

Walthall

LIDDELL

WALKER

Jackson

Smith

Maney

Maney
Winfrey

Stahl

CHEATHAM

Wright

BRAGG
ARMY OF
TENNESSEE

Alexander

Alexander's Bridge

JOHNSON
Willich

Dodge
Turchin

Croft

Brown
Bate

STEWART

Fulton McNair

LAW

HOOD

Benning

Robertson

Gregg

JOHNSON

Park
Trigg

PRESTON

BUCKNER

Wright

Thedford

Kelly

Hall

Hunt

Grace

Thedford's Ford

Hunt

Dalton Ford

West Chickamauga Creek

LEGEND

TROOP MOVEMENTS

Confederate	Union	
▬▬▬	▬▬▬	2:30 - 3:15 PM
▬▬▬	▬▬▬	3:15 - 4:00 PM

LAND FEATURES & PRESERVATION

19th-Century Woodline

19th-Century Structures

19th-Century Roads

19th-Century Roads
no longer in existence

19th-Century Fences

52 Modern Roads

Preserved by the American
Battlefield Trust & other
Partner Organizations

Preserved by Chickamauga
National Military Park

UPDATED JUNE 2020

AMERICAN
BATTLEFIELD
TRUST ★★★

FEET 3,000

MILES 0.75

© American Battlefield Trust. Map prepared by Steven Stanley.
The historic battlefield is shown alongside modern efforts to preserve this land.
Maps are available for download for personal use only at www.battlefields.org/maps.

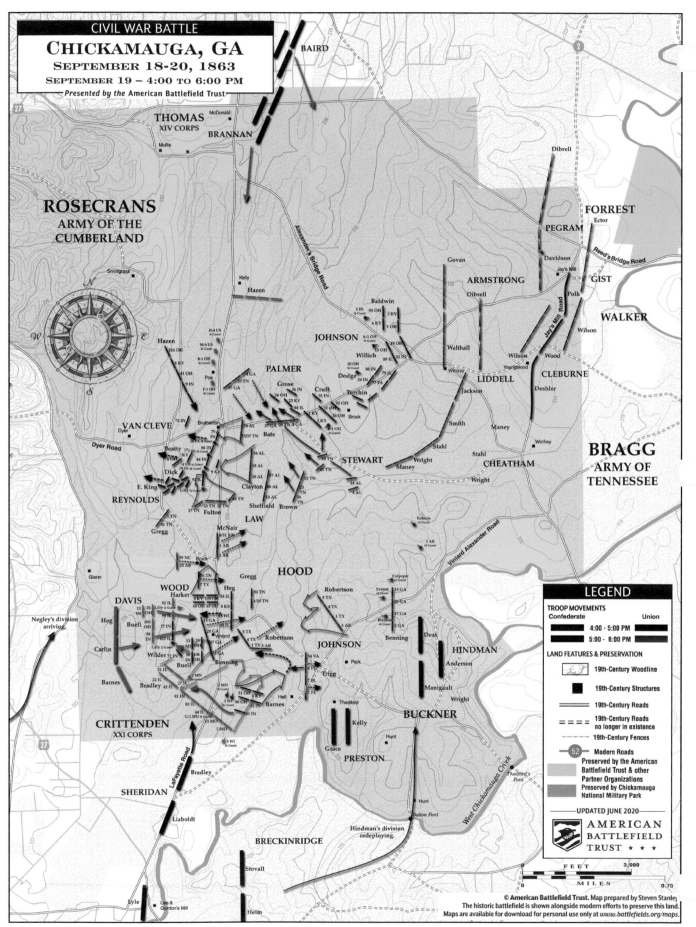

CIVIL WAR BATTLE

CHICKAMAUGA, GA

SEPTEMBER 18-20, 1863
SEPTEMBER 19 – 4:00 TO 6:00 PM

Presented by the American Battlefield Trust

ROSECRANS
ARMY OF THE
CUMBERLAND

THOMAS
XIV CORPS

BRAGG
ARMY OF
TENNESSEE

CRITTENDEN
XXI CORPS

SHERIDAN

LEGEND

TROOP MOVEMENTS
Confederate   Union
4:00 - 5:00 PM
5:00 - 6:00 PM

LAND FEATURES & PRESERVATION

19th-Century Woodline

19th-Century Structures

19th-Century Roads

19th-Century Roads
no longer in existence

19th-Century Fences

52   Modern Roads

Preserved by the American
Battlefield Trust & other
Partner Organizations

Preserved by Chickamauga
National Military Park

— UPDATED JUNE 2020 —

AMERICAN
BATTLEFIELD
TRUST ★ ★ ★

FEET   3,000
0

MILES   0.75

© American Battlefield Trust. Map prepared by Steven Stanley.
The historic battlefield is shown alongside modern efforts to preserve this land.
Maps are available for download for personal use only at *www.battlefields.org/maps.*

56

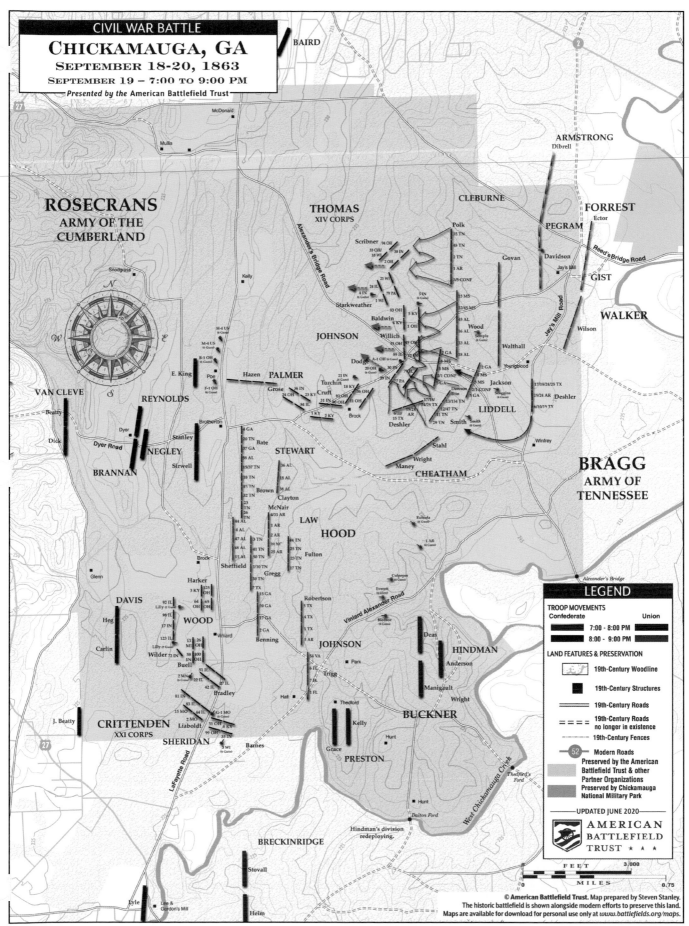

CIVIL WAR BATTLE
CHICKAMAUGA, GA
SEPTEMBER 18-20, 1863
SEPTEMBER 19 – 7:00 TO 9:00 PM
Presented by the American Battlefield Trust

ROSECRANS
ARMY OF THE
CUMBERLAND

THOMAS
XIV CORPS

CLEBURNE

FORREST
Ector

PEGRAM

ARMSTRONG
Dibrell

GIST

WALKER

BRAGG
ARMY OF
TENNESSEE

VAN CLEVE

REYNOLDS

NEGLEY

BRANNAN

PALMER

JOHNSON

Hazen

Turchin

LIDDELL

STEWART

CHEATHAM

DAVIS

WOOD

LAW

HOOD

Wilder

JOHNSON

HINDMAN

Anderson

Manigault

Wright

BUCKNER

CRITTENDEN
XXI CORPS

SHERIDAN

PRESTON

BRECKINRIDGE
Stovall

LEGEND
TROOP MOVEMENTS

Confederate	Union
7:00 - 8:00 PM	
8:00 - 9:00 PM	

LAND FEATURES & PRESERVATION

19th-Century Woodline

19th-Century Structures

19th-Century Roads

19th-Century Roads no longer in existence

19th-Century Fences

52 Modern Roads

Preserved by the American Battlefield Trust & other Partner Organizations

Preserved by Chickamauga National Military Park

UPDATED JUNE 2020

AMERICAN BATTLEFIELD TRUST ★ ★ ★

FEET 3,000

MILES 0.75

© **American Battlefield Trust.** Map prepared by Steven Stanley.
The historic battlefield is shown alongside modern efforts to preserve this land.
Maps are available for download for personal use only at www.battlefields.org/maps.

Hindman's division redeploying.

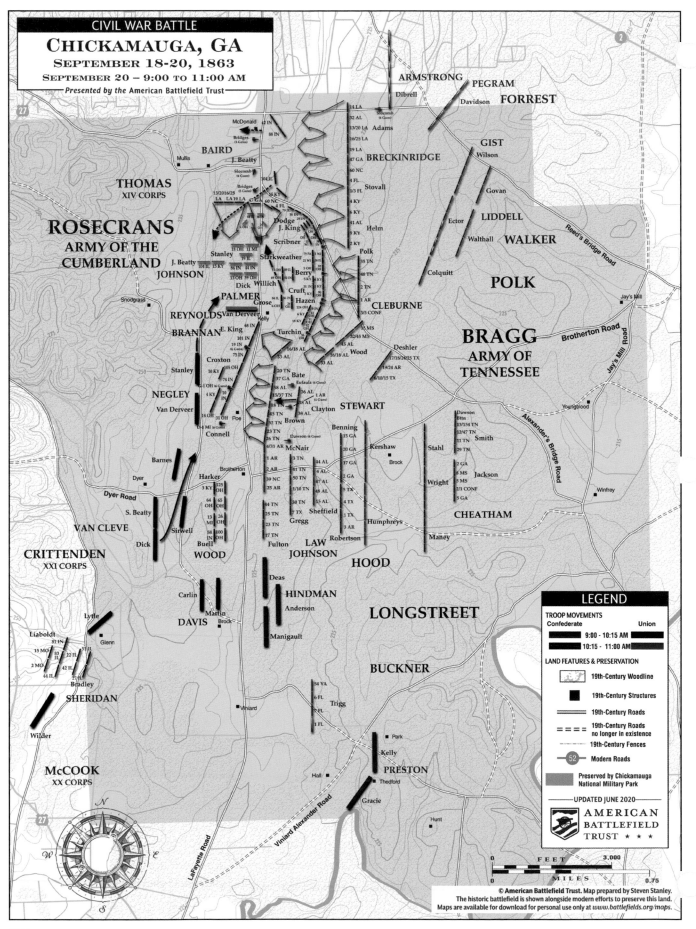

CIVIL WAR BATTLE
CHICKAMAUGA, GA
SEPTEMBER 18-20, 1863
SEPTEMBER 20 – 9:00 TO 11:00 AM
Presented by the American Battlefield Trust

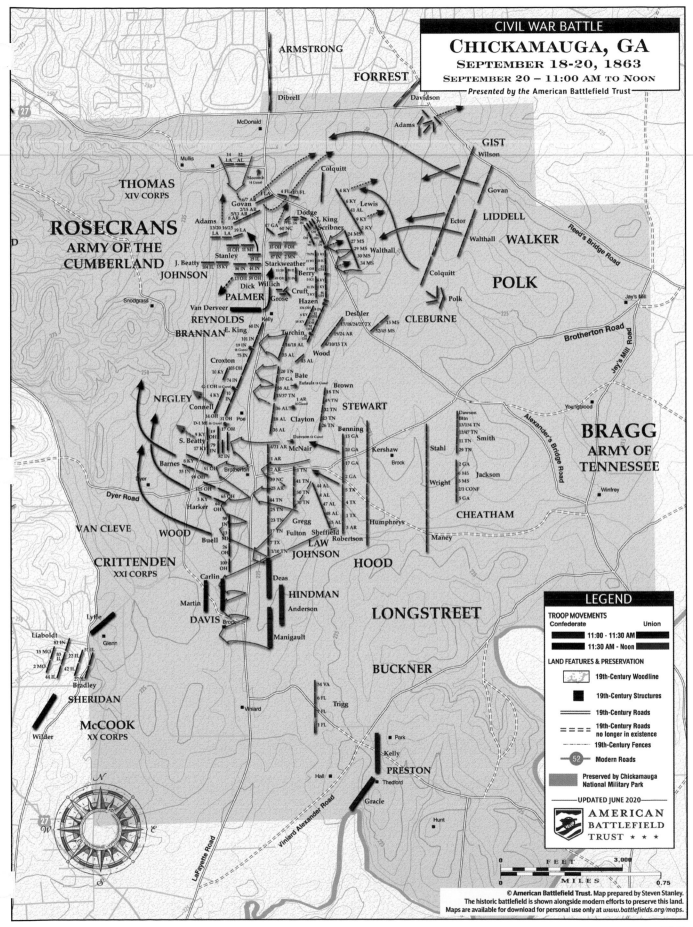

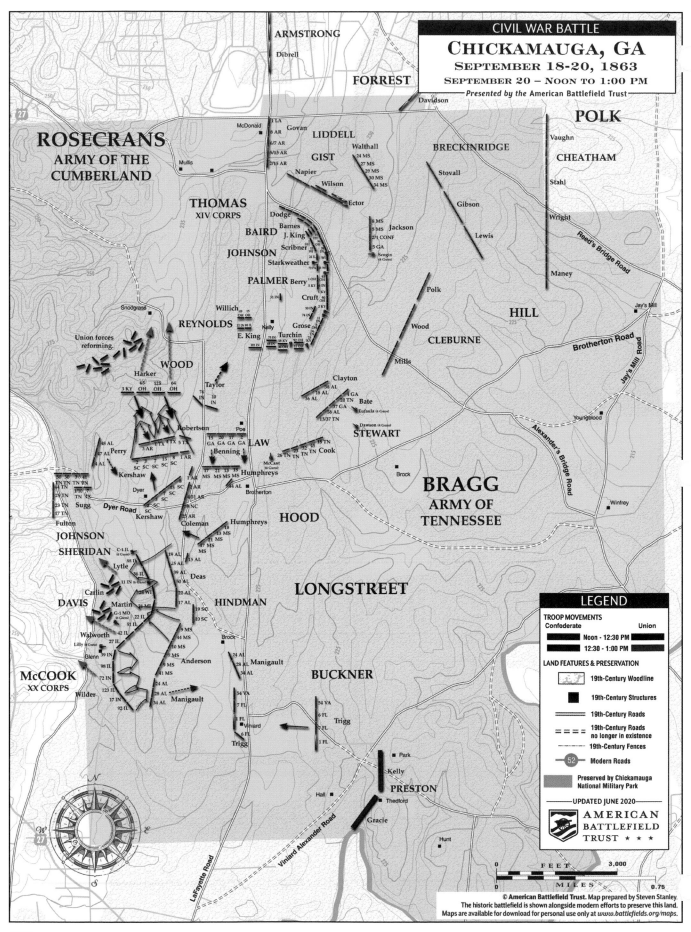

CIVIL WAR BATTLE
CHICKAMAUGA, GA
SEPTEMBER 18-20, 1863
SEPTEMBER 20 – NOON TO 1:00 PM
Presented by the American Battlefield Trust

ROSECRANS
ARMY OF THE
CUMBERLAND

BRAGG
ARMY OF
TENNESSEE

THOMAS
XIV CORPS

McCOOK
XX CORPS

LEGEND

TROOP MOVEMENTS
Confederate   Union
Noon - 12:30 PM
12:30 - 1:00 PM

LAND FEATURES & PRESERVATION

19th-Century Woodline

19th-Century Structures

19th-Century Roads

19th-Century Roads
no longer in existence

19th-Century Fences

52 Modern Roads

Preserved by Chickamauga
National Military Park

UPDATED JUNE 2020

**AMERICAN
BATTLEFIELD
TRUST** ★ ★ ★

FEET   3,000

MILES   0.75

© **American Battlefield Trust.** Map prepared by Steven Stanley.
The historic battlefield is shown alongside modern efforts to preserve this land.
Maps are available for download for personal use only at *www.battlefields.org/maps*.

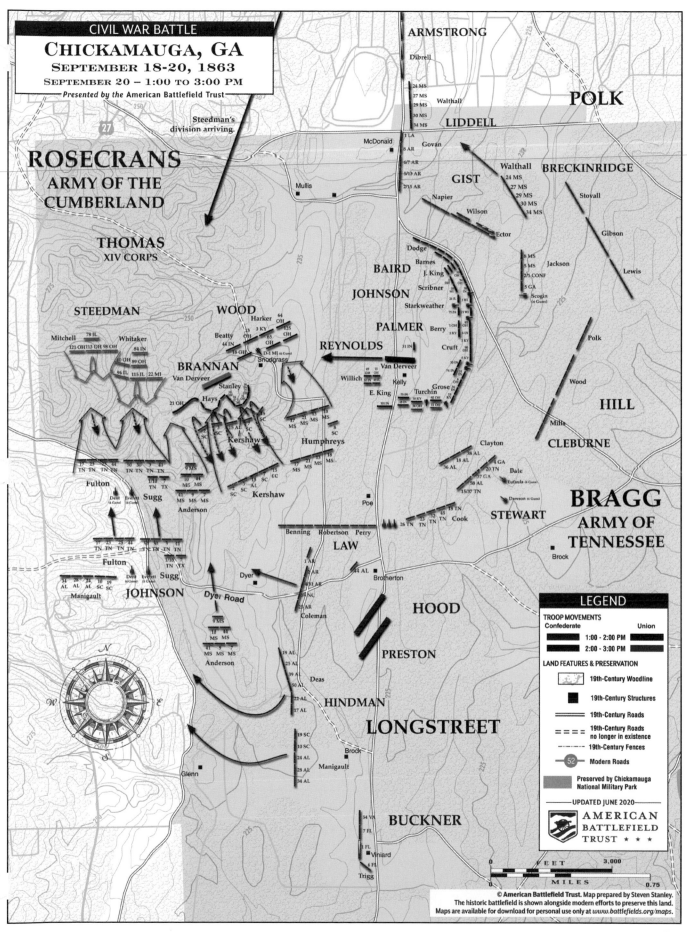

CIVIL WAR BATTLE
CHICKAMAUGA, GA
SEPTEMBER 18-20, 1863
SEPTEMBER 20 – 1:00 TO 3:00 PM
Presented by the American Battlefield Trust

ROSECRANS
ARMY OF THE
CUMBERLAND

THOMAS
XIV CORPS

Steedman's
division arriving.

POLK

ARMSTRONG
Dibrell
24 MS
27 MS   Walthall
29 MS
30 MS
34 MS

LIDDELL

McDonald   1 LA
8 AR   Govan
6/7 AR
5/13 AR   Walthall
2/15 AR   24 MS
GIST   27 MS   BRECKINRIDGE
Napier   29 MS
Wilson   30 MS   Stovall
34 MS
Ector   Gibson

Mullis

BAIRD   Dodge   8 MS   Jackson
Barnes   5 MS   Lewis
J. King   2/5 CONF
JOHNSON   Scribner   5 GA
PALMER   Starkweather   Scogin
Berry   (4 Guns)
1 OH
WOOD   Harker   64   3 KY   Cruft   Polk
Beatty   OH   125
13   3 KY   OH   Van Derveer
BRANNAN   44 IN   65   Reynolds   31 IN
Van Derveer   18 OH   Snodgrass   Willich   Kelly   Wood   HILL
Stanley   E. King   Turchin   CLEBURNE
STEEDMAN   Hays   Humphreys   Grose
Mitchell   78 IL   Whitaker   84 IN   21 OH   Clayton
121 OH 113 OH 98 OH   Kershaw   38 AL   STEWART
40 OH 89 OH   36 AL   18 AL   20 TN   Dale
96 IL 115 IL 22 MI   17   21   15   37 GA   Eufaula (4 Guns)
SC   MS   MS   SC   58 AL   BRAGG
17 25 30 30   15 AL SC   15/37 TN   Dawson (4 Guns)   ARMY OF
TN TN TN TN   SC SC   SC   15 TN   TENNESSEE
1/10 7   10 11   41   15   Poe   45   Cook
TN TX   MS MS   MS SC   15   26 TN TN TN
Fulton   MS MS MS   2   Kershaw   Brock
Dent Everett   SC
(4 Guns)(4 Guns) Sugg   Benning Robertson Perry
Anderson   LAW
17 25 30 41   Dyer   1 AR
TN TN TN TN   5 AR
Fulton   4/31 AR   44 AL   Brotherton
1/18   Everett Sugg   8 NC
TN TX   Dent (4 Guns)   25 AR   HOOD
34 28 24 10 19   JOHNSON   Dyer Road   Coleman
AL AL AL SC SC   PRESTON
Manigault   9 MS   19 AL
MS MS   25 AL
Anderson   39 AL   Deas
50 AL   HINDMAN
22 AL
17 AL   LONGSTREET
19 SC
10 SC
24 AL   Brock
28 AL   Manigault
Glenn   34 AL
54 VA   BUCKNER
7 FL
8 FL
Viniard
6 FL
Trigg

LEGEND
TROOP MOVEMENTS
Confederate   Union
1:00 - 2:00 PM
2:00 - 3:00 PM
LAND FEATURES & PRESERVATION
19th-Century Woodline
19th-Century Structures
19th-Century Roads
19th-Century Roads
no longer in existence
19th-Century Fences
52   Modern Roads
Preserved by Chickamauga
National Military Park
— UPDATED JUNE 2020 —
AMERICAN
BATTLEFIELD
TRUST ★ ★ ★
0   FEET   3,000
0   MILES   0.75
© American Battlefield Trust. Map prepared by Steven Stanley.
The historic battlefield is shown alongside modern efforts to preserve this land.
Maps are available for download for personal use only at www.battlefields.org/maps.

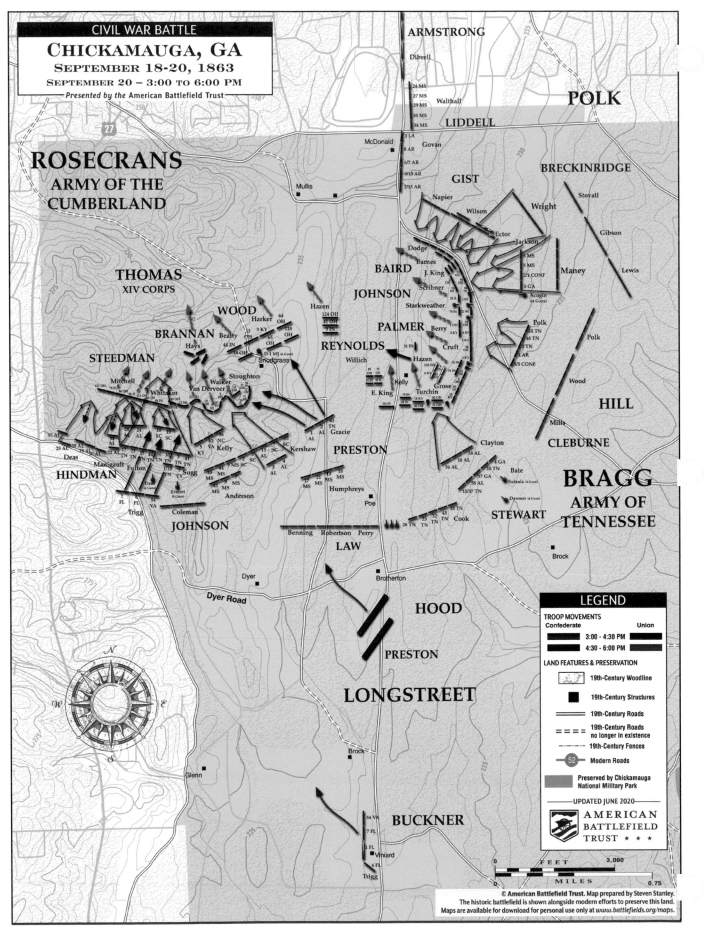

CIVIL WAR BATTLE
CHICKAMAUGA, GA
SEPTEMBER 18-20, 1863
SEPTEMBER 20 – 3:00 TO 6:00 PM
Presented by the American Battlefield Trust

ROSECRANS
ARMY OF THE CUMBERLAND

POLK

LIDDELL

GIST

BRECKINRIDGE

THOMAS
XIV CORPS

BAIRD

JOHNSON

PALMER

REYNOLDS

WOOD

BRANNAN

STEEDMAN

HILL

CLEBURNE

PRESTON

HINDMAN

BRAGG
ARMY OF TENNESSEE

STEWART

JOHNSON

LAW

HOOD

PRESTON

LONGSTREET

BUCKNER

LEGEND
TROOP MOVEMENTS
Confederate | Union
3:00 - 4:30 PM
4:30 - 6:00 PM

LAND FEATURES & PRESERVATION
- 19th-Century Woodline
- 19th-Century Structures
- 19th-Century Roads
- 19th-Century Roads no longer in existence
- 19th-Century Fences
- 52 Modern Roads
- Preserved by Chickamauga National Military Park

— UPDATED JUNE 2020 —

AMERICAN BATTLEFIELD TRUST ★ ★ ★

FEET 3,000
MILES 0.75

BATTLES *of* CHATTANOOGA

(MISSIONARY RIDGE/LOOKOUT MOUNTAIN/TUNNEL HILL)

NOVEMBER 23-25, 1863

TURMOIL GRIPPED THE HIGH COMMANDS OF **THE ARMIES OF THE CUMBERLAND** and Tennessee following the Battle of Chickamauga. Bragg failed to capitalize on his victory and lost the confidence of his army—even as Rosecrans lost the confidence of Abraham Lincoln. Lincoln gave Ulysses S. Grant command over the newly created Military Division of the Mississippi, effectively placing all Federal troops in the Western Theatre under Grant's control. Grant arrived in Chattanooga to find the city besieged, and the Confederates in control of the dominating heights of Lookout Mountain and Missionary Ridge. Grant immediately replaced Rosecrans with George H. Thomas. Reinforcements from the Army of the Tennessee and the Army of the Potomac arrived to bolster the bedraggled Army of the Cumberland.

Meantime, Bragg faced a revolt of sorts from his subordinates. The crisis reached the point where Jefferson Davis arrived and awkwardly allowed his generals to air their grievances. Davis ultimately supported Bragg, but the damage was done. James Longstreet, a Bragg critic, departed Bragg's army for a siege of Knoxville, taking his veteran divisions with him.

On November 23, Grant received word that Bragg was withdrawing some of his brigades. Grant became concerned that Bragg was sending troops to reinforce the siege of Knoxville. Grant countered, sending 14,000 Union troops to engage the rear guard of 600 Confederates at Orchard Knob, where the Federals overran the vastly outnumbered Rebels.

The next day, Maj. Gen. Joseph Hooker struck the Confederate left at Lookout Mountain. Hooker's men drove Confederate Brig. Gen. Edward Walthall's men back. A Confederate counter-attack launched against the surging Union forces, found the Rebels outflanked and they retreated through the fog. That night, Bragg decided to withdraw from Lookout Mountain in order to reinforce Missionary Ridge.

Grant wished for General William T. Sherman to attack Missionary Ridge in coordination with Hooker's attack at Lookout Mountain. However, Sherman's men errantly attacked Billy Goat Hill, which was physically separated from Missionary Ridge. Undaunted, Grant ordered Hooker to advance on Missionary Ridge from the south while Sherman attacked Tunnel Hill, on the northern end of the Confederate position. Thomas's Army of the Cumberland was arrayed against the center of Bragg's line to offer assistance as needed.

On November 25, Sherman's men experienced early successes, but a counter-attack from the Confederates routed the exhausted Federals. On the Union right, Hooker found more success than Sherman. At 2:30 p.m., Grant ordered Thomas to demonstrate against the Confederate center and draw Bragg's attention away from Sherman. Thomas deployed 24,000 men against rifle pits at the base of the Ridge. The Union soldiers charged against the pits and successfully overran the 9,000 defenders. Despite Grant's orders to the contrary, Thomas's men continued their charge straight up the ridge, swarming over the top and overwhelming the Confederate defenders. The Confederate line broke and fled from Missionary Ridge, thus ending the siege of Chattanooga.

Union possession of Chattanooga opened up the Deep South for a Union offensive. The stage was set for Sherman's Atlanta Campaign the following spring, and the victory catapulted Grant to command of all Federal armies.

✳ ✳ PRESERVATION ✳ ✳

To date, the **American Battlefield Trust** has saved **120 acres** at Chattanooga Battlefield.

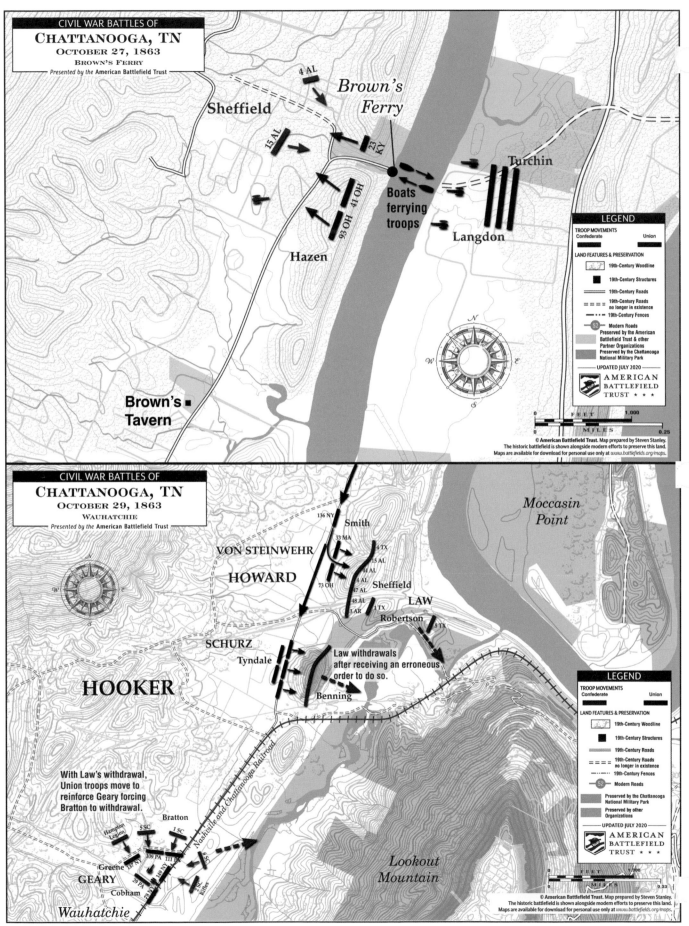

CIVIL WAR BATTLES OF

CHATTANOOGA, TN
OCTOBER 27, 1863
BROWN'S FERRY
Presented by the American Battlefield Trust

Sheffield

4 AL

Brown's Ferry

15 AL

23 KY

Turchin

40 OH

41 OH

93 OH

Boats ferrying troops

Langdon

Hazen

Brown's Tavern

LEGEND

TROOP MOVEMENTS
Confederate   Union

LAND FEATURES & PRESERVATION
19th-Century Woodline
19th-Century Structures
19th-Century Roads
19th-Century Roads no longer in existence
19th-Century Fences
52 Modern Roads
Preserved by the American Battlefield Trust & other Partner Organizations
Preserved by the Chattanooga National Military Park

UPDATED JULY 2020

AMERICAN BATTLEFIELD TRUST ★ ★ ★

FEET 1,000
MILES 0.25

© American Battlefield Trust. Map prepared by Steven Stanley.
The historic battlefield is shown alongside modern efforts to preserve this land.
Maps are available for download for personal use only at www.battlefields.org/maps.

CIVIL WAR BATTLES OF

CHATTANOOGA, TN
OCTOBER 29, 1863
WAUHATCHIE
Presented by the American Battlefield Trust

Moccasin Point

136 NY

Smith

33 MA

4 TX

VON STEINWEHR

15 AL

44 AL

HOWARD

73 OH

4 AL

Sheffield

47 AL

LAW

48 AL

1 TX

5 AR

Robertson

5 TX

SCHURZ

Tyndale

Law withdrawals after receiving an erroneous order to do so.

HOOKER

Benning

With Law's withdrawal, Union troops move to reinforce Geary forcing Bratton to withdrawal.

Bratton

Hampton Legion   5 SC   1 SC

Greene   137 NY   109 PA   111 PA

5 SC

GEARY

29 PA   149 NY   78 NY

Cobham

Wauhatchie

Nashville and Chattanooga Railroad

Lookout Mountain

LEGEND

TROOP MOVEMENTS
Confederate   Union

LAND FEATURES & PRESERVATION
19th-Century Woodline
19th-Century Structures
19th-Century Roads
19th-Century Roads no longer in existence
19th-Century Fences
52 Modern Roads
Preserved by the Chattanooga National Military Park
Preserved by other Organizations

UPDATED JULY 2020

AMERICAN BATTLEFIELD TRUST ★ ★ ★

FEET 1,200
MILES 0.33

© American Battlefield Trust. Map prepared by Steven Stanley.
The historic battlefield is shown alongside modern efforts to preserve this land.
Maps are available for download for personal use only at www.battlefields.org/maps.

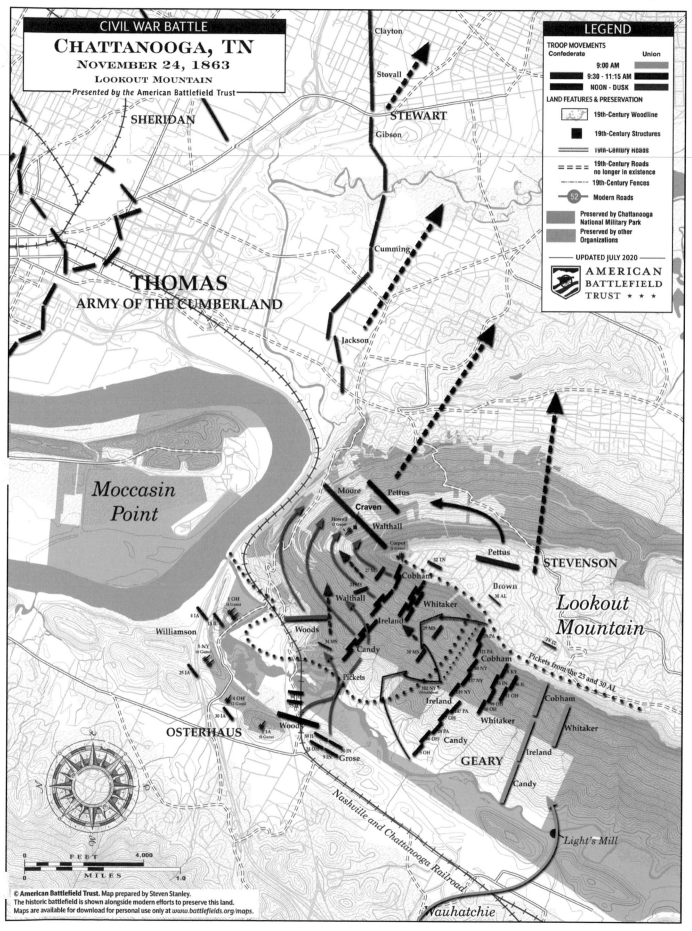

CIVIL WAR BATTLE
CHATTANOOGA, TN
NOVEMBER 24, 1863
LOOKOUT MOUNTAIN
Presented by the American Battlefield Trust

LEGEND

TROOP MOVEMENTS
Confederate · Union
9:00 AM
9:30 - 11:15 AM
NOON - DUSK

LAND FEATURES & PRESERVATION
19th-Century Woodline
19th-Century Structures
19th-Century Roads
19th-Century Roads no longer in existence
19th-Century Fences
52 Modern Roads
Preserved by Chattanooga National Military Park
Preserved by other Organizations

UPDATED JULY 2020

AMERICAN BATTLEFIELD TRUST ★★★

SHERIDAN

Clayton
Stovall
STEWART
Gibson

THOMAS
ARMY OF THE CUMBERLAND

Cumming

Jackson

Moccasin Point

Moore
Pettus
Craven
Walthall
Howell (2 Guns)
Corput (2 Guns)
27 MS
31 MS
Cobham
32 TN
Pettus
STEVENSON
Brown
30 AL
Walthall
Whitaker
1 OH (4 Guns)
4 IA
13 IL
Williamson
Woods
34 MS
Ireland
29 MS
30 MS
Lookout Mountain
1 NY (4 Guns)
Candy
11 PA
Cobham
29 PA
Pickets from the 23 and 30 AL
25 IA
Pickets
102 NY (Skirmish)
137 NY
5 KY
51 OH
7 V IZ
4 OH (2 Guns)
Ireland
149 NY
29 PA
99 OH
149 PA
Cobham
30 IA
147 PA
Whitaker
1 IA (2 Guns)
OSTERHAUS
Woods
29 PA
66 OH
84 IL
Candy
Whitaker
75 IL
59 IL
Ireland
24 IN
59 IN
GEARY
Candy
9 IN
Grose

Nashville and Chattanooga Railroad

Light's Mill

FEET 4,000
MILES 1.0

© **American Battlefield Trust**. Map prepared by Steven Stanley.
The historic battlefield is shown alongside modern efforts to preserve this land.
Maps are available for download for personal use only at *www.battlefields.org/maps.*

Wauhatchie

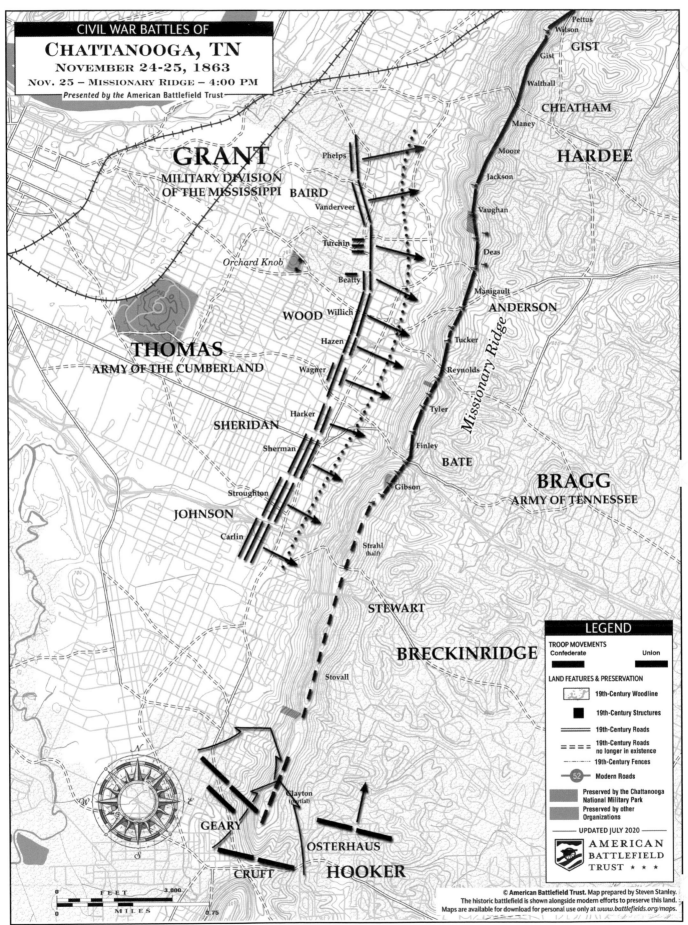

CIVIL WAR BATTLES OF
CHATTANOOGA, TN
NOVEMBER 24-25, 1863
NOV. 25 – MISSIONARY RIDGE – 4:00 PM
Presented by the American Battlefield Trust

GRANT
MILITARY DIVISION
OF THE MISSISSIPPI

THOMAS
ARMY OF THE CUMBERLAND

Orchard Knob

BAIRD

Phelps

Vanderveer

Turchin

Beatty

WOOD

Willich

Hazen

Wagner

Harker

SHERIDAN

Sherman

Stroughton

JOHNSON

Carlin

Strahl
(half)

STEWART

Stovall

BRECKINRIDGE

Pettus
Wilson
GIST
Gist
Walthall
CHEATHAM
Maney
Moore
HARDEE
Jackson
Vaughan
Deas
Manigault
ANDERSON
Tucker
Reynolds
Tyler
Finley
BATE
Gibson

Missionary Ridge

BRAGG
ARMY OF TENNESSEE

GEARY

Clayton
(partial)

OSTERHAUS

CRUFT

HOOKER

LEGEND
TROOP MOVEMENTS
Confederate   Union

LAND FEATURES & PRESERVATION
- 19th-Century Woodline
- 19th-Century Structures
- 19th-Century Roads
- 19th-Century Roads no longer in existence
- 19th-Century Fences
- 52 Modern Roads
- Preserved by the Chattanooga National Military Park
- Preserved by other Organizations

— UPDATED JULY 2020 —

AMERICAN BATTLEFIELD TRUST ★ ★ ★

© American Battlefield Trust. Map prepared by Steven Stanley.
The historic battlefield is shown alongside modern efforts to preserve this land.
Maps are available for download for personal use only at www.battlefields.org/maps.

FEET 3,000
MILES 0.75

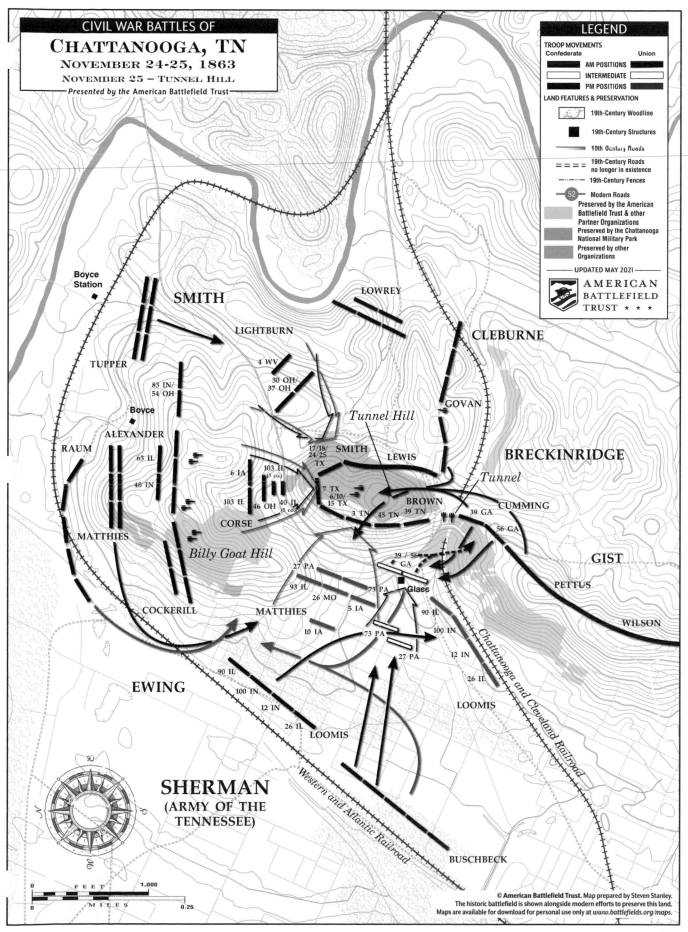

CIVIL WAR BATTLES OF
CHATTANOOGA, TN
NOVEMBER 24-25, 1863
NOVEMBER 25 – TUNNEL HILL
Presented by the American Battlefield Trust

Boyce Station

SMITH

LOWREY

LIGHTBURN

CLEBURNE

4 WV

TUPPER

30 OH / 37 OH

83 IN / 54 OH

GOVAN

Boyce

ALEXANDER

Tunnel Hill

RAUM

17/18/ 24/25 TX

SMITH

LEWIS

BRECKINRIDGE

63 IL

6 1A

103 IL (3 co.)

Tunnel

48 IN

7 TX 6/10/ 15 TX

103 IL

46 OH

40 IL (5 co.)

BROWN

39 GA

CUMMING

MATTHIES

CORSE

3 TN   45 TN   39 TN

56 GA

GIST

Billy Goat Hill

39 / 56 GA

PETTUS

27 PA

93 IL

26 MO

73 PA

Glass

COCKERILL

5 1A

90 IL

WILSON

MATTHIES

10 1A

73 PA

100 IN

12 IN

26 IL

27 PA

90 IL

EWING

100 IN

Chattanooga and Cleveland Railroad

12 IN

26 IL

LOOMIS

LOOMIS

SHERMAN
(ARMY OF THE TENNESSEE)

Western and Atlantic Railroad

BUSCHBECK

FEET   1,000
0
MILES   0.25
0

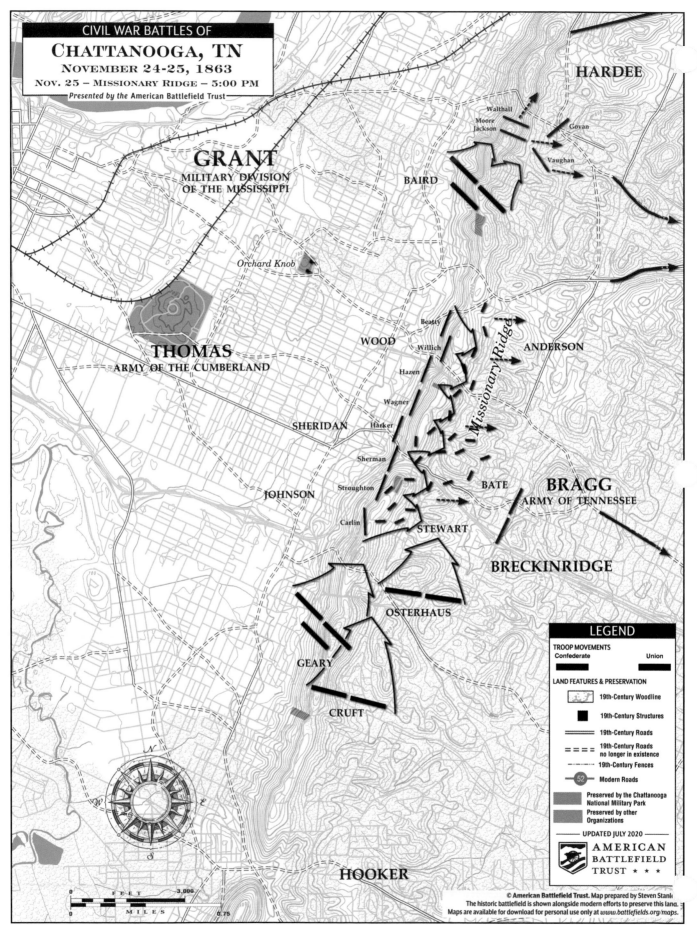

CIVIL WAR BATTLES OF
CHATTANOOGA, TN
NOVEMBER 24-25, 1863
NOV. 25 – MISSIONARY RIDGE – 5:00 PM
Presented by the American Battlefield Trust

HARDEE

Walthall
Moore
Jackson
Govan

Vaughan

GRANT
MILITARY DIVISION
OF THE MISSISSIPPI

BAIRD

Orchard Knob

Beatty

THOMAS
ARMY OF THE CUMBERLAND

WOOD

Willich

Anderson

Missionary Ridge

Hazen

Wagner

SHERIDAN

Harker

Sherman

Stroughton

BATE

BRAGG
ARMY OF TENNESSEE

JOHNSON

Carlin

Stewart

BRECKINRIDGE

OSTERHAUS

GEARY

CRUFT

LEGEND

TROOP MOVEMENTS
Confederate   Union

LAND FEATURES & PRESERVATION

19th-Century Woodline

19th-Century Structures

19th-Century Roads

19th-Century Roads
no longer in existence

19th-Century Fences

52 Modern Roads

Preserved by the Chattanooga
National Military Park

Preserved by other
Organizations

— UPDATED JULY 2020 —

AMERICAN
BATTLEFIELD
TRUST ★ ★ ★

HOOKER

N

FEET   3,000

MILES   0.75

© American Battlefield Trust. Map prepared by Steven Stanley
The historic battlefield is shown alongside modern efforts to preserve this land.
Maps are available for download for personal use only at www.battlefields.org/maps.

BATTLE *of* ROCKY FACE RIDGE

MAY 7-13, 1864

THE DAWN OF 1864 BROUGHT RENEWED VIGOR TO THE UNION WAR EFFORT. The victories of 1863, a new overall Union commander, and the November presidential election looming on the horizon all blended together into an urgency heretofore unseen in the war. In March, Ulysses S. Grant was promoted to command all Federal armies, and Sherman assumed command of the Military Division of Mississippi. Grant sought to apply pressure to the Confederate armies across all theaters of the war.

The Confederates, too, felt an urgency. With the pending northern presidential election, there was a glimmer of hope that the Southern Confederacy could gain independence through the northern voters. If Lincoln were replaced with a northern "Peace Democrat," independence for the South would almost be inevitable. But to win over the northern voters, the Confederate high command had to both survive the coming campaign season and make it so bloody that the voters of the north could not stomach the ever-growing casualty lists.

After the Confederate defeat at Chattanooga, Jefferson Davis relieved Bragg of command. Davis then reluctantly turned to Gen. Joseph E. Johnston. Johnston had amassed a long and relatively unimpressive resume during the war, yet the Confederate people and Southern soldiers felt a confidence in Johnston—a confidence Davis did not share. Johnston maneuvered his army into a blocking position in north Georgia. To the Confederates, the next logical Union step toward victory after the fall of Chattanooga was an offensive on the vital rail and supply center of Atlanta.

In the first week of May, Sherman led 100,000 men—divided between three armies—into Georgia. While the capture of Atlanta was a goal of the spring offensive, the destruction of Johnston's army was the higher priority.

After pushing back brief resistance at Tunnel Hill on May 7, Sherman approached Johnston's 60,000 Confederates entrenched west of Dalton, Georgia, along an imposing summit known locally as Rocky Face Ridge. A head-on assault risked disaster. Instead, Sherman ordered Maj. Gen. James B. McPherson's Army of the Tennessee to make a wide march around the southern tip of the ridge and strike the railhead at Resaca, Georgia, cutting the Confederate retreat and resupply line. Meantime, Maj. Gen. George Thomas's Army of the Cumberland and Maj. Gen. John Schofield's Army of the Ohio would launch diversionary attacks on the northern and western faces of the ridge to draw Johnston's attention away from his vulnerable southern flank.

The fighting on Rocky Face Ridge began in earnest on May 8, with Union columns pressing towards Mill Creek Gap from the west and from Dug Gap to the south. Hurling rocks when they ran out of ammunition, the Confederates held their position, but the Federals successfully kept Johnston's men and his attention away from his southern sector.

On May 9, McPherson moved through Snake Creek Gap 17 miles south and formed for an attack on Resaca. The Confederates here were vastly outnumbered—some 4,000 men versus McPherson's 25,000—and the rest of the army was pinned down on the ridge. Still, their stubborn resistance cowed McPherson, and he refused to order the kind of full-scale attack that might have taken the town and broken Johnston's supply line. On May 10, Sherman began to pull his men out of their lines opposing the Rocky Face, while Johnston matched Sherman's maneuver, withdrawing into another fortified ring around Resaca where the fighting would continue.

✳ ✳ PRESERVATION ✳ ✳

To date, the **American Battlefield Trust** has saved **926 acres** at Rocky Face Ridge Battlefield.

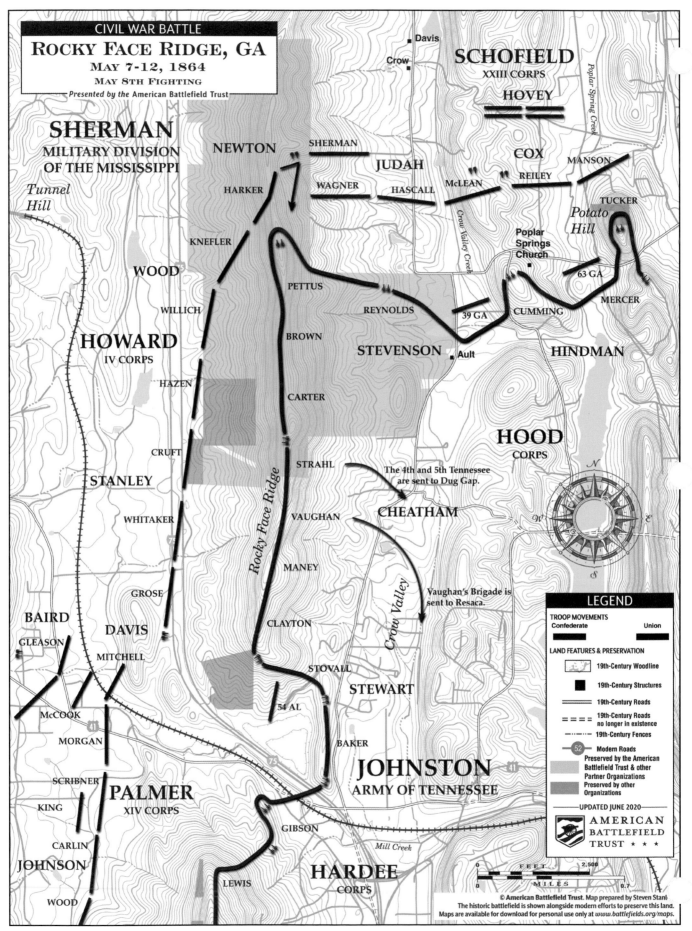

CIVIL WAR BATTLE

ROCKY FACE RIDGE, GA
MAY 7-12, 1864
MAY 8TH FIGHTING
Presented by the American Battlefield Trust

SCHOFIELD
XXIII CORPS

HOVEY

Davis
Crow

SHERMAN
MILITARY DIVISION
OF THE MISSISSIPPI

Tunnel Hill

NEWTON

SHERMAN
JUDAH
COX
MANSON

HARKER
WAGNER
HASCALL
McLEAN
REILEY
TUCKER

Potato Hill

KNEFLER

PETTUS

Poplar Springs Church

63 GA

WOOD

WILLICH

REYNOLDS

39 GA
CUMMING
MERCER

HOWARD
IV CORPS

BROWN

STEVENSON
Ault

HINDMAN

HAZEN

CARTER

CRUFT

STRAHL

The 4th and 5th Tennessee are sent to Dug Gap.

HOOD
CORPS

STANLEY

WHITAKER

VAUGHAN

CHEATHAM

Rocky Face Ridge

MANEY

Vaughan's Brigade is sent to Resaca.

GROSE

Crow Valley

CLAYTON

BAIRD

DAVIS

GLEASON

MITCHELL

STOVALL

STEWART

McCOOK

54 AL

MORGAN

BAKER

JOHNSTON
ARMY OF TENNESSEE

PALMER
XIV CORPS

SCRIBNER

KING

CARLIN

GIBSON

JOHNSON

WOOD

LEWIS

HARDEE
CORPS

Mill Creek

LEGEND

TROOP MOVEMENTS
Confederate   Union

LAND FEATURES & PRESERVATION

19th-Century Woodline

19th-Century Structures

19th-Century Roads

19th-Century Roads no longer in existence

19th-Century Fences

52 Modern Roads

Preserved by the American Battlefield Trust & other Partner Organizations

Preserved by other Organizations

UPDATED JUNE 2020

AMERICAN BATTLEFIELD TRUST ★ ★ ★

0   FEET   2,500

MILES

0   0.7

© American Battlefield Trust. Map prepared by Steven Stanl
The historic battlefield is shown alongside modern efforts to preserve this land.
Maps are available for download for personal use only at www.battlefields.org/maps.

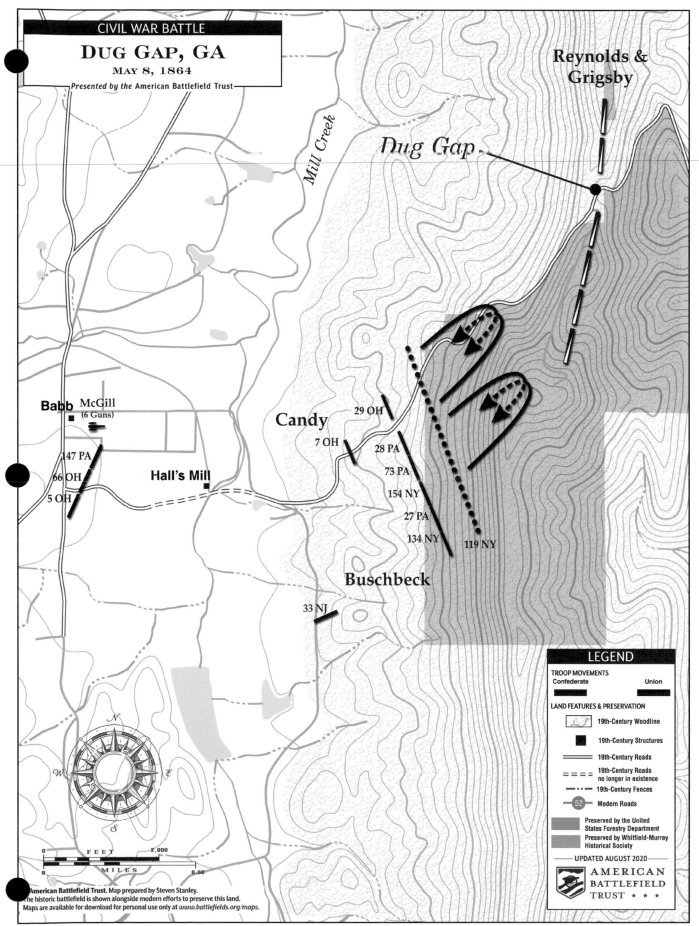

CIVIL WAR BATTLE

DUG GAP, GA

MAY 8, 1864

Presented by the American Battlefield Trust

Reynolds & Grigsby

Dug Gap

Mill Creek

Babb McGill (6 Guns)

147 PA

66 OH

5 OH

Candy

29 OH

7 OH

28 PA

73 PA

154 NY

27 PA

134 NY

119 NY

Hall's Mill

Buschbeck

33 NJ

LEGEND

TROOP MOVEMENTS

Confederate   Union

LAND FEATURES & PRESERVATION

19th-Century Woodline

19th-Century Structures

19th-Century Roads

19th-Century Roads no longer in existence

19th-Century Fences

52 Modern Roads

Preserved by the United States Forestry Department

Preserved by Whitfield-Murray Historical Society

— UPDATED AUGUST 2020 —

AMERICAN BATTLEFIELD TRUST ★ ★ ★

N
W E
S

FEET 2,000
MILES 0.50

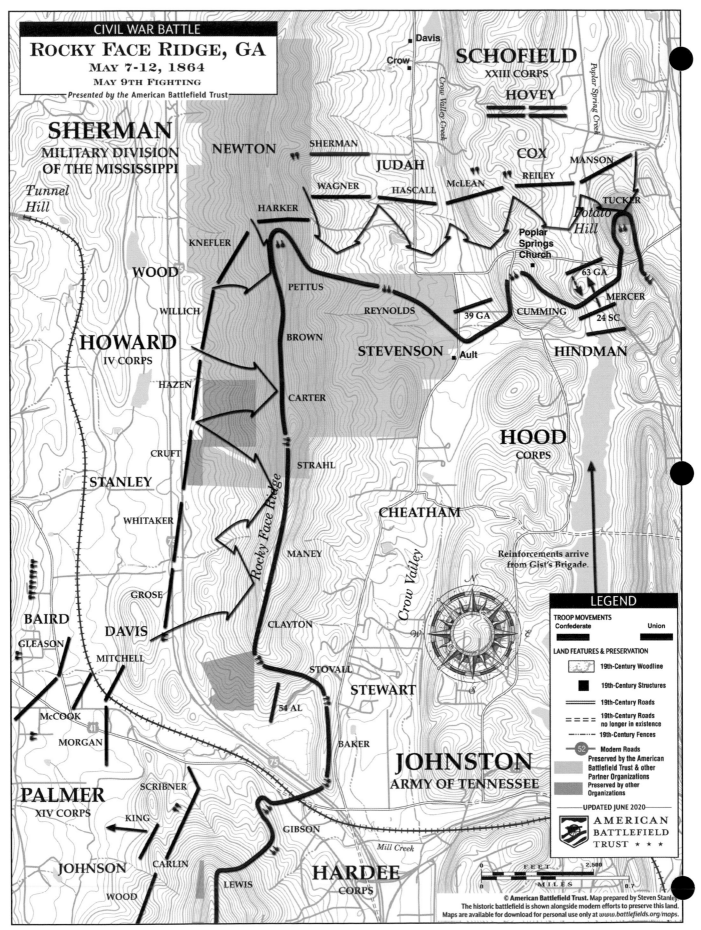

CIVIL WAR BATTLE
ROCKY FACE RIDGE, GA
MAY 7-12, 1864
MAY 9TH FIGHTING
Presented by the American Battlefield Trust

SHERMAN
MILITARY DIVISION
OF THE MISSISSIPPI

Tunnel Hill

NEWTON

SHERMAN

SCHOFIELD
XXIII CORPS

HOVEY

Davis
Crow

Crow Valley Creek

Poplar Spring Creek

JUDAH

WAGNER

HARKER

HASCALL

McLEAN

COX

REILEY

MANSON

TUCKER

KNEFLER

Potato Hill

WOOD

PETTUS

Poplar Springs Church

63 GA

WILLICH

REYNOLDS

39 GA

CUMMING

MERCER

HOWARD
IV CORPS

BROWN

24 SC

HAZEN

STEVENSON

Ault

HINDMAN

CARTER

CRUFT

HOOD
CORPS

STANLEY

STRAHL

Rocky Face Ridge

WHITAKER

CHEATHAM

MANEY

Reinforcements arrive from Gist's Brigade.

GROSE

Crow Valley

BAIRD

CLAYTON

GLEASON

DAVIS

MITCHELL

STOVALL

STEWART

LEGEND

McCOOK

54 AL

TROOP MOVEMENTS
Confederate   Union

MORGAN

BAKER

LAND FEATURES & PRESERVATION

19th-Century Woodline

JOHNSTON
ARMY OF TENNESSEE

19th-Century Structures

PALMER
XIV CORPS

SCRIBNER

19th-Century Roads

KING

19th-Century Roads
no longer in existence

GIBSON

19th-Century Fences

52   Modern Roads
Preserved by the American
Battlefield Trust & other
Partner Organizations
Preserved by other
Organizations

JOHNSON

CARLIN

Mill Creek

UPDATED JUNE 2020

AMERICAN
BATTLEFIELD
TRUST ★ ★ ★

WOOD

LEWIS

HARDEE
CORPS

0   FEET   2,500

MILES

0   0.7

© American Battlefield Trust. Map prepared by Steven Stanley.
The historic battlefield is shown alongside modern efforts to preserve this land.
Maps are available for download for personal use only at www.battlefields.org/maps.

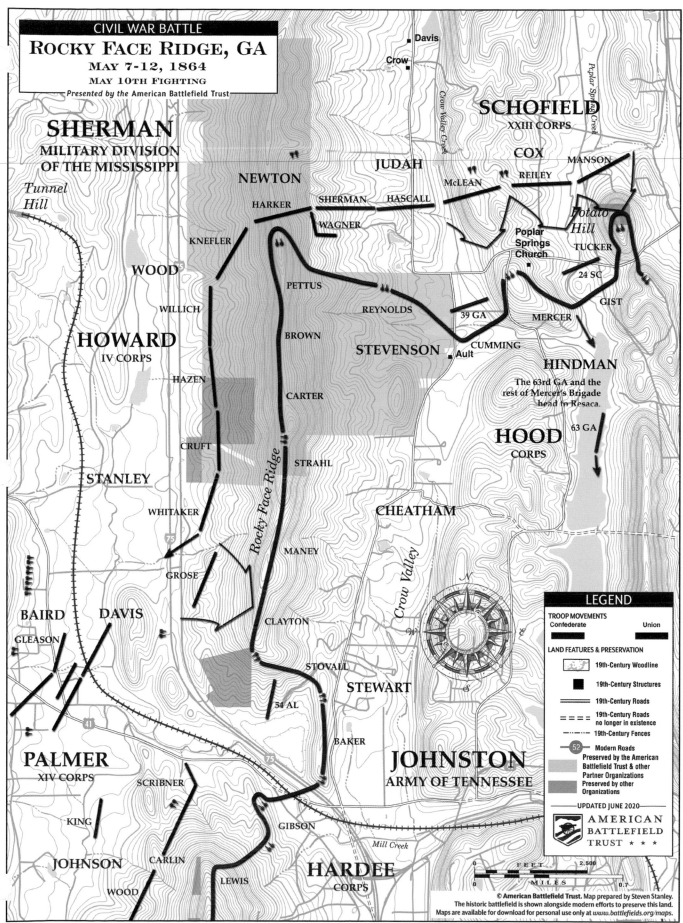

CIVIL WAR BATTLE

ROCKY FACE RIDGE, GA
MAY 7-12, 1864
MAY 10TH FIGHTING
Presented by the American Battlefield Trust

SCHOFIELD
XXIII CORPS

SHERMAN
MILITARY DIVISION
OF THE MISSISSIPPI

Tunnel Hill

Davis

Crow

Crow Valley Creek

Poplar Spring Creek

COX

MANSON

JUDAH

McLEAN

REILEY

NEWTON

HARKER

SHERMAN

HASCALL

WAGNER

Potato Hill

KNEFLER

Poplar Springs Church

TUCKER

WOOD

WILLICH

PETTUS

24 SC

HOWARD
IV CORPS

REYNOLDS

39 GA

MERCER

GIST

BROWN

STEVENSON

CUMMING

Ault

HAZEN

CARTER

HINDMAN

The 63rd GA and the rest of Mercer's Brigade head to Resaca.

CRUFT

STRAHL

HOOD
CORPS

63 GA

STANLEY

CHEATHAM

WHITAKER

MANEY

Rocky Face Ridge

Crow Valley

GROSE

BAIRD

DAVIS

CLAYTON

GLEASON

STOVALL

STEWART

54 AL

BAKER

JOHNSTON
ARMY OF TENNESSEE

PALMER
XIV CORPS

SCRIBNER

KING

GIBSON

Mill Creek

JOHNSON

CARLIN

LEWIS

WOOD

HARDEE
CORPS

LEGEND

TROOP MOVEMENTS
Confederate   Union

LAND FEATURES & PRESERVATION

19th-Century Woodline

19th-Century Structures

───── 19th-Century Roads

═══ 19th-Century Roads no longer in existence

── · ── 19th-Century Fences

52 Modern Roads

Preserved by the American Battlefield Trust & other Partner Organizations

Preserved by other Organizations

— UPDATED JUNE 2020 —

AMERICAN BATTLEFIELD TRUST ★ ★ ★

0   FEET   2,500
0   MILES   0.7

© American Battlefield Trust. Map prepared by Steven Stanley.
The historic battlefield is shown alongside modern efforts to preserve this land.
Maps are available for download for personal use only at *www.battlefields.org/maps*.

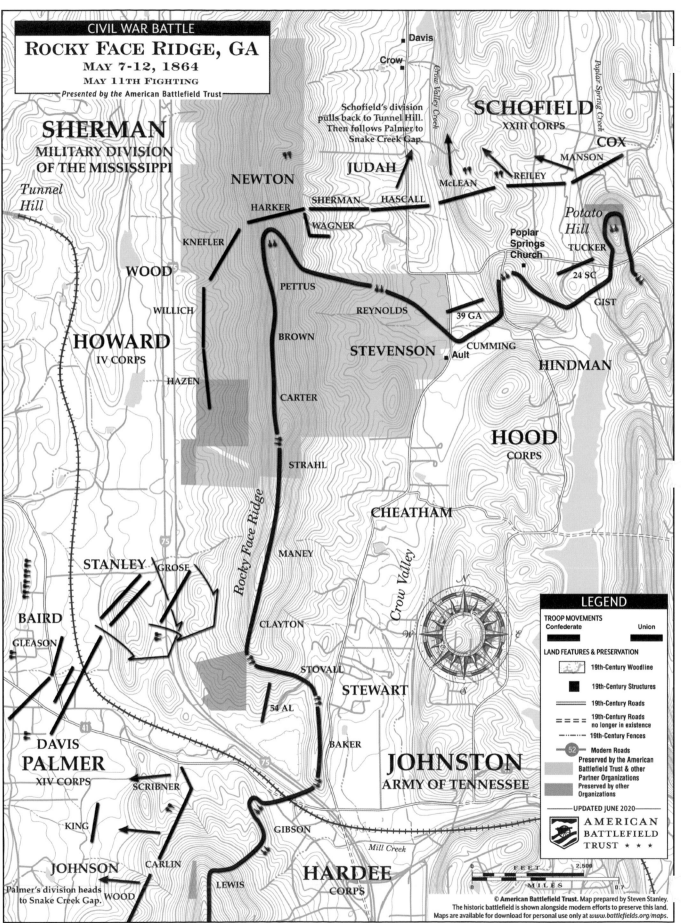

CIVIL WAR BATTLE
ROCKY FACE RIDGE, GA
MAY 7-12, 1864
MAY 11TH FIGHTING
Presented by the American Battlefield Trust

SHERMAN
MILITARY DIVISION
OF THE MISSISSIPPI

Tunnel Hill

SCHOFIELD
XXIII CORPS

Schofield's division pulls back to Tunnel Hill. Then follows Palmer to Snake Creek Gap.

Davis

Crow

COX

MANSON

NEWTON

JUDAH

McLEAN

REILEY

HARKER

SHERMAN

HASCALL

WAGNER

KNEFLER

Potato Hill

TUCKER

WOOD

PETTUS

Poplar Springs Church

24 SC

WILLICH

REYNOLDS

39 GA

GIST

BROWN

CUMMING

HOWARD
IV CORPS

STEVENSON

Ault

HINDMAN

HAZEN

CARTER

HOOD
CORPS

STRAHL

CHEATHAM

MANEY

Rocky Face Ridge

Crow Valley

STANLEY

GROSE

CLAYTON

BAIRD

GLEASON

STOVALL

STEWART

54 AL

BAKER

DAVIS
PALMER
XIV CORPS

JOHNSTON
ARMY OF TENNESSEE

SCRIBNER

KING

GIBSON

JOHNSON

CARLIN

Mill Creek

Palmer's division heads to Snake Creek Gap.

WOOD

LEWIS

HARDEE
CORPS

LEGEND
TROOP MOVEMENTS
Confederate — Union

LAND FEATURES & PRESERVATION
- 19th-Century Woodline
- 19th-Century Structures
- 19th-Century Roads
- 19th-Century Roads no longer in existence
- 19th-Century Fences
- 52 Modern Roads
- Preserved by the American Battlefield Trust & other Partner Organizations
- Preserved by other Organizations

—UPDATED JUNE 2020—

AMERICAN BATTLEFIELD TRUST ★ ★ ★

FEET 0 — 2,500
MILES 0 — 0.7

© American Battlefield Trust. Map prepared by Steven Stanley.
The historic battlefield is shown alongside modern efforts to preserve this land.
Maps are available for download for personal use only at www.battlefields.org/maps.

BATTLE *of* RESACA

MAY 13 15, 1864

ON MAY 5, CONFEDERATE GEN. JOSEPH E. JOHNSTON ORDERED Brig. Gen. James Cantey's infantry brigade to Resaca, a hamlet along the Western & Atlantic Railroad on the north bank of the Oostanaula River, five and a half miles east of Snake Creek Gap. Canty fortified the railroad and wagon bridges, and defended a treeless ridge known as the "Bald Hill." Johnston bolstered this force on May 8, with Col. J. Warren Grigsby's brigade of cavalry. That day, Sherman had attacked Johnston on Rocky Face Ridge 17 miles to the north, and Johnston needed the Resaca bridges to supply his army, or to provide a safe route of retreat toward Atlanta.

Major General James B. McPherson had his troops marching on May 9 with orders to strike the railroad at Resaca and to cut off Johnston. When Grigsby's troopers approached, the Federals drove them back. A division of Federal infantry under Brig. Gen. Thomas Sweeny drove the Confederates across Camp Creek and back to Canty's main line. Sweeny's troops occupied Bald Hill and from there could see Resaca and the railroad bridge over the Oostanaula.

McPherson arrived and instructed Sweeny to hold Bald Hill while he sent men to the north looking for an approach to the railroad. But McPherson fretted that Johnston would send troops to drive him back, and he ordered Sweeny back to Snake Creek Gap. The Union infantry withdrew, abandoning Bald Hill. When Sherman learned this, he ordered McPherson to halt and dig in while he brought the rest of the army through Snake Creek Gap.

By May 14, Johnston's Confederate army was positioned north and west of Resaca, stretching four miles, with its left on the Oostanaula and the right extending to the Conasauga River. Sherman's forces marching from Snake Creek Gap paralleled the Rebel lines. As they did, Sherman ordered attacks to keep the Rebels occupied while Sweeny's division crossed the Oostanaula four miles downstream from Resaca at Lay's Ferry, beyond the Confederate left, to threaten the railroad.

Late on the morning of May 14, Federals of Maj. Gens. John Schofield's XXIII Corps and Oliver O. Howard's IV Corps attacked across Camp Creek but failed to dislodge their opponents. Stiff resistance by Major Generals Patrick Cleburne's and Thomas Hindman's divisions helped repel the attacks, with Maj. Gen. William Bate's division bearing the brunt of the fighting.

The next morning, Maj. Gen. Carter Stevenson positioned a battery to counter the Federal artillery. Stevenson ordered the "Cherokee Battery" of four Napoleons to be placed 20 yards in front of his entrenched infantry. Soldiers constructed an earthen lunette for the guns, but before they could connect it to their main line with rifle pits, Federals attacked the Confederate position, and two Federal regiments of Brig. Gen. John Ward's brigade stormed up to the Rebel earthworks. The Federals received heavy fire and withdrew, leaving the battery unmanned. Neither side could move forward to claim the cannons. After dark, Brig. Gen. John Geary ordered troops to sneak forward, quietly dig through the earthwork, and with ropes drag the four guns back into Union lines.

While all this was taking place on Johnston's right, Sweeny's division crossed the Oostanaula on pontoon bridges below the Confederate left. Realizing he had been flanked, Johnston ordered his troops to withdraw on the night of May 15-16. After crossing to the south bank of the Oostanaula, Johnston's men attempted to burn the bridges, but they were quickly repaired by Sherman's men, and the Federals were one step closer to Atlanta.

✳ ✳ PRESERVATION ✳ ✳

To date, the **American Battlefield Trust** has saved **1,044 acres** at Resaca Battlefield.

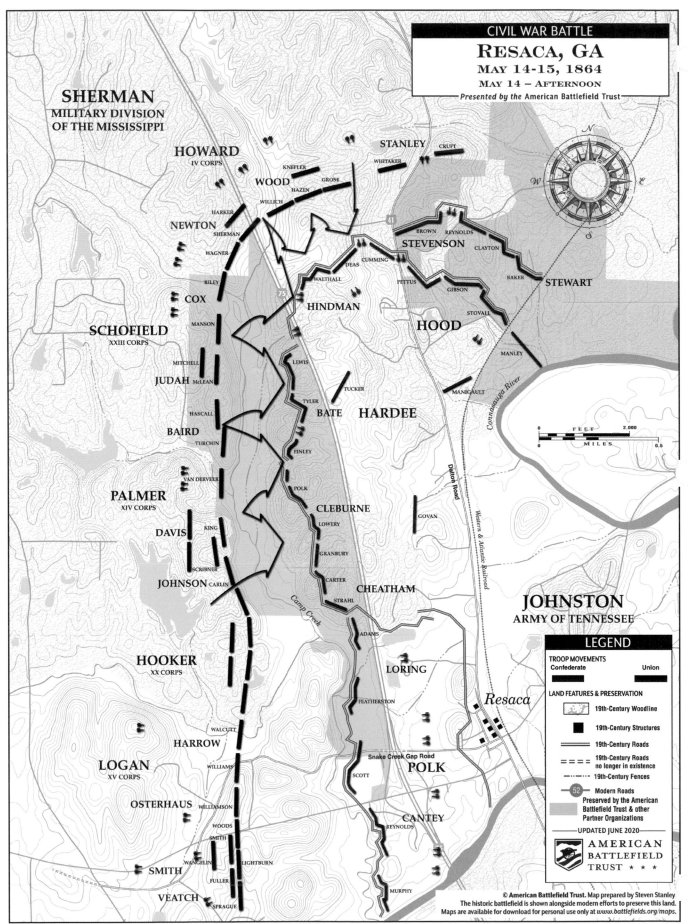

CIVIL WAR BATTLE

RESACA, GA

MAY 14-15, 1864

MAY 14 – AFTERNOON

Presented by the American Battlefield Trust

SHERMAN
MILITARY DIVISION
OF THE MISSISSIPPI

HOWARD
IV CORPS

STANLEY
CRUFT

KNEFLER
WHITAKER
WOOD
GROSE
HAZEN
WILLICH

HARKER
NEWTON
SHERMAN
WAGNER

RILEY

COX

MANSON

SCHOFIELD
XXIII CORPS

MITCHELL
JUDAH McLEAN

HASCALL

BAIRD
TURCHIN

VAN DERVEER

PALMER
XIV CORPS

DAVIS
KING

JOHNSON CARLIN

SCRIBNER

HOOKER
XX CORPS

WALCUTT

HARROW

WILLIAMS

LOGAN
XV CORPS

OSTERHAUS
WILLIAMSON

WOODS

SMITH

WANGELIN LIGHTBURN

SMITH
FULLER

VEATCH
SPRAGUE

BROWN REYNOLDS
STEVENSON
CLAYTON

CUMMING
DEAS
WALTHALL
PETTUS
GIBSON BAKER
STEWART

HINDMAN
STOVALL

HOOD

MANLEY

LEWIS

TUCKER
MANIGAULT

TYLER

BATE HARDEE

FINLEY

POLK

CLEBURNE
LOWERY

GOVAN

GRANBURY

CARTER
CHEATHAM

STRAHL

ADAMS

Camp Creek

LORING

FEATHERSTON

Snake Creek Gap Road
POLK
SCOTT

CANTEY
REYNOLDS

MURPHY

Conasauga River

Dalton Road

Western & Atlantic Railroad

Resaca

JOHNSTON
ARMY OF TENNESSEE

LEGEND

TROOP MOVEMENTS
Confederate   Union

LAND FEATURES & PRESERVATION

19th-Century Woodline

19th-Century Structures

19th-Century Roads

19th-Century Roads
no longer in existence

19th-Century Fences

52 Modern Roads

Preserved by the American
Battlefield Trust & other
Partner Organizations

—UPDATED JUNE 2020—

AMERICAN
BATTLEFIELD
TRUST ★ ★ ★

FEET 2,000
MILES 0.5

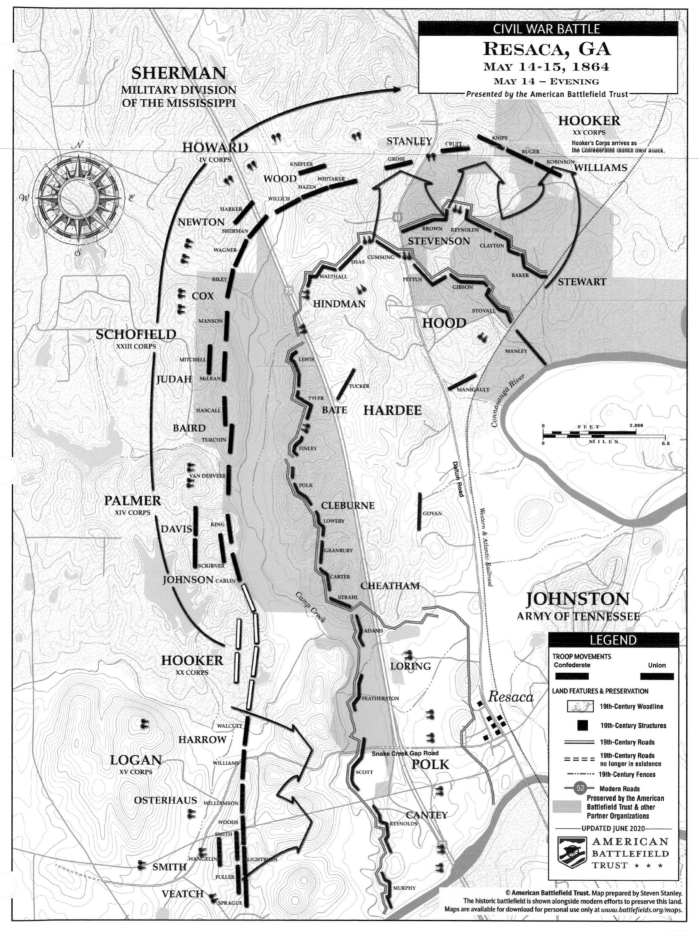

SHERMAN
MILITARY DIVISION
OF THE MISSISSIPPI

CIVIL WAR BATTLE
RESACA, GA
MAY 14-15, 1864
MAY 14 – EVENING
Presented by the American Battlefield Trust

HOOKER
XX CORPS
Hooker's Corps arrives as
the Confederates launch their attack.

HOWARD
IV CORPS

STANLEY

KNIPE
CHULT
RUGER
ROBINSON

WILLIAMS

KNEFLER
WOOD
HAZEN
WHITAKER
GROSE

WILLICH

HARKER
NEWTON
SHERMAN

BROWN
REYNOLDS
STEVENSON
CLAYTON

WAGNER

CUMMING
DEAS

BAKER

STEWART

RILEY

WALTHALL
HINDMAN
PETTUS
GIBSON

COX

MANSON

STOVALL

HOOD

SCHOFIELD
XXIII CORPS

MITCHELL
JUDAH
McLEAN

LEWIS

MANLEY

HASCALL

TUCKER

MANIGAULT

BAIRD

TURCHIN

TYLER
BATE
HARDEE

VAN DERVEER

FINLEY

PALMER
XIV CORPS

POLK

DAVIS
KING

CLEBURNE

LOWERY

GOVAN

SCRIBNER

GRANBURY

JOHNSON CARLIN

CARTER
CHEATHAM
STRAHL

JOHNSTON
ARMY OF TENNESSEE

ADAMS

HOOKER
XX CORPS

LORING

FEATHERSTON

Resaca

WALCUTT
HARROW

WILLIAMS

LOGAN
XV CORPS

Snake Creek Gap Road
SCOTT
POLK

OSTERHAUS
WILLIAMSON

WOODS

SMITH

CANTEY
REYNOLDS

WANGELIN
LIGHTBURN

SMITH

FULLER

VEATCH

MURPHY

SPRAGUE

LEGEND
TROOP MOVEMENTS
Confederate   Union

LAND FEATURES & PRESERVATION

19th-Century Woodline

19th-Century Structures

19th-Century Roads

19th-Century Roads
no longer in existence

19th-Century Fences

52 Modern Roads

Preserved by the American
Battlefield Trust & other
Partner Organizations

—UPDATED JUNE 2020—

AMERICAN
BATTLEFIELD
TRUST ★ ★ ★

© American Battlefield Trust. Map prepared by Steven Stanley.
The historic battlefield is shown alongside modern efforts to preserve this land.
Maps are available for download for personal use only at www.battlefields.org/maps.

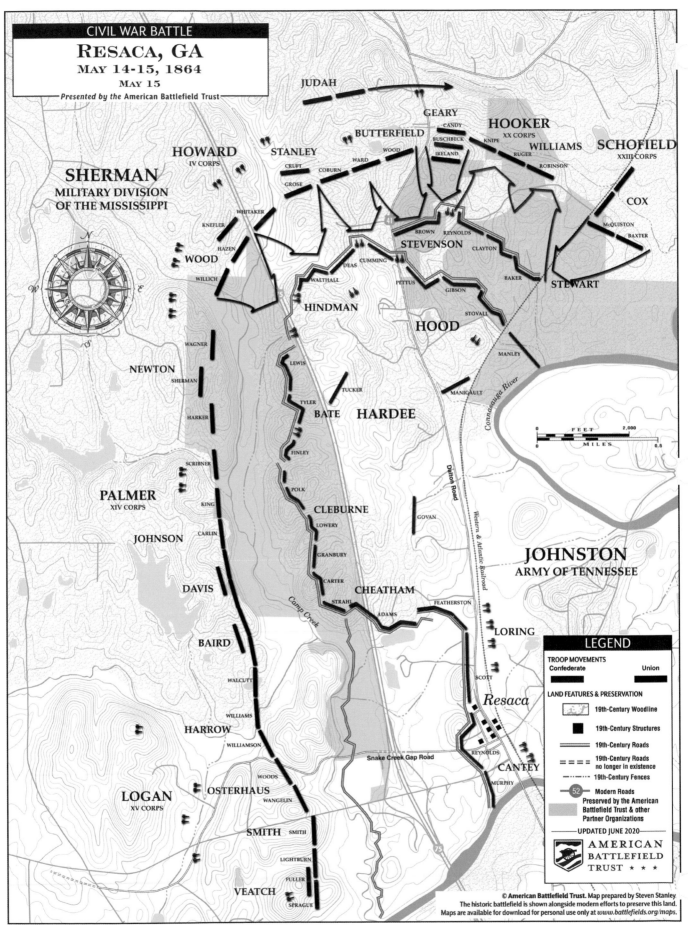

CIVIL WAR BATTLE
RESACA, GA
MAY 14-15, 1864
MAY 15
Presented by the American Battlefield Trust

JUDAH

GEARY

BUTTERFIELD

HOOKER
XX CORPS

CANDY
BUSCHBECK
IRELAND

KNIPE

WILLIAMS

SCHOFIELD
XXIII CORPS

HOWARD
IV CORPS

STANLEY

WOOD
COBURN
WARD

RUGER

ROBINSON

COX

SHERMAN
MILITARY DIVISION
OF THE MISSISSIPPI

CRUFT
GROSE

WHITAKER

KNEFLER

HAZEN

WOOD

WILLICH

BROWN

REYNOLDS

STEVENSON

CLAYTON

McQUISTON

BAXTER

DEAS

CUMMING

PETTUS

BAKER

STEWART

WALTHALL

GIBSON

HINDMAN

STOVALL

HOOD

WAGNER

MANLEY

NEWTON

SHERMAN

LEWIS

TUCKER

MANIGAULT

HARKER

TYLER

BATE

HARDEE

FINLEY

SCRIBNER

POLK

PALMER
XIV CORPS

KING

CLEBURNE

GOVAN

JOHNSTON
ARMY OF TENNESSEE

JOHNSON

CARLIN

LOWERY

GRANBURY

DAVIS

CARTER

CHEATHAM

BAIRD

STRAHL

ADAMS

FEATHERSTON

LORING

WALCUTT

SCOTT

WILLIAMS

HARROW

WILLIAMSON

Resaca

Snake Creek Gap Road

REYNOLDS

WOODS

LOGAN
XV CORPS

OSTERHAUS

WANGELIN

CANTEY

MURPHY

SMITH   SMITH

LIGHTBURN

FULLER

VEATCH

SPRAGUE

Conasauga River

Dalton Road

Western & Atlantic Railroad

Camp Creek

LEGEND

TROOP MOVEMENTS
Confederate   Union

LAND FEATURES & PRESERVATION

19th-Century Woodline

19th-Century Structures

19th-Century Roads

19th-Century Roads
no longer in existence

19th-Century Fences

52 Modern Roads

Preserved by the American
Battlefield Trust & other
Partner Organizations

—UPDATED JUNE 2020—

AMERICAN
BATTLEFIELD
TRUST ★ ★ ★

FEET   2,000
MILES   0.5

© American Battlefield Trust. Map prepared by Steven Stanley.
The historic battlefield is shown alongside modern efforts to preserve this land.
Maps are available for download for personal use only at www.battlefields.org/maps.

BATTLE *of* KENNESAW MOUNTAIN

JUNE 22-27, 1864

MILE BY MILE, SHERMAN AND JOHNSTON SLOWLY MADE THEIR WAY toward Atlanta. Along the way, the armies clashed at New Hope Church, Pickett's Mill, and Marietta. Johnston employed Fabian tactics as a means of slowing and stretching Sherman's armies, withdrawing in the face of Sherman's successive flanking maneuvers, while Sherman tried to avoid pitched battles that necessitated head-on assaults against fortified positions. This all changed at Kennesaw Mountain.

By June 19, Johnston's main forced occupied a seven-mile-long defensive line. The position was well fortified, taking on a crescent-shaped battle formation, with the imposing Kennesaw Mountain rising more than 1,800 feet in elevation above Marietta, Georgia, and the surrounding terrain—and just 25 miles outside of Atlanta.

Fighting on June 22 at Kolb's Farm convinced Sherman that Johnston's line was overstretched. The Yankee commander formulated a plan of attack—a frontal attack—the first major frontal attack he ordered during the campaign. On June 24, Sherman issued attack orders that called for the Army of the Tennessee and the Army of the Cumberland to assault the Confederate right and center respectively. The Army of the Ohio would act as a diversion on the Confederate left. If all went well, Johnston's army would be dispersed or destroyed, with the door to Atlanta swinging wide open. But it was not to be.

At 8 a.m. on June 27, more than fifty cannons opened fire along the Army of the Tennessee front. Troops of the Federal XV and XVII Corps skirmished in the dense undergrowth to prevent the Rebels from shifting forces to Little Kennesaw and Pigeon Hill. Three brigades of Maj. Gen. John Logan's XV Corps moved forward but, despite overrunning some of the rifle pits fronting them, could not penetrate the principal Confederate defenses. Most Federals became mired in the undergrowth and devastated by punishing musketry as they attempted to ascend the slope. Well-directed fire Confederate artillery fire on Little Kennesaw and a Confederate counterattack eventually drove off the Yankees.

At the center of the Union line, the opposing armies were only 400 yards apart. Portions of Howard's IV Corps and Maj. Gen. John M. Palmer's XIV Corps of the Army of the Cumberland entered the fray. Facing them was perhaps Johnston's best division, that of Maj. Gen. Patrick R. Cleburne's, which had built nearly impregnable abatis and entrenchments along the divisional front. Brigadier General George Maney's Tennessee brigade held a position jutting forward in a salient on a rise now known as Cheatham's Hill. Federal artillery shelled the Rebel works for fifteen minutes before the infantry advanced, only to be stalled at the abatis around 50 yards short of the enemy works. By 10 a.m., the Union attack became disorganized, and the men fell back. Some men of Col. John Mitchell's brigade made it up the slope to Maney's entrenched salient, where the lines became so close that the Tennesseans threw rocks at the advancing Federals. Eventually, Mitchell's men retreated and found cover within yards of the Confederate works. Afterward, the combatants dubbed the area of the most brutal fighting the "Dead Angle."

By noon, the Union attack had failed. Although the survivors of the assaulting columns spent the next five days in advanced works just yards from the Confederate position, there was no more heavy fighting at Kennesaw. On July 2, Sherman maneuvered a force around Johnston's left flank, forcing the Confederates to fall back once again closer to Atlanta.

✳ ✳ PRESERVATION ✳ ✳

To date, the **American Battlefield Trust** has saved **4 acres** at Kennasaw Mountain Battlefield.

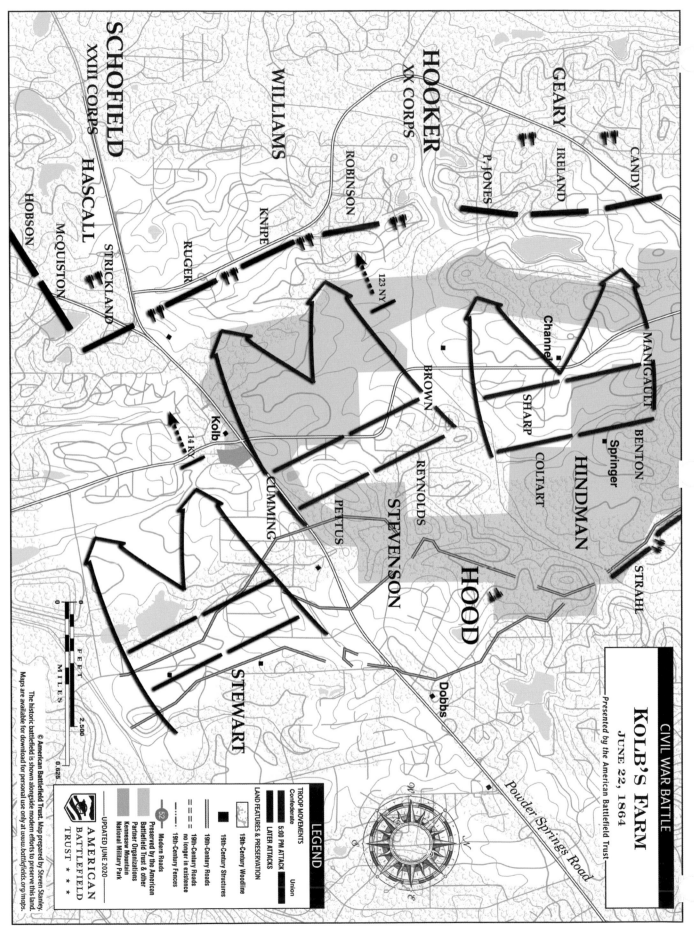

CIVIL WAR BATTLE

KOLB'S FARM
JUNE 22, 1864

Presented by the American Battlefield Trust

LEGEND

TROOP MOVEMENTS
Confederate   Union

5:00 PM ATTACK

LATER ATTACKS

LAND FEATURES & PRESERVATION

19th-Century Woodline

19th-Century Structures

52 Modern Roads
19th-Century Roads
19th-Century Roads
no longer in existence
19th-Century Fences

Preserved by the American
Battlefield Trust & other
Partner Organizations
Kennesaw Mountain
National Military Park

UPDATED JUNE 2020

AMERICAN
BATTLEFIELD
TRUST ★ ★ ★

SCHOFIELD
XXIII CORPS

HOOKER
XX CORPS

HASCALL

HOBSON
McQUISTON
STRICKLAND

WILLIAMS
RUGER
KNIPE
ROBINSON

GEARY
P.JONES
IRELAND
CANDY

123 NY

Kolb

14 KY

CUMMING

BROWN
PETTUS
REYNOLDS

STEVENSON

Channel
SHARP
COLTART

MANIGAULT
BENTON
Springer

HINDMAN

STRAHL

HOOD

STEWART

Dobbs

Powder Springs Road

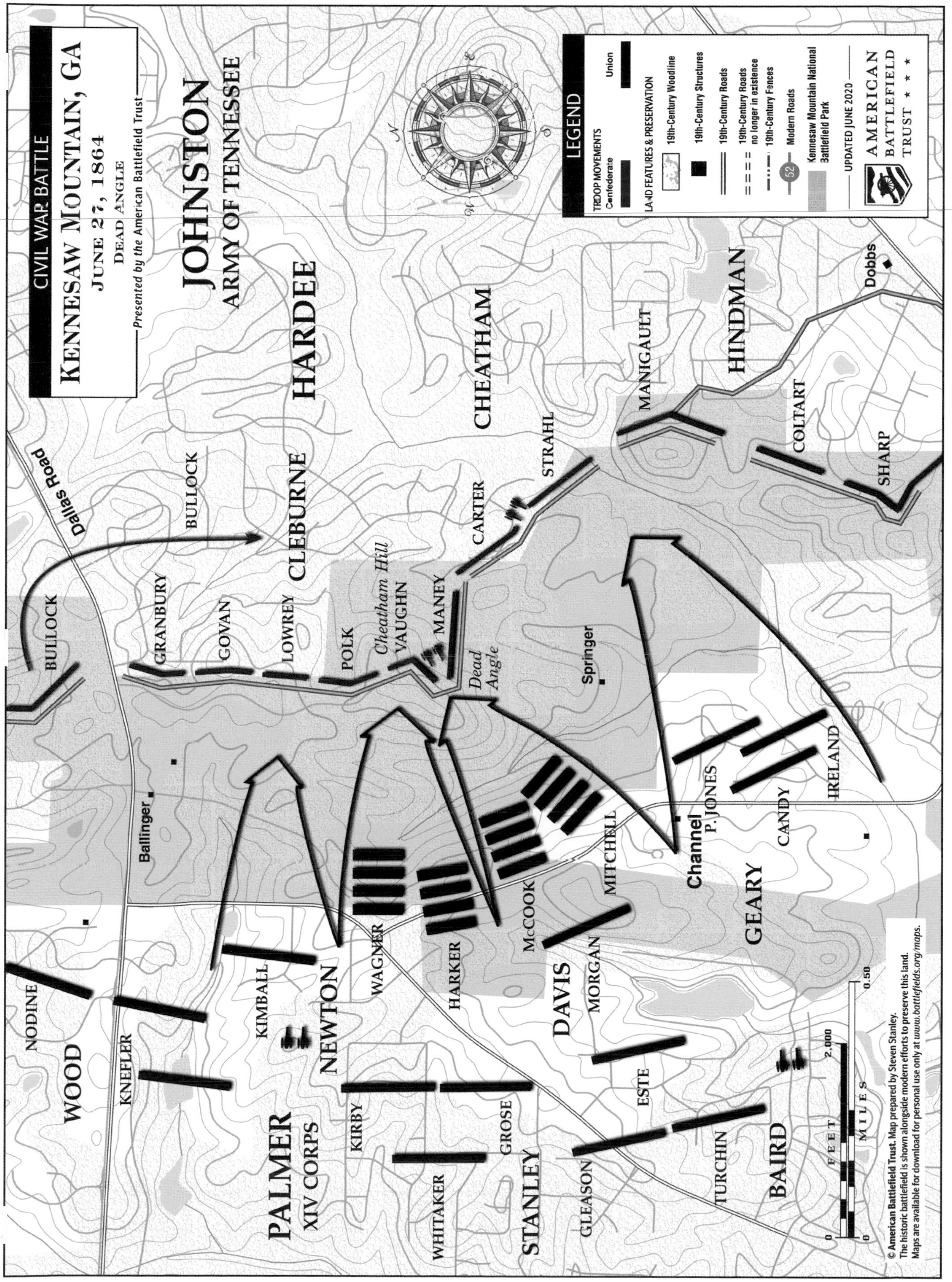

CIVIL WAR BATTLE

KENNESAW MOUNTAIN, GA
JUNE 27, 1864
DEAD ANGLE

Presented by the American Battlefield Trust

JOHNSTON
ARMY OF TENNESSEE

HARDEE

CLEBURNE

CHEATHAM

HINDMAN

MANIGAULT

COLTART

SHARP

Dobbs

STRAHL

CARTER

BULLOCK

Dallas Road

BULLOCK

GRANBURY

GOVAN

LOWREY

POLK

Cheatham Hill

VAUGHN

MANEY

Dead Angle

Springer

P. JONES

IRELAND

Channel

GEARY

CANDY

McCOOK

MITCHELL

HARKER

WAGNER

Ballinger

NODINE

WOOD

KNEELER

KIMBALL

NEWTON

KIRBY

WHITAKER

GROSE

STANLEY

DAVIS

MORGAN

ESTE

GLEASON

TURCHIN

BAIRD

PALMER
XIV CORPS

LEGEND

TROOP MOVEMENTS
- Confederate
- Union

LAND FEATURES & PRESERVATION
- 19th-Century Woodline
- 19th-Century Structures
- 19th-Century Roads
- 19th-Century Roads no longer in existence
- 19th-Century Fences
- 52 — Modern Roads
- Kennesaw Mountain National Battlefield Park

UPDATED JUNE 2020

AMERICAN BATTLEFIELD TRUST ★ ★ ★

© American Battlefield Trust. Map prepared by Steven Stanley.
The historic battlefield is shown alongside modern efforts to preserve this land.
Maps are available for download for personal use only at *www.battlefields.org/maps*.

FEET 2,000

MILES 0.50

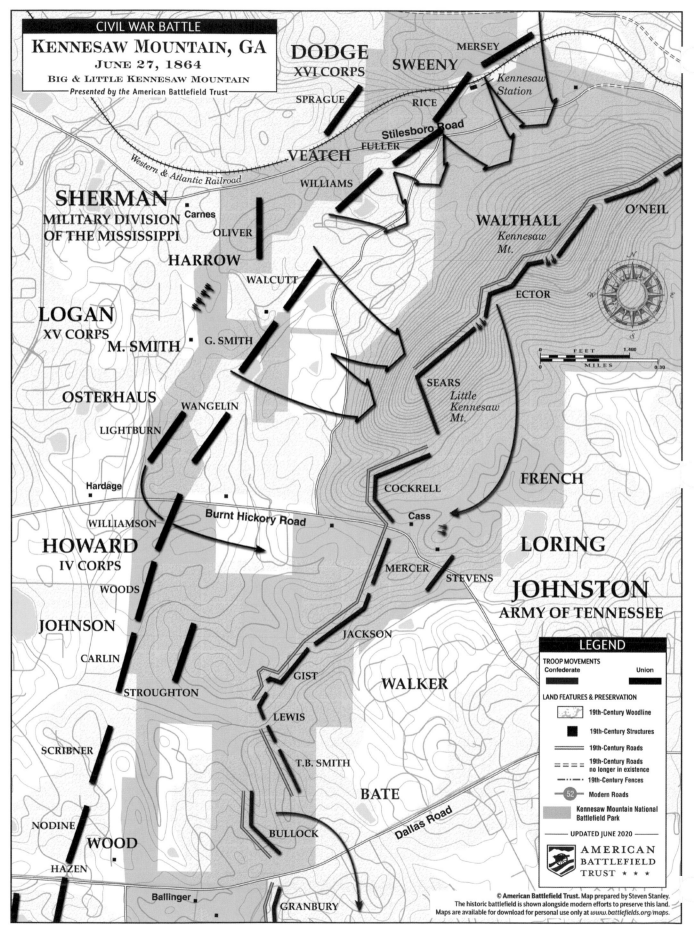

CIVIL WAR BATTLE
KENNESAW MOUNTAIN, GA
JUNE 27, 1864
BIG & LITTLE KENNESAW MOUNTAIN
Presented by the American Battlefield Trust

DODGE
XVI CORPS

SPRAGUE

MERSEY

SWEENY

Kennesaw Station

RICE

VEATCH

Stilesboro Road

FULLER

WILLIAMS

WALTHALL

O'NEIL

SHERMAN
MILITARY DIVISION
OF THE MISSISSIPPI

Kennesaw Mt.

Carnes

OLIVER

HARROW

WALCUTT

ECTOR

LOGAN
XV CORPS

M. SMITH

G. SMITH

SEARS
Little Kennesaw Mt.

OSTERHAUS

WANGELIN

LIGHTBURN

FRENCH

COCKRELL

Hardage

Cass

WILLIAMSON

Burnt Hickory Road

LORING

HOWARD
IV CORPS

MERCER

STEVENS

WOODS

JOHNSTON
ARMY OF TENNESSEE

JOHNSON

CARLIN

JACKSON

WALKER

STROUGHTON

GIST

LEWIS

SCRIBNER

T.B. SMITH

NODINE

BATE

WOOD

BULLOCK

Dallas Road

HAZEN

Ballinger

GRANBURY

LEGEND

TROOP MOVEMENTS
Confederate   Union

LAND FEATURES & PRESERVATION

19th-Century Woodline

19th-Century Structures

19th-Century Roads

19th-Century Roads no longer in existence

19th-Century Fences

52 Modern Roads

Kennesaw Mountain National Battlefield Park

— UPDATED JUNE 2020 —

AMERICAN
BATTLEFIELD
TRUST ★ ★ ★

© American Battlefield Trust. Map prepared by Steven Stanley.
The historic battlefield is shown alongside modern efforts to preserve this land.
Maps are available for download for personal use only at *www.battlefields.org/maps*.

BATTLE *of* PEACHTREE CREEK

JULY 20, 1864

DURING THE FIRST WEEK OF JULY 1864, GEN. JOSEPH E. JOHNSTON'S CONFEDERATE army fell back from its defensive position on Kennesaw Mountain with Sherman's armies in pursuit. Johnston's destination was the fortifications along the west bank of the Chattahoochee River. The Chattahoochee was the Rubicon of the Confederacy of sorts, as it was the last natural defensive barrier to the west of Atlanta, yet once again, Sherman outflanked Johnston's army by sending men around the Confederate right. Once over the river, the Federal Armies of the Tennessee and of the Ohio pushed east toward Decatur and the Georgia Railroad, while the Army of the Cumberland headed south toward Peach Tree Creek, just four miles north of Atlanta.

The Confederate crisis was at its boiling point, and with no indication that Johnston was going to take the fight to the enemy, on July 17, Davis sacked his senior commander and replaced him with John Bell Hood, who fancied himself a pupil of Robert E. Lee and Stonewall Jackson. However, Hood lacked the strategic insight of Lee and the tactical acumen of Jackson and would prove to be a destructive force hitherto unseen by the Confederacy—and not in any way they needed.

As Thomas's army moved forward, his IV and XX Corps held the center and left, with the XIV Corps on the right.

Hood planned to take the fight to the enemy. On July 20, the Confederate Army of Tennessee would engage with, isolate, and destroy the Army of the Cumberland before Sherman's other two armies could render assistance. If the Confederates struck hard, with luck they might wreck half of Sherman's force before the rest of it could respond.

Things went wrong for Hood from the start. A Union force threatened the Confederate right east of Atlanta. In reaction, Hood had to move his whole line in that direction. This had a domino effect, as Lt. Gens. William J. Hardee's and Alexander P. Stewart's corps spent an additional 90 minutes shifting to new positions a half-mile to their right. By this time, the last of the Army of the Cumberland had crossed Peach Tree Creek and began entrenching.

Hardee, on the right, did not advance until nearly 3:30 p.m., sending Maj. Gen. William H. T. Walker's division against the Federal left. As Walker's men advanced, the Yankees opened on them with musketry and cannon fire. The Southerners made repeated charges until about 6 p.m. without breaching the enemy works. Brigadier General George Maney attacked next, taking up Walker's assault. For a while, Confederate attackers overlapped the Union line, but a quick adjustment shored up the Federals, and all of Hardee's attacks failed.

Major General William W. Loring's division of Stewart's corps took up the attack next, moving down the valley of Tanyard Creek (Early's Creek), without success. Another Confederate force managed to overrun a portion of the Union lines, but this success was short lived.

Major General Edward C. Walthall's Confederate division created a crisis on the other Federal flank. Another brief breakthrough was quickly repulsed by the Yankees. Walthall's left brigade, under Brig. Gen. Daniel Reynolds, drove in skirmishers of Brig. Gen. Alpheus Williams's division and even took a portion of its main lines. Federal counterattacks and enfilading fire forced Walthall back, causing his attack to fall apart. As darkness approached, Stewart ordered his troops back into their trenches.

By 6:00 p.m., the Battle of Peach Tree Creek was over. Hood's attack had failed.

✳ ✳ PRESERVATION ✳ ✳

To date, the **American Battlefield Trust** has not saved any land at Peachtree Creek Battlefield.

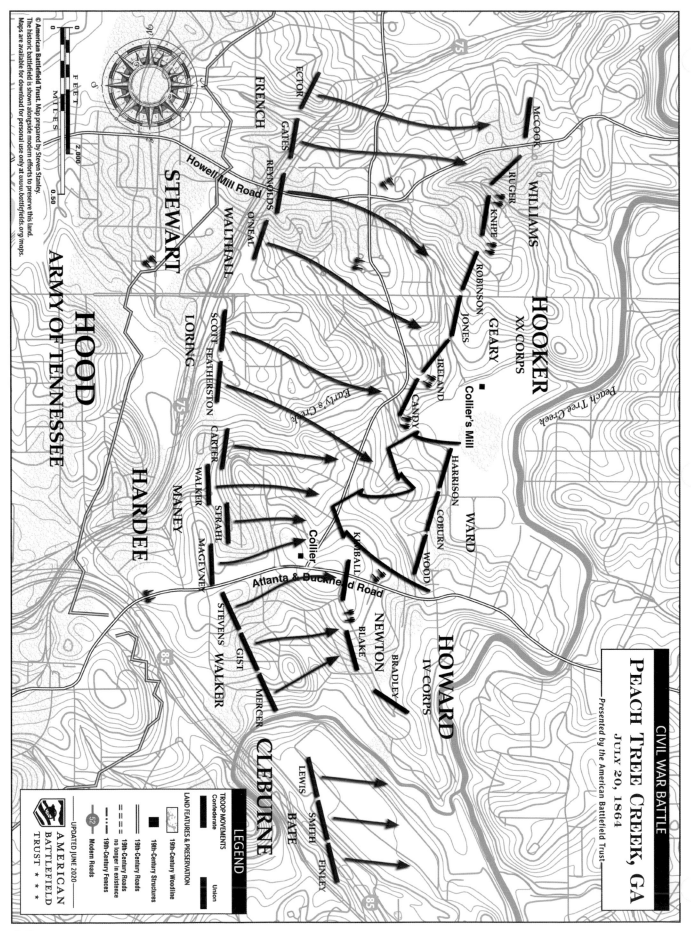

PEACH TREE CREEK, GA

CIVIL WAR BATTLE

JULY 20, 1864

Presented by the American Battlefield Trust

BATTLE *of* ATLANTA
(BALD HILL/LEGGETT'S HILL)

JULY 22, 1864

ON JULY 21, 1864, WILLIAM T. SHERMAN'S THREE ARMIES WERE SEPARATED on the outskirts of Atlanta. John Bell Hood received reports that the left flank of Maj. Gen. James B. McPherson's Army of the Tennessee was in the air. McPherson's army was facing Atlanta from the east astride the Georgia Railroad. Hood seized the opportunity and ordered Hardee's corps to drop back from its lines north of the city into the main fortified perimeter on the night of July 21-22; the remaining corps of Alexander P. Stewart and Maj. Gen. Benjamin F. Cheatham would follow. Hardee's corps would march through and out of the city, guided by Confederate cavalry. Once in position, the corps would strike McPherson's left-rear, while Confederate cavalry of Maj. Gen. Joseph Wheeler attacked McPherson's wagon trains at Decatur. Cheatham would support Hardee from the east edge of Atlanta. It was an ambitious plan, calling for a 15-mile night march by Hardee's troops and a dawn attack on the 22nd. But a late start, the exhaustion of the men, a hot night, and dusty roads combined to bring the four assault divisions not nearly far enough into McPherson's rear.

On the Union left, a Union XVI Corps division under Brig. Gen. Thomas W. Sweeny was positioned in the path of Hardee's opening assault. Instead of overrunning hospital tents and wagon trains in McPherson's rear, Confederate troops ran instead face-to-face into veteran Yankee infantry.

McPherson, having left Sherman's headquarters just before the firing started, was on this part of the field watching Sweeny contend with the Rebels. He rode off to see how Maj. Gen. Frank Blair's XVII Corps was doing, which had been struck by Maj. Gen. Patrick Cleburne's hard-hitting division. McPherson and his staff were riding down a wagon road when they unexpectedly ran into part of Cleburne's line. "He (McPherson) checked his horse, raised his hat in salute, wheeled to the right and dashed off to the rear in a gallop," an observed recalled. The Rebels fired on McPherson, felling the general—a bullet hole in the back, near the heart.

Cleburne's attack initially overran part of the Union line, capturing two guns and several hundred prisoners. Then the Southerners ran up against infantry and artillery on a treeless hilltop occupied by Brig. Gen. Mortimer Leggett's division, which stopped them cold. Brig. Gen. George Maney's Confederate division joined in the fight, but Leggett held onto his hill.

Around 3:00 p.m., Hood ordered Cheatham's corps to launch an attack from Atlanta's eastern line of works. Cheatham's fierce but uncoordinated assaults against the line held by the Federal XV Corps met with initial success, overrunning the Yankees at the Troup Hurt House and capturing artillery, but a Union counterattack forced it back.

The Battle of Atlanta, the bloodiest of Sherman's Atlanta Campaign, was over. Confederate losses on July 22 added up to about 5,500, while the Federals sustained 3,700 casualties. Hood's effort to roll up Sherman's left flank had failed.

Sherman's armies would move on, northwest and then west of Atlanta, fighting again at Ezra Church on July 28. Worn out after that, both armies settled in for a siege of the city that consumed all of August. On September 1, 1864, Hood abandoned the city of Atlanta, and Sherman's forces marched into the city the next day. The gateway to the Deep South—and the sea—lay open.

✳ ✳ PRESERVATION ✳ ✳

To date, the **American Battlefield Trust** has not saved any land at Atlanta Battlefield.

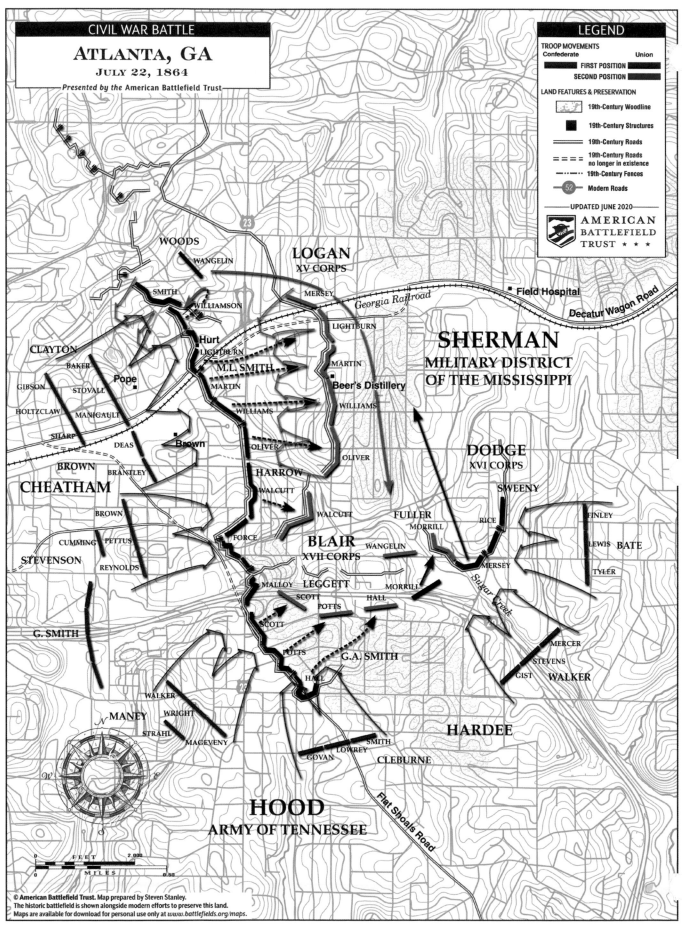

CIVIL WAR BATTLE

ATLANTA, GA
JULY 22, 1864
Presented by the American Battlefield Trust

LEGEND

TROOP MOVEMENTS
Confederate · Union
FIRST POSITION
SECOND POSITION

LAND FEATURES & PRESERVATION
19th-Century Woodline
19th-Century Structures
19th-Century Roads
19th-Century Roads no longer in existence
19th-Century Fences
52 Modern Roads

UPDATED JUNE 2020

AMERICAN BATTLEFIELD TRUST ★ ★ ★

BATTLE *of* MOBILE BAY

AUGUST 5, 1864

BY THE SUMMER OF 1864, THE BLOCKADE OF CONFEDERATE PORTS WAS NEARLY at its zenith. Mobile, Alabama, was one of only two major operational ports in the Confederacy (the other being Wilmington, North Carolina). Mobile Bay was massive, spanning some 413 square miles. However, while the bay itself was vast, it only had two narrow Gulf-facing entry points or ship channels. The first was a split between Dauphin Island and the Fort Morgan Peninsula running east to west. The second entry point, Grant's Pass, was a narrow opening on the northside of Dauphin Island, between the island and the mainland at Cedar Point. From the mouth of Mobile Bay to the city of Mobile is roughly 31 miles as the crow flies. The defenses near the mouth of the bay were formidable. A British foray into this area during the War of 1812 illustrated the importance of properly fortifying the bay. Thus, three forts defended the shipping channels, the largest being Fort Morgan, a 46-gun, star-shaped fortification constructed in 1834 protecting the deepest channel from its eastern side. On the west side of the channel, on Dauphin Island, the smaller and newer Fort Gaines boasted 26 guns. Fort Powell guarded Grant's Pass at the western entrance of Mobile Bay with 16 guns.

To supplement these defenses, the Confederates had blocked part of the main channel with torpedoes (floating wooden barrels of explosives like modern naval mines) and assembled a small flotilla consisting of the ironclad CSS *Tennessee* and three gunboats inside the bay. They were commanded by the veteran Adm. Franklin Buchanan, former commander of the ironclad CSS *Virginia*.

Tasked with closing the port was Rear Adm. David G. Farragut. Farragut devised a combined Army-Navy operation that would entail landing some 1,500 soldiers commanded by Maj. Gen. Gordon Granger on Dauphin Island to lay siege to Fort Gaines. Granger's force established a beachhead on August 3 and laid siege to Fort Gaines while Farragut assembled his fleet of four ironclad monitors and more than a dozen wooden ships offshore. Early in the morning of August 5, 1864, the Federal fleet passed into the harbor.

Farragut split his ships into two parallel columns: the ironclads sailing nearest Fort Morgan and the wooden ships on the far side. Farragut ordered the larger wooden ships lashed together to a smaller ship so that the larger vessels could serve as shields, and so the ships would be able to tow each other if one became crippled. Farragut personally observed much of the battle while lashed to the rigging of his flagship, the USS *Hartford*.

The ships steamed through the narrow width of the channel that had not been mined while passing under the guns of the fort. The ironclad USS *Tecumseh* struck a torpedo and sank almost instantly, and cautious Union captains began stopping their ships while still within range of Fort Morgan. At this juncture, Farragut allegedly bellowed, "Damn the torpedoes! Full speed ahead!"

The *Hartford* made it through the minefield with the rest of the fleet following in its wake. Once into the expansive bay, Farragut engaged with the Confederate ships. The Federals quickly captured or drove away the Rebel gunboats, but despite the overwhelming odds, the *Tennessee*, Buchanan's flagship, moved forward to meet the northerners. Buchanan was soon surrounded by Federal ships.

Eventually, Buchanan was injured, and his ship was disabled after three hours of fighting. While the city of Mobile would not fall until 1865, Fort Gaines surrendered on August 8 and Fort Morgan fell on August 23. Farragut's victory at Mobile Bay cut off one of the last of the Confederate's deep-water ports and helped to secure President Abraham Lincoln's reelection in November.

✷ ✷ PRESERVATION ✷ ✷

To date, the **American Battlefield Trust** has not saved any land in the Mobile Bay Area.

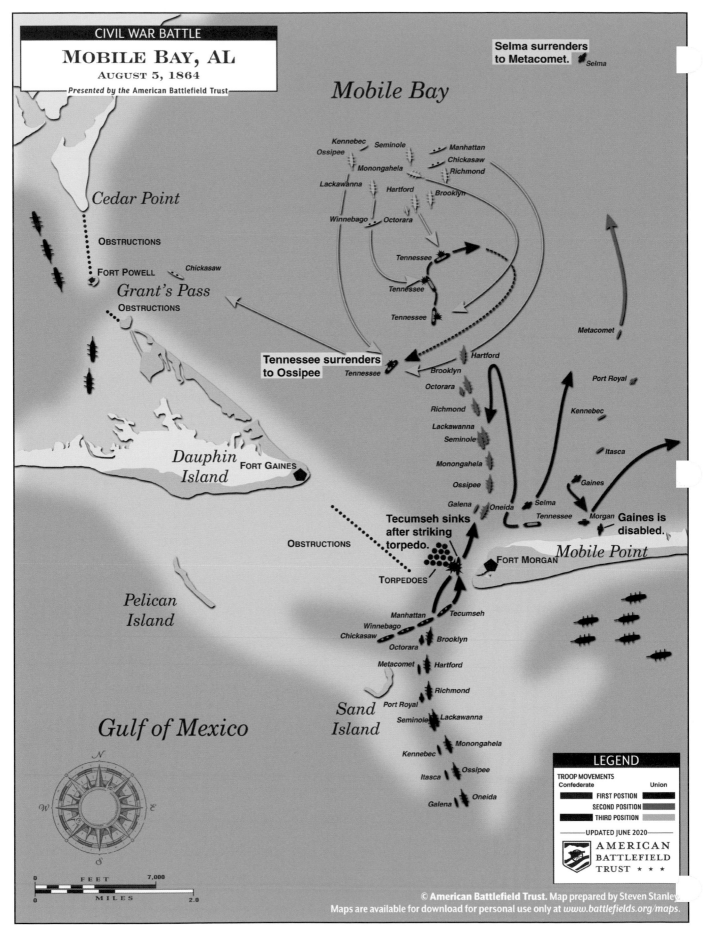

CIVIL WAR BATTLE

MOBILE BAY, AL

AUGUST 5, 1864

Presented by the American Battlefield Trust

Selma surrenders
to Metacomet.
Selma

Mobile Bay

Kennebec
Seminole
Ossipee
Monongahela
Manhattan
Chickasaw
Richmond
Lackawanna
Hartford
Brooklyn
Winnebago
Octorara

Cedar Point

OBSTRUCTIONS

FORT POWELL
Chickasaw

Grant's Pass

OBSTRUCTIONS

Tennessee
Tennessee
Tennessee
Tennessee

Metacomet

**Tennessee surrenders
to Ossipee**
Tennessee
Hartford
Brooklyn
Octorara
Richmond
Lackawanna
Seminole
Monongahela
Ossipee
Galena
Oneida
Selma
Tennessee
Morgan

Port Royal
Kennebec
Itasca
Gaines

**Gaines is
disabled.**

*Dauphin
Island*
FORT GAINES

**Tecumseh sinks
after striking
torpedo.**

OBSTRUCTIONS

TORPEDOES

FORT MORGAN   *Mobile Point*

*Pelican
Island*

Manhattan   Tecumseh
Winnebago
Chickasaw
Octorara   Brooklyn
Metacomet   Hartford
Port Royal   Richmond
*Sand
Island*   Seminole   Lackawanna
Kennebec   Monongahela
Itasca   Ossipee
Galena   Oneida

Gulf of Mexico

N
W   E
S

FEET   7,000
MILES   2.0

LEGEND

TROOP MOVEMENTS
Confederate   Union
FIRST POSTION
SECOND POSITION
THIRD POSITION

UPDATED JUNE 2020

AMERICAN
BATTLEFIELD
TRUST ★ ★ ★

BATTLE *of* FRANKLIN

NOVEMBER 30, 1864

AFTER THE FALL OF ATLANTA, GENERAL JOHN BELL HOOD AND HIS 39,000-MAN Army of Tennessee tried to divert the attention William T. Sherman and his armies. While aggressive maneuvers, pitched battles, and a siege did not stop Sherman, Hood felt that his next best option of slowing Sherman was to threaten his supply lines. This strategy, too, would end in Confederate failure.

Hood maneuvered his army into Georgia, into Alabama, and finally into Middle Tennessee. While Sherman half-heartedly pursued Hood at first, it didn't take the Yankee commander long to realize that his armies could live off of the land untouched by the hard hand of war in the Deep South. Thus, Sherman delegated the responsibility of dealing with Hood to ro veteran commanders, George Thomas and John Schofield—and their nearly 62,000 Federal soldiers.

Hood's army dashed into Middle Tennessee in November. He stole marches on Schofield and Thomas—all the while aiming for the Union supply depot at Nashville. Hood hoped to destroy Schofield's force, and then turn on Thomas. Dual victories in this sector could draw Sherman out of Georgia or, in a very long shot, Federal troops away from the Eastern Theater.

Hood managed to divide Schofield's army and surround a portion of it in the riverside town of Columbia, Tennessee. Unfortunately for Hood, the Confederate's failed to snap the trap shut at Spring Hill, and Schofield's army escaped to Franklin, Tennessee, arriving early on November 30.

While Schofield set his army to work fortifying its position, Hood moved his army to the outskirts of the town. The Confederate commander focused on the destruction of Schofield's force at all costs. The Rebel army of some 27,000 men faced the prospect of making a frontal assault over two miles of open ground against a roughly equal foe entrenched behind three lines of breastworks. Unmoved by his subordinates' objections, Hood ordered the assault.

The Confederate ranks stepped off near 4 p.m. and were immediately torn apart by cannon and small-arms fire. Nevertheless, the line swept forward and quickly overlapped and overwhelmed two poorly positioned Federal brigade's half a mile in front of the main line. Charging and yelling mere yards behind the broken Federal men, the Confederates in the center were able to cross the last half-mile of their assault largely unopposed. The Rebels slammed into the Union center with full momentum and splintered the defenders around the Carter House.

Thousands of men now surged into a deadly vortex of combat. The quick reaction of Col. Emerson Opdycke's Federal brigade, which hurled itself forward into the breach, prevented full-scale disaster. More Confederates entered the fray as butternut soldiers of Alexander P. Stewart's corps crashed against the western portion of the Federal main line. The Confederates retreated, reformed, and renewed the attack as many as six times but could not dislodge the Union defenders. As the sun set, with his attempt on the right stalled and the hand-to-hand fighting in the center raging into its third hour, Hood sent forward his left wing. A torchlit assault by the men of Benjamin F. Cheatham's corps soon came to grief.

The Confederates pulled back across the broad front, leaving thousands of dead and wounded behind. The Battle of Franklin decimated the Army of Tennessee. Fourteen general officers and 55 regimental commanders were listed among the Confederate casualty rolls. Undaunted, Hood continued the campaign to Nashville, where Schofield and Thomas united their forces for the climactic battle of Hood's career.

✳ ✳ PRESERVATION ✳ ✳

To date, the **American Battlefield Trust** has saved **180 acres** at Franklin Battlefield.

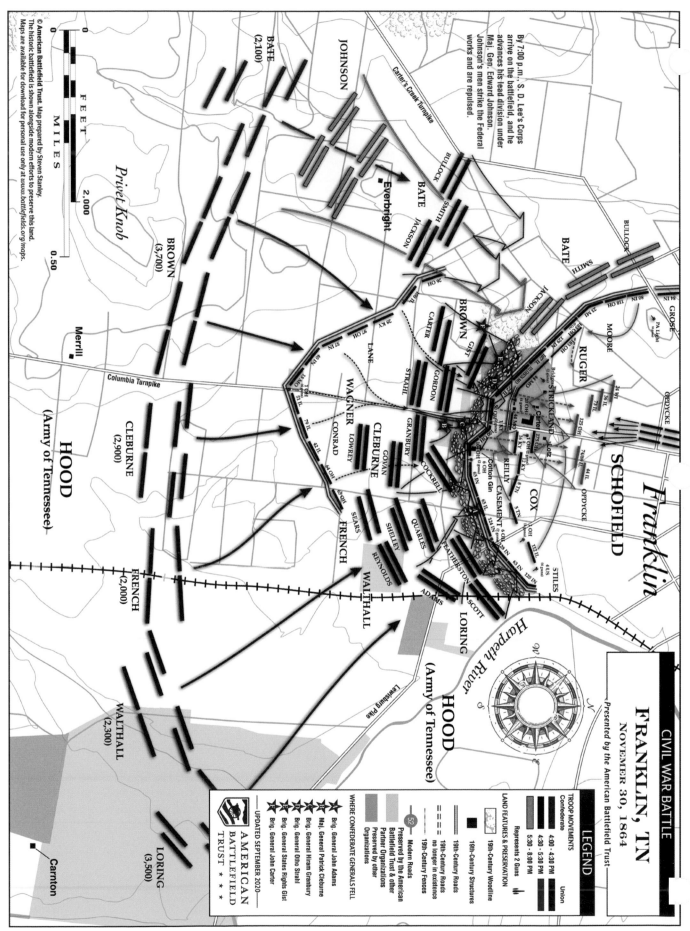

© American Battlefield Trust. Map prepared by Steven Stanley.
Maps are available for download for personal use only at www.battlefields.org/maps.
The historic battlefield is shown alongside modern efforts to preserve this land.

By 7:00 p.m., S. D. Lee's Corps arrive on the battlefield, and he advances his lead division under Maj. Gen. Edward Johnson. Johnson's men strike the Federal works and are repulsed.

Privet Knob

Carter's Creek Turnpike

JOHNSON

BATE (2,100)

BULLOCK

SMITH

JACKSON

Everbright

BROWN (3,700)

Merrill

Columbia Turnpike

CLEBURNE (2,900)

HOOD (Army of Tennessee)

FRENCH (2,000)

WALTHALL (2,300)

LORING (3,500)

Carnton

LANE

WAGNER

CONRAD

LOWREY

GOVAN

CLEBURNE

GRANBURY

COCKRELL

SEARS

SHELLEY

FRENCH

QUARLES

REYNOLDS

WALTHALL

FEATHERSTON

ADAMS

SCOTT

LORING

HOOD (Army of Tennessee)

CARTER

STRAHL

GORDON

BROWN

GIST

STRICKLAND

Carter

REILLY

CASEMENT

COX

MOORE

RUGER

GROSE

SCHOFIELD

STILES

Franklin

Harpeth River

Lewisburg Pike

FRANKLIN, TN
NOVEMBER 30, 1864
Presented by the American Battlefield Trust

CIVIL WAR BATTLE

UPDATED SEPTEMBER 2020

AMERICAN BATTLEFIELD TRUST

LEGEND

TROOP MOVEMENTS
Confederate
Union

4:00 - 4:30 PM
4:30 - 5:30 PM
5:30 - 8:00 PM

Represents 2 Guns

LAND FEATURES & PRESERVATION
19th-Century Woodline
19th-Century Structures
19th-Century Roads no longer in existence
19th-Century Roads in existence
19th-Century Fences
Modern Roads
Preserved by the American Battlefield Trust & other Partner Organizations
Preserved by other Organizations

WHERE CONFEDERATE GENERALS FELL
Brig. General John Adams
Maj. General Patrick Cleburne
Brig. General Hiram Granbury
Brig. General Otho Strahl
Brig. General States Rights Gist
Brig. General John Carter

BATTLE of NASHVILLE

DECEMBER 15 - 16, 1864

JOHN BELL HOOD PARTICIPATED IN SOME OF THE MOST BRUTAL AND iconic actions of the Civil War, including the breakthrough at Gaines' Mill, the hellacious fighting at the Cornfield at Antietam, and the drive to Snodgrass Hill at Chickamauga. Hood had also served under some of the most famous generals in the south: Lee, Longstreet, Johnston, and Jackson. Since mid-July of 1864, though, this proud general's name was linked to Confederate disaster after disaster, and in the waning weeks of 1864, he was leading an unrelenting campaign. The missed opportunity at Spring Hill gave way to a disaster on an epic scale at Franklin, and now the Confederate Army of Tennessee faced the united and fortified Armies of the Ohio and of the Cumberland near Nashville.

Outnumbered by a factor of more than two-to-one, Hood resolutely and mistakenly stuck to the offensive. His grand strategy included the taking of Tennessee's capital, Nashville, and then moving farther north into his home state of Kentucky to gather provisions and volunteers, and then planned to turn east to join Robert E. Lee's beleaguered forces in Virginia. The reality of the situation passed Hood by, and he was simply grasping at non-existent straws.

Hood reached Nashville on December 2, hoping to draw the Union forces into a costly attack. The overall Federal commander in Nashville, Maj. Gen. George H. Thomas, received telegrams from Ulysses S. Grant and Abraham Lincoln urging him to strike the Confederate army. Thomas delayed the attack for nearly two weeks, citing freezing temperatures, full-blown ice storms, and limited cavalry support.

On December 15, Thomas launched a demonstration on the Confederate right across the line of the Nashville & Chattanooga Railroad. At the same time, his main assault fell on a cluster of redoubts on the Confederate left. The diversionary assault force was a true hodgepodge of units and men. The troops were pieced together from undersized units of the Army of Georgia, Army of the Tennessee, United States Colored Troops, and other seemingly homeless units. Yet, this force performed its job and struck the Confederate right, although the action failed to draw Hood's attention for long.

On the Confederate left, Thomas swung the bulk of his forces out of the defensive of Nashville in a grand-wheeling offensive. Confederate Redoubts #1-#5 fell as the Federals outflanked and overwhelmed the left of Hood's line. What remained of Hood's army retreated two miles farther south during the night and established a new defensive line.

Thomas renewed the attack on the afternoon of December 16. He followed the pattern of the first day, hoping to pin the Confederate right while smashing the left. This time the diversion was more successful. The Southerners defending Peach Orchard Hill repulsed the four-brigade Union attack, but they could not spare any reinforcements to bolster other parts of their lines.

The Confederate left was anchored on Compton's Hill. In the shadows of the setting sun, Brig. Gen. John McArthur, on his own initiative, ordered his three brigades to charge the hill. McArthur's attack broke the Confederate line and soon threatened to sweep up Hood's whole army. Col. William Shy of the 20th Tennessee died defending the hill, and the prominence was renamed in his honor.

Hood ordered his army off the field, ending offensive operations. In six months of campaigning, the Army of Tennessee had lost nearly 75% of its fighting force and ceased to be a serious threat to the Federals. The fall of the Southern Confederacy was now only a matter of time.

✳ ✳ PRESERVATION ✳ ✳

To date, the **American Battlefield Trust** has not saved any land at Nashville Battlefield.

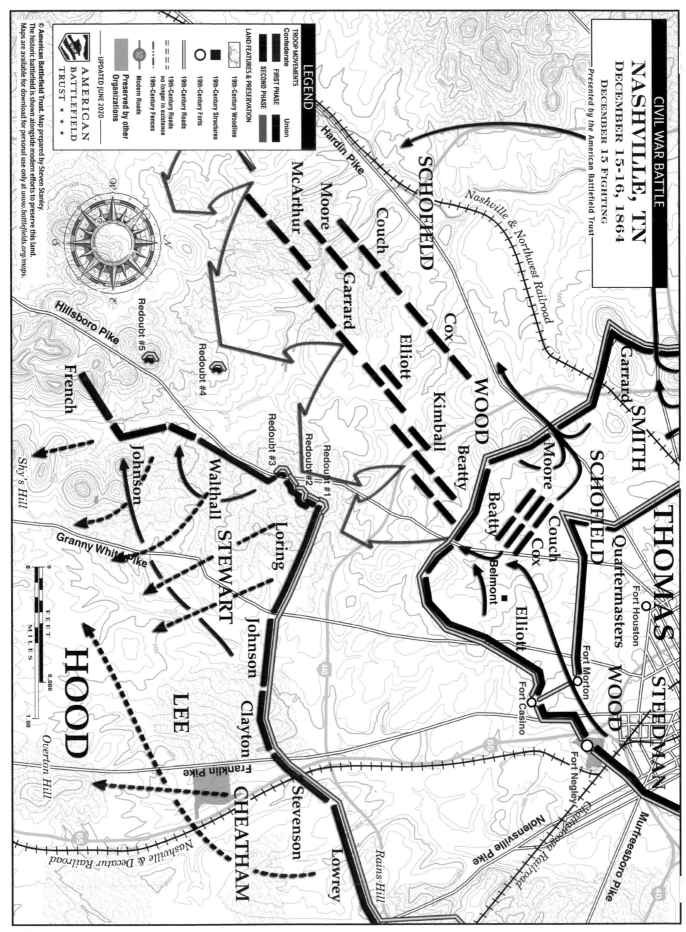

CIVIL WAR BATTLE

NASHVILLE, TN
DECEMBER 15-16, 1864
DECEMBER 15 FIGHTING

Presented by the American Battlefield Trust

LEGEND

TROOP MOVEMENTS

Confederate

Union

FIRST PHASE

SECOND PHASE

LAND FEATURES & PRESERVATION

19th-Century Woodline

19th-Century Structures

19th-Century Forts

19th-Century Roads no longer in existence

19th-Century Roads still in existence

19th-Century Fences

Modern Roads

Preserved by other Organizations

52

UPDATED JUNE 2020

AMERICAN BATTLEFIELD TRUST ★ ★ ★

FEET

MILES

6,000

1.50

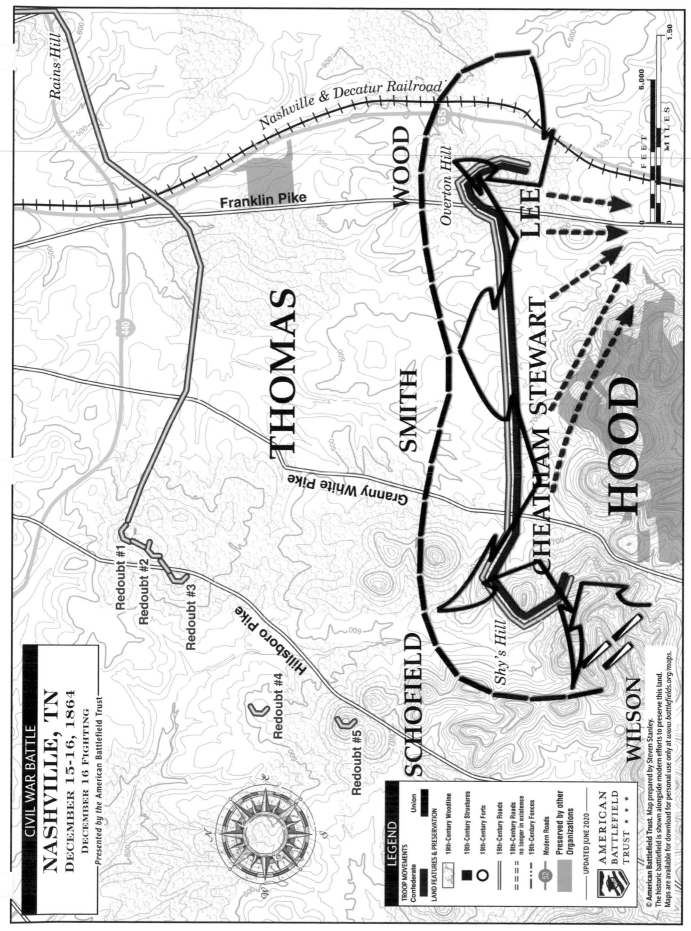

Rains Hill

Nashville & Decatur Railroad

WOOD

Franklin Pike

Overton Hill

LEE

THOMAS

SMITH

CHEATHAM STEWART

HOOD

Granny White Pike

Redoubt #1

Redoubt #2

Redoubt #3

Hillsboro Pike

Shy's Hill

SCHOFIELD

Redoubt #4

Redoubt #5

WILSON

CIVIL WAR BATTLE

NASHVILLE, TN

DECEMBER 15-16, 1864

DECEMBER 16 FIGHTING

Presented by the American Battlefield Trust

LEGEND

TROOP MOVEMENTS
Confederate   Union

LAND FEATURES & PRESERVATION
19th-Century Woodline
19th-Century Structures
19th-Century Forts
19th-Century Roads
19th-Century Roads
no longer in existence
19th-Century Fences
Modern Roads
52
Preserved by other
Organizations

AMERICAN
BATTLEFIELD
TRUST ★ ★ ★

UPDATED JUNE 2020

FEET

MILES

6,000

1.50

SECOND BATTLE *of* FORT FISHER

JANUARY 15, 1865

AFTER THE UNION ARMY AND NAVY SEALED OFF MOBILE BAY IN August of 1864, only one major port remained opened for the Confederacy: Wilmington, North Carolina. Access to the port of Wilmington was via the Cape Fear River, which ran in a north-south direction on the city's west side before emptying into the Atlantic Ocean some 20 miles south of the city. A peninsula of land on the east side of the river sheltered the river and ships from the Federal North Atlantic Blockading Squadron. Bolstering the area's natural defense were a series of Confederate fortifications, with the primary fortification being Fort Fisher, an upside-down L-shaped fort that was dubbed (as many others were) the "Gibraltar of the Confederacy."

The southern defenders of Wilmington and Fort Fisher were overseen by a troupe of Confederate castaways: Braxton Bragg, Alfred Colquitt, William Lamb, William H.C. Whiting, and Robert Hoke. Of the quintet, Hoke was the only capable commander in the sector. Luckily for the Confederates, the Union did not send their best and brightest to Wilmington, either—at least initially. Major General Benjamin F. Butler, a political general through and through, performed poorly in the Eastern and Western Theaters of the war. But his political connections made him such a problem for the Union high command that he had to receive prominent positions.

The first Battle of Fort Fisher (Dec. 23-27, 1864) was more of a Gallipoli than a Normandy. An ill-timed naval bombardment tipped off the Confederate defenders. A Federal ship packed with tons of explosives failed to make contact with Fort Fisher's defenses and harmlessly blew up at sea. And when the Federal infantry did land, they were quickly evacuated. Butler was sacked.

In January of 1865, a second attempt was made to secure Fort Fisher, and this time the Federals placed two capable men in command: Maj. Gen. Alfred Terry

and Rear Adm. David D. Porter. Terry collected nearly 10,000 Union army soldiers while Porter arrayed 58 ships offshore in roughly three lines of battle. Porter would pummel the Confederate defenses and land the army on shore. Once ashore, a division of United States Colored Troops (USCT) would advance north up the peninsula and assume a blocking position—their primary mission was to hold back any Confederate reinforcements from Hoke's division. A second force of Union infantry would establish a line facing south and attack the landward wall of Fort Fisher. A third force of sailors and United States Marines, some 2,000 in all, would land and attack the seaward wall of the fort. In terms of ships and men, the assault on Fort Fisher was the largest and most complex amphibious operation in U.S. history until World War II.

On January 13, Terry's soldiers established a beachhead north of Fort Fisher. On January 15, the Union Navy pounded the Confederate defenses south of Wilmington. Three successive waves of sailors and marines were to attack the eastern seawall. Like something from an Errol Flynn movie, the 2,000 sea dogs and leathernecks crashed into the defenses with pistols and cutlasses in hand in one great wave of humanity. The 1,900 Confederate defenders focused on this initial assault as the division of Brig. Gen. Adelbert Ames smashed into the land wall. The battle was intense and furious. Seven of Ames's thirteen regimental commanders were killed or wounded, and all three of his brigade commanders fell as casualties, too.

Whiting pleaded with Bragg for reinforcements. Bragg refused, but sent Colquitt to the fort with orders to relive Whiting. By the time Colquitt arrived, Confederates were evacuating the fort and Whiting and Lamb lay wounded. After hours of battle, the Confederate's surrendered the fort, and Wilmington fell to Union soldiers roughly one month later. The last Confederate port was locked shut.

✳ ✳ **PRESERVATION** ✳ ✳

To date, the **American Battlefield Trust** has not saved any land at Fort Fisher Battlefield.

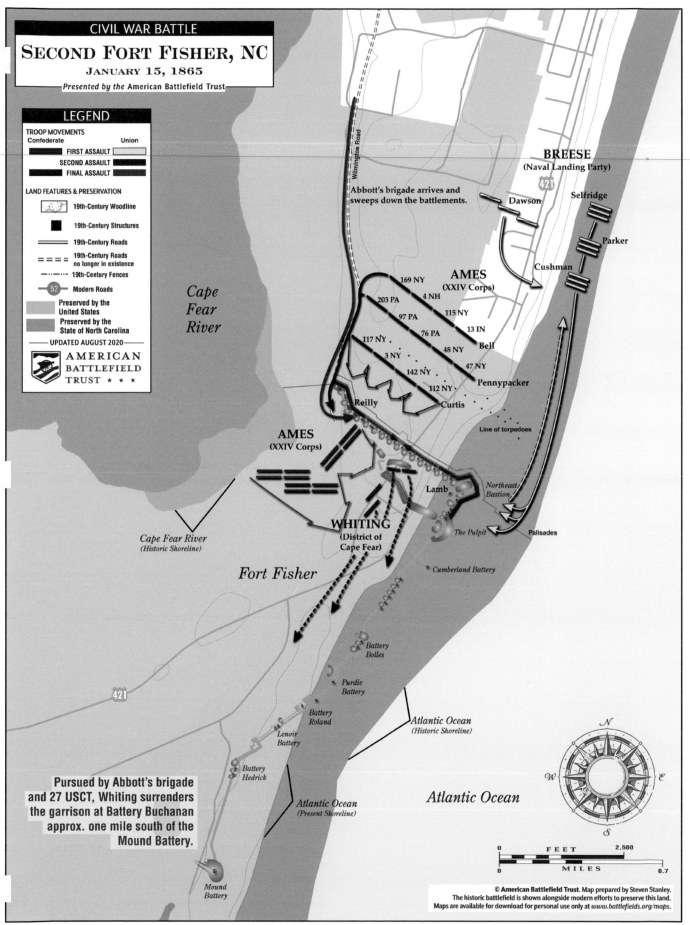

CIVIL WAR BATTLE
SECOND FORT FISHER, NC
JANUARY 15, 1865
Presented by the American Battlefield Trust

LEGEND

TROOP MOVEMENTS
Confederate — Union
- FIRST ASSAULT
- SECOND ASSAULT
- FINAL ASSAULT

LAND FEATURES & PRESERVATION
- 19th-Century Woodline
- 19th-Century Structures
- 19th-Century Roads
- 19th-Century Roads no longer in existence
- 19th-Century Fences
- 52 Modern Roads
- Preserved by the United States
- Preserved by the State of North Carolina

— UPDATED AUGUST 2020 —

AMERICAN BATTLEFIELD TRUST ★ ★ ★

Cape Fear River

BREESE (Naval Landing Party)

421

Abbott's brigade arrives and sweeps down the battlements.

Dawson
Selfridge
Cushman
Parker

169 NY
4 NH
203 PA
97 PA
115 NY
117 NY
76 PA
13 IN
3 NY
48 NY
Bell
142 NY
47 NY
112 NY
Pennypacker
Reilly
Curtis

AMES (XXIV Corps)

Line of torpedoes

AMES (XXIV Corps)

Lamb
Northeast Bastion

WHITING (District of Cape Fear)

The Pulpit
Palisades

Cape Fear River (Historic Shoreline)

Fort Fisher

Cumberland Battery

Battery Bolles

Purdie Battery

Battery Roland

Lenoir Battery

Atlantic Ocean (Historic Shoreline)

421

Battery Hedrick

Pursued by Abbott's brigade and 27 USCT, Whiting surrenders the garrison at Battery Buchanan approx. one mile south of the Mound Battery.

Atlantic Ocean (Present Shoreline)

Atlantic Ocean

Mound Battery

N
W — E
S

FEET 2,500
MILES 0.7

© **American Battlefield Trust**. Map prepared by Steven Stanley.
The historic battlefield is shown alongside modern efforts to preserve this land.
Maps are available for personal use only at *www.battlefields.org/maps*.

BATTLE *of* AVERASBORO

(AVERASBOROUGH)

MARCH 16, 1865

MAJOR GENERAL WILLIAM T. SHERMAN REMAINED **ACTIVE FOLLOWING THE FALL** of Atlanta. Once his armies were reorganized, Sherman and his armies cut a swath across Georgia during his March to the Sea. The march destroyed Georgia's capacity for making war by inflicting more than $100 million in damages. The city of Savannah was offered to President Lincoln as a Christmas gift. Next, Sherman and his armies unleashed their wrath upon the birthplace of secession: South Carolina. The state capital of Columbia was burned, railroads and rolling stock destroyed, and throngs of slaves freed. The Confederate forces in the Carolinas could do little to slow Sherman.

By March of 1865, the overall Confederate command in this region (two military departments) fell once again on the shoulders of Gen. Joseph E. Johnston. Jefferson Davis was reluctant to restore Johnston, but with the Confederacy shrinking by the day, Davis had little choice. In turn, Johnston knew that there was little that he could do to stop Sherman on his own. He determined to gather all of the Confederate forces he could muster—including the smashed ruins of Hood's army—and then move north toward Robert E. Lee and the besieged rebel armies around Richmond and Petersburg. The combined weight of Confederate arms would hopefully be enough to thwart the Yankees.

Sherman's armies moved in two wings as they drove north through North Carolina. The left wing moved toward the state capital at Raleigh, while the right wing drove toward the road junction at Goldsboro, NC.

On the afternoon of March 15, 1865, Sherman's cavalry screen under Brig. Gen. Hugh Judson Kilpatrick came up against Lt. Gen. William Hardee's corps, consisting of two infantry divisions commanded by William B. Taliaferro and Lafayette McLaws, and a division of cavalry under Maj. Gen. Joseph Wheeler. The Confederates were deployed across the Raleigh Road near Averasboro, 40 miles south of Raleigh. Hardee's orders were to delay Sherman's 25,000-man left wing of Maj. Gen. Henry W. Slocum so that Johnston could consolidate his remaining forces to defend the road networks connecting Raleigh and Goldsboro. Hardee posted his 6,000-man corps in a well-chosen position astride the road, with the Cape Fear River anchoring his right flank and the Black River swamps to the east anchoring his left.

After reconnoitering the Confederate defenses, Kilpatrick withdrew and called for infantry support. During the night, two divisions of the Brig. Gen. Alpheus Williams's XX Corps arrived to confront Hardee's men arrayed across the plantation of the John C. Smith family. At dawn on March 16, Williams's infantry advanced against McLaws's division on the Confederate left and drove back the rebel skirmishers but was stopped by the main Confederate line and a sharp Rebel counterattack. Around mid-morning, Williams renewed his advance with reinforcements on his left and drove Taliaferro's Confederates from two lines of works but was repulsed upon reaching a third line of defenders. Late that afternoon, two divisions from Maj. Gen. Jefferson C. Davis's Union XIV Corps arrived on the field and attempted to flank the Confederate right where they were stopped with significant casualties by Wheeler's dismounted cavalry. Sporadic fighting continued into the evening with little result.

Around 8:30 p.m., Hardee withdrew from the battlefield and retreated north toward Smithfield, leaving his campfires burning to conceal his departure. The penultimate battle for the Carolinas set the stage for Sherman's and Johnston's last major battle of the Civil War.

✳ ✳ PRESERVATION ✳ ✳

To date, the **American Battlefield Trust** has saved **520 acres** at Averasboro Battlefield.

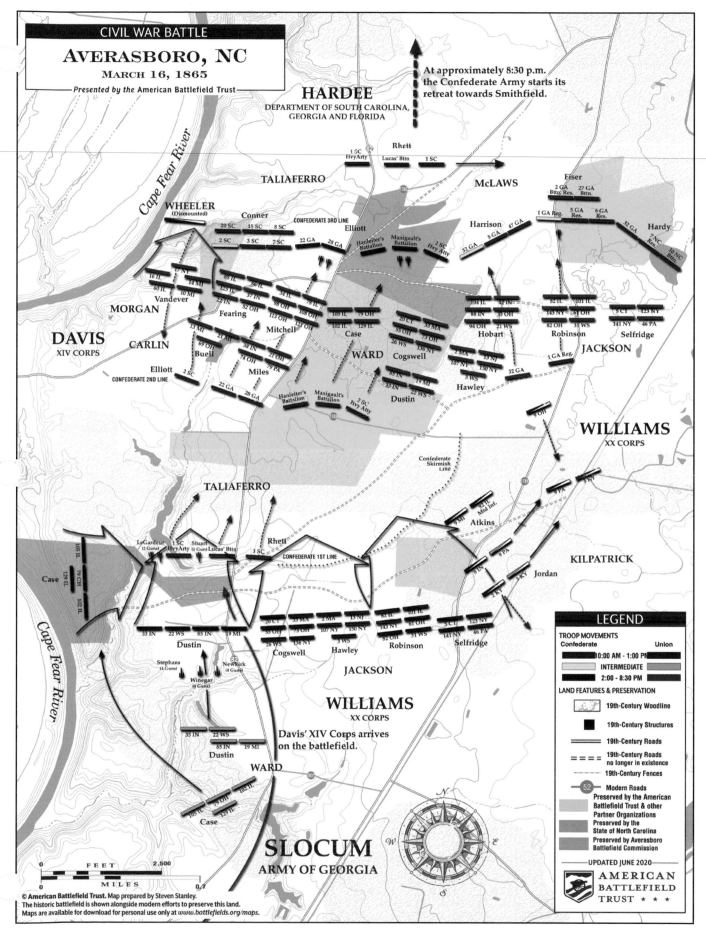

BATTLE *of* BENTONVILLE

MARCH 19 - 21, 1865

THE BATTLE OF BENTONVILLE WAS A VERITABLE WHO'S-WHO OF DISCARDED CONFEDERATE leaders: Joe Johnston, Braxton Bragg, Lafayette McLaws, Alfred Colquitt, Evander Law, and William B. Taliaferro were just some of the hapless commanders on the field. The 22,000-man army that Johnston commanded looked much more impressive on paper. The army consisted of the remnants of the Army of Tennessee, the Department of North Carolina, and the Department of South Carolina, Georgia & Florida, with other castoffs joining along the way.

In the aftermath of the Battle of Averasboro, Sherman continued his march through the Carolinas, destroying railroads and disrupting supply lines on its way to join Lt. Gen. Ulysses S. Grant's army near Petersburg & Richmond. On March 19, as the respective Federal wings approached Goldsboro, North Carolina, Maj. Gen. Henry W. Slocum's wing encountered Johnston's hodgepodge army. Johnston's forces concentrated at Bentonville with the hope of falling upon Slocum's wing before the Federal wing of Maj. Gen. Oliver O. Howard could come to Slocum's support.

Convinced that he faced only a paltry Confederate cavalry force, Slocum launched an attack to disperse them. In turn, the Yankees were driven back. Slocum then established a makeshift defensive line northeast of the Harper house and called for reinforcements. Meantime, Johnston's army arrayed itself to deal a blow to Slocum. It took the Confederates the better part of the day to bring their offensive to life. After 3 p.m., the Rebel line surged forward. Maj. Gen. Robert F. Hoke's division of the Army of Northern Virginia attacked the right of Slocum's line, driving back Slocum's men and overrunning the Union XIV Corps field hospital. While on the Union left, the remnants of the Confederate Army of Tennessee crashed into the weak Federal line. While many of the Federal units were driven back, Brig. Gen. James D. Morgan's Union division held out against the onslaught, and eventually Union reinforcements arrived to support a counterattack. The Confederates reached their high-water mark at the Morris Farm, where Union forces formed a defensive line. After several Confederate attacks failed to dislodge the Union defenders, the rebels pulled back to their original lines. Nightfall brought the first day's fighting to a close in a tactical draw.

The next day, Howard's right wing arrived to reinforce Slocum, which put the Confederates at a numerical disadvantage. Sherman expected Johnston to retreat and was inclined to let him do so. Although Johnston began evacuating his wounded, he refused to give up his tenuous position, guarding his only route of escape across Mill Creek. Outnumbered, his only hope for success was to entice Sherman into attacking his entrenched position, something Sherman was unlikely to do.

The next day, Johnston remained in position and skirmishing resumed. Heavy fighting erupted south of the Goldsboro Road in an area later called the "Bull Pen" between Morgan's and Hoke's men. Under a heavy rainfall, Union Maj. Gen. Joseph A. Mower led a "little reconnaissance" toward the Mill Creek Bridge. When Mower discovered the weakness of the Confederate left flank, Mower launched an attack against the small force holding the bridge. A Confederate counterattack, combined with Sherman's order for Mower to withdraw, ended the advance, allowing Johnston's army to retain control of their only means of supply and retreat. Johnston's men retreated across the bridge that evening, ending the battle. Sherman pursued Johnston's army toward Raleigh—capturing the city on April 13. The war in the Western Theater was drawing to a close.

✳ ✳ PRESERVATION ✳ ✳

To date, the **American Battlefield Trust** has saved **1,867 acres** at Bentonville Battlefield.

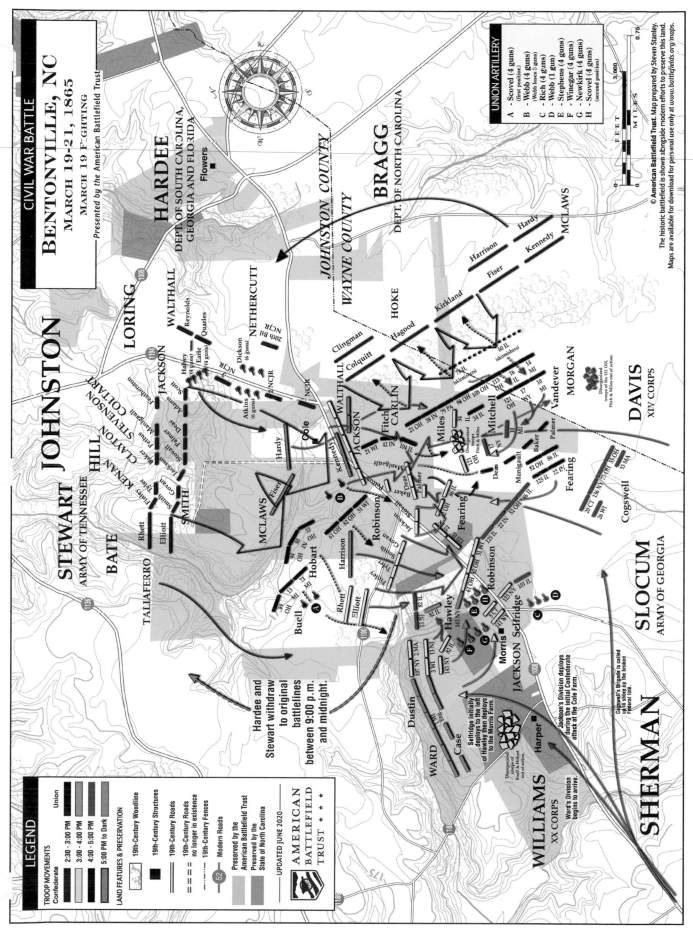

CIVIL WAR BATTLE

BENTONVILLE, NC
MARCH 19-21, 1865
MARCH 19 FIGHTING
Presented by the American Battlefield Trust

LEGEND

TROOP MOVEMENTS

Confederate | Union
- 2:30 - 3:00 PM
- 3:00 - 4:00 PM
- 4:00 - 5:00 PM
- 5:00 PM to Dark

LAND FEATURES & PRESERVATION
- 19th-Century Woodline
- 19th-Century Structures
- 19th-Century Roads
- 19th-Century Roads no longer in existence
- 19th-Century Fences
- 52 Modern Roads
- Preserved by the American Battlefield Trust
- Preserved by the State of North Carolina

— UPDATED JUNE 2020 —

AMERICAN BATTLEFIELD TRUST ★ ★ ★

UNION ARTILLERY
- A - Scovel (4 guns) (first position)
- B - Webb (4 guns) (Webb loses 3 guns)
- C - Rich (4 guns)
- D - Webb (1 gun)
- E - Stephens (4 guns)
- F - Winegar (4 guns)
- G - Newkirk (4 guns)
- H - Scovel (4 guns) (second position)

© American Battlefield Trust. Map prepared by Steven Stanley.
The historic battlefield is shown a Brigade-scale modern efforts to preserve this land.
Maps are available for download for personal use only at *www.battlefields.org/maps*.

Hardee and Stewart withdraw to original battlelines between 9:00 p.m. and midnight.

Selfridge initially deploys to the left of Hawley then deploys to the Morris Farm.

Jackson's Division deploys during the initial Confederate attack at the Cole Farm.

Cogswell's Brigade is called up to shore up the broken Federal line.

Ward's Division begins to arrive.

Disorganized troops of Buell & Hibbert out of action.

Disorganized troops of the 121 OH, Fitch & Miles out of action.

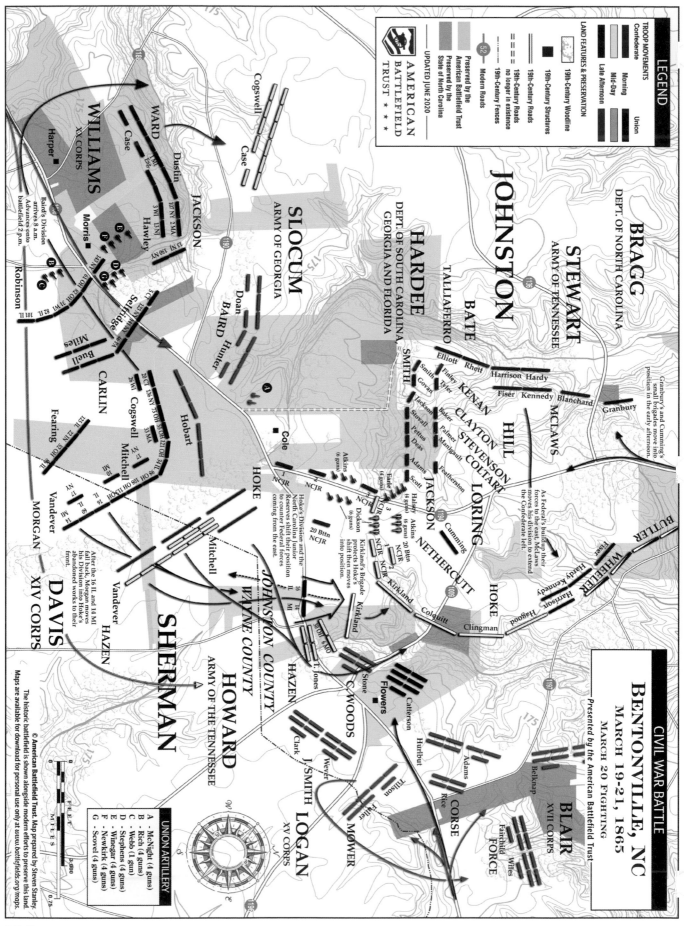

LEGEND

TROOP MOVEMENTS

Confederate | Union
- Morning
- Mid-Day
- Late Afternoon

LAND FEATURES & PRESERVATION
- 19th-Century Woodline
- 19th-Century Structures
- 19th-Century Roads
- 19th-Century Roads no longer in existence
- Modern Roads
- 19th-Century Fences
- Preserved by the American Battlefield Trust
- Preserved by the State of North Carolina

UPDATED JUNE 2020

AMERICAN BATTLEFIELD TRUST

CIVIL WAR BATTLE

BENTONVILLE, NC

MARCH 19-21, 1865

MARCH 20 FIGHTING

Presented by the American Battlefield Trust

UNION ARTILLERY
- A — McNight (4 guns)
- B — Rich (4 guns)
- C — Webb (1 gun)
- D — Stephens (4 guns)
- E — Winegar (4 guns)
- F — Newkirk (4 guns)
- G — Scovel (4 guns)

© American Battlefield Trust. Map prepared by Steven Stanley. The historic battlefield is shown alongside modern efforts to preserve this land. Maps are available for download for personal use only at www.battlefields.org/maps.

BRAGG
DEPT. OF NORTH CAROLINA

STEWART
ARMY OF TENNESSEE

JOHNSTON

BATE

HARDEE
DEPT. OF SOUTH CAROLINA, GEORGIA AND FLORIDA

HILL

LORING

BUTLER

WHEELER

As Federal's buildup their forces to the east, McLaws moves his division to extend the Confederate left.

Granbury's and Cumming's small brigades move into position in the early afternoon.

SLOCUM
ARMY OF GEORGIA

WILLIAMS
XX CORPS

WARD

JACKSON

BAIRD

CARLIN

DAVIS
XIV CORPS

MORGAN

SHERMAN

HOKE

JOHNSTON COUNTY

WAYNE COUNTY

HOWARD
ARMY OF THE TENNESSEE

LOGAN
XV CORPS

J. SMITH

BLAIR
XVII CORPS

FORCE

CORSE

MOWER

Hoke's Division and the North Carolina Junior Reserves shift their position to counter Federal forces coming from the east.

Kirkland's Brigade protects Hoke's flank then moves into position.

After the 16 IL and 14 MI fall back, Morgan moves his Division into Hoke's abandoned works to their front.

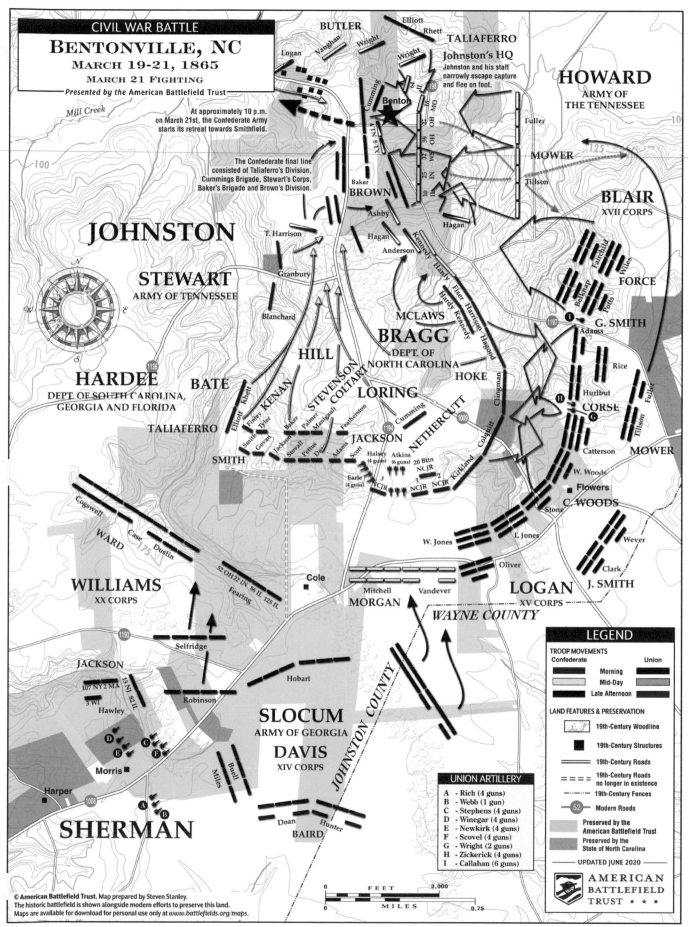

CIVIL WAR BATTLE
BENTONVILLE, NC
MARCH 19-21, 1865
MARCH 21 FIGHTING
Presented by the American Battlefield Trust

At approximately 10 p.m. on March 21st, the Confederate Army starts its retreat towards Smithfield.

The Confederate final line consisted of Taliaferro's Division, Cummings Brigade, Stewart's Corps, Baker's Brigade and Brown's Division.

Mill Creek

BUTLER

Logan Vaughan Wright Wright Elliott Rhett

TALIAFERRO

Johnston's HQ
Johnston and his staff narrowly escape capture and flee on foot.

Benton

Cumming

BROWN

Baker

Ashby

Hagan Hagan

T. Harrison

Anderson

JOHNSTON

STEWART
ARMY OF TENNESSEE

Granbury

Blanchard

MCLAWS

BRAGG
DEPT. OF NORTH CAROLINA

HILL

HOKE

KENAN STEVENSON COLTART LORING

HARDEE
DEPT. OF SOUTH CAROLINA, GEORGIA AND FLORIDA

BATE

Elliott Rhett

Finley Tyler

Smith Govan

Jackson Baker Palmer Manigault Featherston

Stovall Pettus Dea Adams

Scott

Cumming

NETHERCUTT

TALIAFERRO

SMITH

JACKSON

Halsey (4 guns) Atkins (6 guns) 20 Bttn NCJR

Earle (4 guns) 3 NCJR 2 NCJR Kirkland

Colquitt Clingman

HOWARD
ARMY OF THE TENNESSEE

Fuller

MOWER

Tillson

BLAIR
XVII CORPS

Belknap Fairchild Wiles Potts FORCE

G. SMITH

Adams

Rice

Hurlbut

CORSE

Tillson Fuller

Catterson MOWER

W. Woods

Flowers

C. WOODS

Stone Wever

Clark

J. SMITH

W. Jones I. Jones

Oliver

LOGAN
XV CORPS

Cogswell WARD Case Dustin

52 OH 22 IN 86 IL 125 IL Fearing

Cole

Mitchell Vandever

MORGAN

WAYNE COUNTY

WILLIAMS
XX CORPS

Selfridge

JACKSON

107 NY 2 MA 13 NJ 82 IL
3 WI
Hawley

D E C F

Morris

Harper

SHERMAN

Robinson

Hobart

SLOCUM
ARMY OF GEORGIA

Buell

Miles

DAVIS
XIV CORPS

Doan Hunter

BAIRD

A B

JOHNSTON COUNTY

LEGEND
TROOP MOVEMENTS

Confederate		Union
	Morning	
	Mid-Day	
	Late Afternoon	

LAND FEATURES & PRESERVATION

19th-Century Woodline

19th-Century Structures

19th-Century Roads

19th-Century Roads no longer in existence

19th-Century Fences

52 — Modern Roads

Preserved by the American Battlefield Trust

Preserved by the State of North Carolina

— UPDATED JUNE 2020 —

UNION ARTILLERY
A - Rich (4 guns)
B - Webb (1 gun)
C - Stephens (4 guns)
D - Winegar (4 guns)
E - Newkirk (4 guns)
F - Scovel (4 guns)
G - Wright (2 guns)
H - Zickerick (4 guns)
I - Callahan (6 guns)

AMERICAN BATTLEFIELD TRUST ★★★

FEET 0 _____ 3,000
MILES 0 _____ 0.75

SIEGE *and* BATTLE *of* SPANISH FORT *and* FORT BLAKELY

MARCH 27 - APRIL 9, 1865

WITHOUT A DOUBT, REAR ADM. DAVID G. FARRAGUT'S AUDACIOUS battle to take Mobile Bay in August of 1864 is one of the most famous actions of the Civil War, and while Mobile Bay had been closed to blockade-running traffic since August 1864, the city of Mobile remained under Confederate control well into 1865.

In the wake of Sherman's March to the Sea and his Carolinas Campaign, and John Bell Hood's disastrous Middle Tennessee Campaign, Union forces largely had free reign to mop up Confederate resistance. By March 1865, Union Maj. Gen. Edward R. S. Canby prepared to advance on the remaining Confederate strongholds along the Gulf of Mexico coast, and the city of Mobile was one of Canby's targets.

Key to the defenses of Mobile were two Confederate posts on the eastern shore of Mobile Bay: Spanish Fort, directly opposite the city, and Fort Blakely (also spelled Blakeley), five miles to the north. Spanish Fort was occupied by about 3,000 men and mounted 47 guns behind earthen redoubts. Many of those guns were trained westward across the bay, and nearby swamps and frequent high water prevented construction of substantial defenses outside the main fort. Nearby Fort Blakely, at the mouth of the Blakely (now the Tensaw) River, was manned by 2,500 men and around 40 guns. The three-mile-long earthen fortifications were defended by veteran soldiers. A series of nine earthen redoubts fronted by abatis and felled trees were supported by primitive land mines and telegraph wire strung between tree stumps. Confederate Brig. Gen. St. John R. Liddell commanded the garrison there and was the senior commander of both forts.

In the last week of March, two Federal infantry columns converged on both garrisons. One column, commanded by Maj. Gen. Frederick Steele, moved northwest from Pensacola, Florida, with orders to take Fort Blakely. Canby's XVI and XIII Corps moved on Spanish Fort. By March 27, Canby had encircled the Confederate defenders there and, after a brief firefight, ordered his men to dig in rather than risk a frontal assault. Three armored Rebel gunboats supported the infantry inside Spanish Fort.

Canby surrounded Spanish Fort with around 90 guns. On April 8, an artillery barrage preceded an attack on the lightly defended northern edge of the fort. Canby's men dislodged the Confederate defenders and the fort was evacuated that evening. Many of the Confederates fled to Mobile, and around 1,000 escaped into Fort Blakely. Canby's men rounded up and additional 500 prisoners.

Meantime, Steele's column from Pensacola had arrived outside Fort Blakely on April 1 and laid siege to the garrison for a week. The Federals concentrated around 16,000 men for an attack on the fort on April 9. Included in Canby's force were around 5,000 United States Colored Troops, one of the largest concentrations of USCTs in the entire war. The Union assault began around 5 p.m. Heavy hand-to-hand fighting raged all along the defensive line. The Union's overwhelming numbers eventually breached the Confederate earthworks. Liddell surrendered his men to Canby just six hours after Gen. Robert E. Lee surrendered his army to Ulysses S. Grant at Appomattox, Virginia.

The siege and capture of Fort Blakely was the last major battle in the Western Theater during the American Civil War. The mayor of Mobile surrendered the city without a fight on April 12, and all Confederate forces in the area surrendered to Canby on May 4, 1865.

✳ ✳ PRESERVATION ✳ ✳

To date, the **American Battlefield Trust** has saved **126 acres** at Fort Blakeley Battlefield.

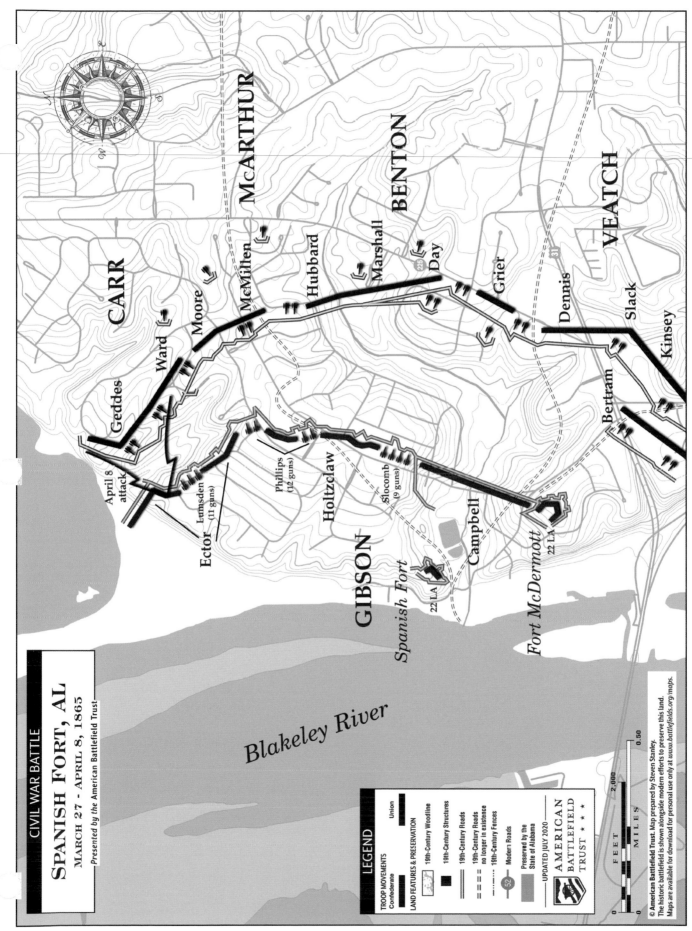

CIVIL WAR BATTLE

SPANISH FORT, AL

MARCH 27 - APRIL 8, 1865

Presented by the American Battlefield Trust

CARR

McARTHUR

BENTON

VEATCH

GIBSON

Geddes
Ward
Moore
McMillen
Hubbard
Marshall
Day
Grier
Dennis
Slack
Kinsey
Bertram

April 8 attack

Ector
Lumsden (11 guns)
Phillips (12 guns)
Holtzclaw
Slocomb (9 guns)
Campbell
Fort McDermott
22 LA

Spanish Fort
22 LA

Blakeley River

LEGEND

TROOP MOVEMENTS
Confederate   Union

LAND FEATURES & PRESERVATION
19th-Century Woodline
19th-Century Structures
19th-Century Roads
19th-Century Roads no longer in existence
19th-Century Fences
52 Modern Roads
Preserved by the State of Alabama
— UPDATED JULY 2020 —

AMERICAN
BATTLEFIELD
TRUST ★ ★ ★

FEET 0   2,000
MILES 0   0.50

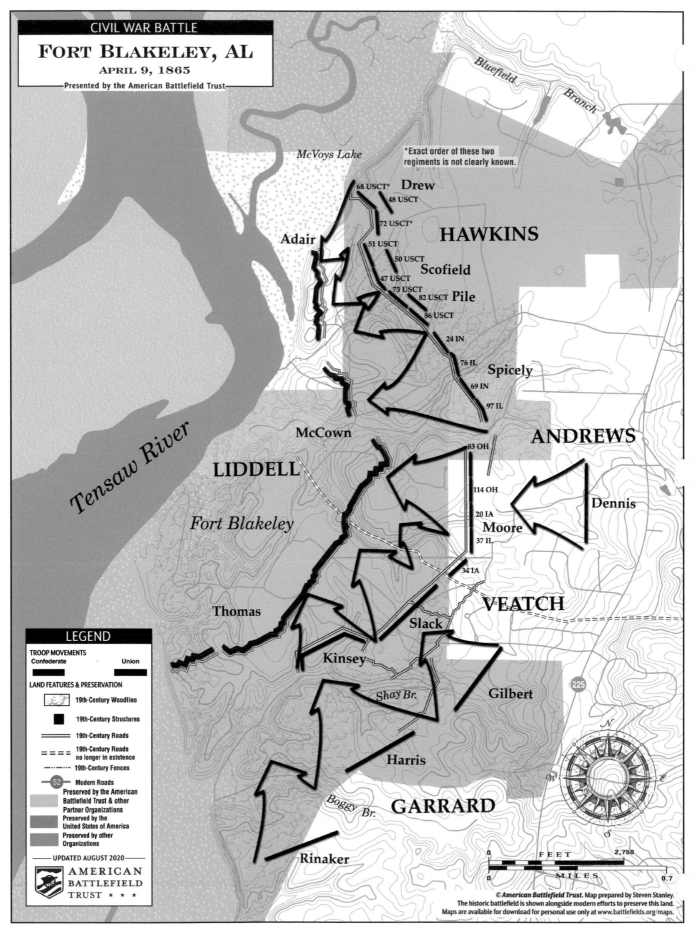

CIVIL WAR BATTLE

FORT BLAKELEY, AL
APRIL 9, 1865
Presented by the American Battlefield Trust

*Exact order of these two regiments is not clearly known.

McVoys Lake

68 USCT* Drew
48 USCT

72 USCT* HAWKINS
51 USCT

Adair

50 USCT Scofield
47 USCT
73 USCT 82 USCT Pile
86 USCT

24 IN

76 IL Spicely
69 IN

97 IL

McCown 83 OH ANDREWS

LIDDELL

Tensaw River

114 OH
20 IA Dennis
Moore
37 IL

Fort Blakeley

34 IA

Thomas VEATCH

Slack

Kinsey

Shay Br. Gilbert

225

Harris

Boggy Br. GARRARD

Rinaker

LEGEND

TROOP MOVEMENTS
Confederate   Union

LAND FEATURES & PRESERVATION

19th-Century Woodline

19th-Century Structures

19th-Century Roads

19th-Century Roads no longer in existence

19th-Century Fences

52 Modern Roads

Preserved by the American Battlefield Trust & other Partner Organizations

Preserved by the United States of America

Preserved by other Organizations

UPDATED AUGUST 2020

AMERICAN BATTLEFIELD TRUST ★ ★ ★

FEET 2,750

MILES 0.7

© *American Battlefield Trust.* Map prepared by Steven Stanley.
The historic battlefield is shown alongside modern efforts to preserve this land.
Maps are available for download for personal use only at www.battlefields.org/maps.

EPILOGUE: BENNETT PLACE

APRIL 26, 1865

GENERAL JOSEPH JOHNSTON AWOKE TO GRIM NEWS EARLY ON THE MORNING of April 11, 1865. General Robert E. Lee had surrendered the Army of Northern Virginia at Appomattox Court House. This change in events left Johnston as the senior field general for the Confederacy and what was left of his army the last hopes of the Southern Confederacy. Grant's armies in Virginia were now free to swoop into North Carolina and link with Sherman's armies now in pursuit of Johnston's forces. The writing was on the wall.

Yet, Confederate President Jefferson Davis remained unconvinced that Lee's surrender was a fatal blow to the Confederacy and the war effort. Johnston tried to bring Davis back to reality and reasoned that the Confederate forces were now outnumbered eighteen to one, and the South had little economic, agricultural, or industrial capacity to carry on the war. "[I]t would be the greatest of human crimes to continue the war," argued Johnston. Joe Johnston then opened communications with William T. Sherman. The two generals agreed to meet on April 17 at James Bennett's farm near Durham Station (today Durham, North Carolina) to discuss cessation of hostilities.

As Sherman departed, he received a telegram from Secretary of War Edwin Stanton: President Lincoln was dead at the hands of the assassin John Wilkes Booth.

Sherman and Johnston had never met before, despite both serving in the Old Army. After exchanging pleasantries, Sherman handed Johnston the telegram announcing Lincoln's assassination. Johnston told Sherman he believed "the event was the greatest possible calamity to the South." Johnston then offered to negotiate the terms of the surrender of all the remaining armies in exchange for amnesty for Davis and his cabinet. Sherman initially rejected that offer as he had promised Grant he would not deviate from the terms Grant offered Lee at Appomattox.

On April 18 Johnston and Sherman met once again at the Bennett House. Johnston wanted Sherman's explicit assurance for the protection of his soldiers' Constitutional rights. Sherman assured him that Lincoln's 1863 Amnesty Proclamation and the terms of the Appomattox surrender allowed for a full pardon of all Confederate soldiers. Sherman and Johnston eventually reached an extraordinarily lenient agreement, suspending hostilities pending approval of the terms by the new United States President Andrew Johnson. Sherman's negotiations with Johnston and Confederate Secretary of War John C. Breckenridge aligned with Sherman's policy of a hard war followed by soft terms of peace. However, President Andrew Johnson angrily rejected these April 18 terms and sent Grant to Raleigh to oversee the resumption of hostilities on April 26.

At Johnston's request, he and Sherman met again at the Bennett Place on April 26 without Grant. Under Johnston and Sherman's authority, terms that closely resembled the Appomattox surrender were drafted, which Johnston slightly amended. President Johnson and his cabinet approved these terms. Under these final terms, Johnston's army and his naval force would cease all hostilities, and all officers and men were to be paroled under an oath to not take up arms against the United States. Soldiers could retain their horses and other private property, and the Union army would provide field, rail, and water transportation home to the paroled men. Separate from this agreement, Sherman also promised 250,000 rations to the newly paroled troops.

The surrender at Bennett Place was the largest surrender of the entire war, which included approximately 90,000 Confederates stationed in North Carolina, South Carolina, Georgia, and Florida. However, Bennett Place was not the last Confederate surrender. That occurred on June 23, 1865, with General Stand Watie's Indian Territory troops and, in November 1865, the surrender of the blockade runner CSS *Shenandoah*. The long road of war was over—and the dawn of a difficult peace broke across a reunified United States.

APPENDIX A
A SHORT HISTORY OF THE BATTLEFIELD PRESERVATION MOVEMENT

THE IDEA OF PROTECTING AMERICA'S BATTLEFIELDS IS NOT NEW. In the mid-19th century, portions of the Revolutionary War battlefields at places like Bunker Hill and Yorktown were set aside as a means of remembrance. Civil War veterans began erecting memorials to their units, actions, and fallen comrades almost as soon as the guns fell silent. Veterans reunions catalyzed battlefield preservation, as, at these gatherings, the men of the blue and the gray discussed creating open-air classrooms where the military could visit and learn the lessons from battles of the past.

By 1900, five national military parks — at Antietam, Chickamauga and Chattanooga, Gettysburg, Shiloh and Vicksburg — had been established under the auspices of the War Department. Gradually, additional parks were created at places like Cowpens, Guilford Court House, Fort McHenry, Fort Donelson and Petersburg, all of which were transferred to the control of the National Park Service in 1933. The so-called "cannonball circuit" continued to grow through the Civil War centennial commemoration in the 1960s, but federal battlefield preservation efforts then began to stall.

In the years following the Second World War, the pace of urban and suburban development in America dramatically escalated, leading to the destruction of battlefield land virtually across the map. The destruction was particularly devastating at battlefields adjacent to major cities. Witnessing commercial and residential construction destroying these historic sites, local preservation and park friends groups began to take shape and advocate for their protection. But there was no unified voice and success was both scattered and limited; entire battlefields like Chantilly and Salem Church, both Civil War sites in central Virginia, were all but swallowed by sprawl.

In July 1987, twenty or so stalwart souls met in Fredericksburg, Va., to discuss what could be done to protect the rapidly disappearing battlefields around them. Calling themselves the Association for the Preservation of Civil War Sites (APCWS), they decided the only way to save these sites for posterity was to buy the physical landscapes themselves.

In 1999, seeking to increase the scope of preservation opportunities that could be pursued, that first group merged with another organization sharing its vision to form the Civil War Preservation Trust. On the eve of the war's sesquicentennial commemoration in 2011, the group shortened its name to the Civil War Trust.

By mastering the art of seeking out public-private partnerships to maximize efficiency, and by working with developers to find win-win solutions, the Civil War Trust became the number one entity saving battlefield land in America, protecting land at a rate four times that of the National Park Service.

In 2014, responding to a clear need from the National Park Service, the Civil War Trust launched Campaign 1776, a limited scope project to lend its considerable expertise and clout to the protection of battlefields associated with the Revolutionary War and the War of 1812.

In May 2018, having concluded its 30th anniversary year, the group unveiled a new organizational structure, in which the Civil War Trust and the Revolutionary War Trust would operate as land preservation divisions under the banner of a broader American Battlefield Trust. With the mission to — Preserve. Educate. Inspire. — The American Battlefield Trust continues to be the leader in the land preservation community.

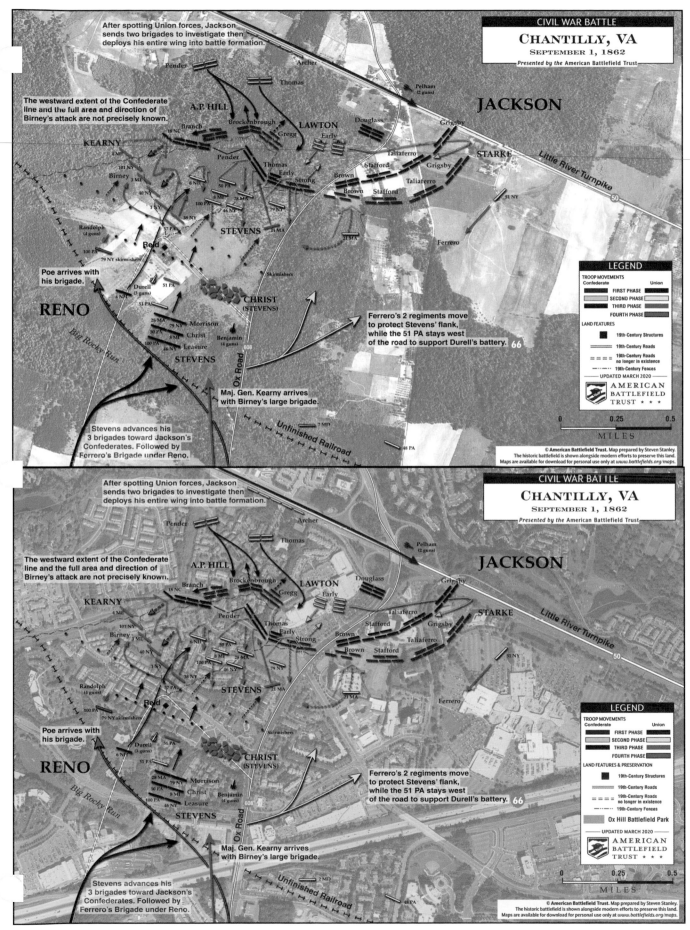

APPENDIX B
DETERMINING THE LAND
THAT WE SAVE

FOR MORE THAN 30 YEARS, THE AMERICAN BATTLEFIELD TRUST has been working to save hallowed battlefield land associated with the Revolutionary War, War of 1812, and American Civil War. To date, the American Battlefield Trust has preserved more than 53,000 acres of battlefield land in 24 states associated with 143 battles spanning the first 100 years of our nation's history.

The American Battlefield Trust preserves significant battlefield land in perpetuity by only working with willing sellers and utilizing well-established conservation strategies, chiefly through "fee simple" transactions and conservation easements. In order to determine the suitability of a particular property, we first consult the landmark studies prepared by the American Battlefield Protection Program ("ABPP"), an arm of the National Park Service. These robust reports commissioned by Congress examined more than 13,000 battles and skirmishes from the Revolutionary War, War of 1812, and Civil War and identified the 627 principle sites most worthy of preservation.

Once we determine whether a prospective property is part of an ABPP-listed site, we utilize our Geographic Information System ("GIS") computerized mapping capabilities to locate the property in relation to the historic landscape. If a property is within the recognized boundary of an eligible battlefield, we next determine what conservation strategy is best suited to the project, recognizing that each opportunity presents a unique situation. Thus, we oversee each prospective land deal on a case-by-case basis.

Fee simple transactions transfer full ownership of a property. The Trust generally pays fair market value for land, but landowners can sell for less and receive tax benefits from their charitable contribution of the difference. Some landowners choose to negotiate a life estate—meaning they retain the right to live at and use the property until their death—or a leaseback option where the land trust gains control upon the death of the landowner. We also work to identify conservation buyers who take ownership of the property after placing permanent restrictions on its development potential.

Conservation Easements are legal agreements wherein a qualified land trust or state entity formally restricts future activities on the land to protect its conservation values in perpetuity. Ownership of the land does not change hands. This is an attractive option that protects family land in perpetuity without selling it, while also providing benefits on federal and state income taxes, estate taxes, and property taxes. Each easement is negotiated individually, but in general, they disallow new structures not necessary for an agricultural operation, restrict changes to topography, and limit the ability to subdivide a property.

Once the American Battlefield Trust determines the best preservation strategy, the Trust must determine how to pay for the transaction. Funding for battlefield preservation projects generally comes from member donations being leveraged against federal and state matching grants—most notably National Park Service Battlefield Land Acquisition Grants. However, contributions by other nonprofit organizations, foundation grants, and landowner donations also play significant roles.

For more information about our current preservation efforts, please visit our website www.battlefields.org.

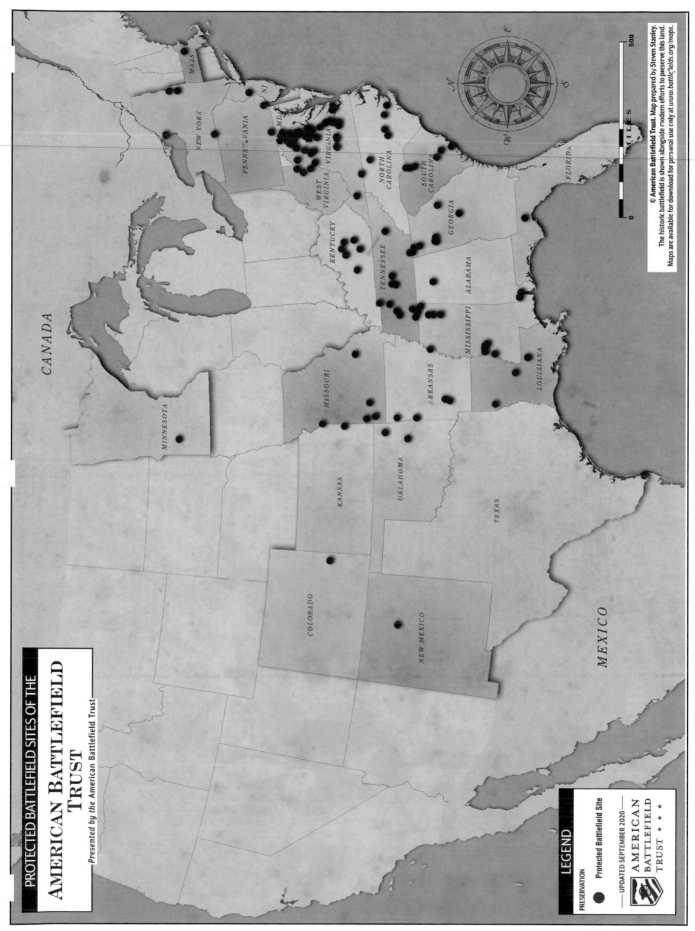

PROTECTED BATTLEFIELD SITES OF THE

AMERICAN BATTLEFIELD TRUST

Presented by the American Battlefield Trust

LEGEND

PRESERVATION

● Protected Battlefield Site

—— UPDATED SEPTEMBER 2020 ——

AMERICAN
BATTLEFIELD
TRUST ★ ★ ★

© American Battlefield Trust. Map prepared by Steven Stanley.
The historic battlefield is shown alongside modern efforts to preserve this land.
Maps are available for download for personal use only at www.battlefields.org/maps.

MILES

0   500

BATTLE MAPS OF THE CIVIL WAR: THE WESTERN THEATER
MAPS FROM THE AMERICAN BATTLEFIELD TRUST ⸗ VOLUME 2

PROJECT TEAM

ADMINISTRATION AND MANAGEMENT DEPARTMENT

David Duncan
President

Steve Wyngarden
Chief Administrative Officer

Ruth Hudspeth
Senior Financial Advisor

DEVELOPMENT DEPARTMENT

Amanda Murray
Deputy Director of Development

POLICY & COMMUNICATIONS DEPARTMENT

Mary Koik
Director of Communications

DIGITAL OPERATIONS DEPARTMENT

Wendy Woodford
Design Lead

REAL ESTATE DEPARTMENT

Jon Mitchell
GIS Specialist

HISTORY & EDUCATION DEPARTMENT

Garry Adelman
Chief Historian

Kristopher White
Deputy Director of Education

Steven Stanley
Historical Map Designer

PRESERVATION IS PUTTING THIS BATTLEFIELD BACK ON THE MAP

Franklin Battlefield
Franklin, Tenn.
MIKE TALPLACIDO

AND YOU CAN HELP SAVE OTHERS BEFORE THEY'RE LOST.

Please send me free information on preserving America's Battlefields.

Name

Address _____ State ___ Zip ___

Email

Phone

AMERICAN BATTLEFIELD TRUST ★ ★ ★
PRESERVE. EDUCATE. INSPIRE.

Mail the coupon to: 1156 15th St. NW, Suite 900, Washington, DC 20005 or go to www.battlefields.org/about

Map prepared for the Civil War Trust by Steven Stanley